INSIDE THE
HOUSE OF
COMMONS

INSIDE THE HOUSE OF COMMONS

Behind the Scenes
at Westminster

John Biffen

GRAFTON BOOKS
A Division of the Collins Publishing Group

LONDON GLASGOW
TORONTO SYDNEY AUCKLAND

Grafton Books
A Division of the Collins Publishing Group
8 Grafton Street, London W1X 3LA

Published by Grafton Books 1989

British Library Cataloguing in Publication Data

Biffen, John
  Inside the House of Commons: behind the scenes
  at Westminster.
  1. Great Britain. Parliament. House of Commons.
  Procedure
  I. Title
  328.41'05

ISBN 0–246–13479–8
ISBN 0–246–13501–8 (Pbk)

Printed and bound in Great Britain by
Butler & Tanner Ltd, Frome and London

CONTENTS

INTRODUCTION

When I became a Treasury Minister I knew that my days as a low-profile politician had ended. One morning my private secretary came to me, a touch of excitement in his voice. 'Chief Secretary,' he said, 'you are in *Private Eye*.' I was not alone. Fellow Ministers Geoffrey Howe and Nigel Lawson were also featured. It seemed that the Treasury team had colourful private lives that ill matched their public austerity. Only Lord Cockfield was blameless. It was superb imaginative journalism.

Since then I have managed to revert to a more sober, self-effacing role. In that spirit I have written *Inside the House of Commons*. It is a straightforward book: the title faithfully records its contents. It is not a coded party political message or a disguised autobiography. There is no shortage of the latter available elsewhere. A generation of politicians are now giving us their world view – 'How I shaped our national fortunes and broke the political mould.' I do not despise this form of wholesome family entertainment, but I also share Aneurin Bevan's view of political autobiography, that he liked his fiction straight. Neither do I intend to publish a political diary. The Cabinet diarists of the 1960s all managed to report the same event with an engaging variety of recollection. As 'Rab' Butler so aptly put it, 'truth is many-sided'. So, after nearly twenty-eight years as an MP, eight of which have been spent in Cabinet, I have set myself the task of writing about the House of Commons, rather than my own career there; and for the layman, rather than the historian, the academic or the pundit.

For me politics has always meant the House of Commons rather than Whitehall. I still recall vividly my first visit to Westminster in 1948 when I was just eighteen. A friend of my parents took me to the Commons where I met his MP, Harry White, who sat for Derbyshire North-East, and White's fellow Labour Member, Arthur Jenkins, who represented Pontypool and whose son Roy was to become a Labour Chancellor of the Exchequer and first leader of the SDP. I saw the Palace of Westminster from the river, an imposing prospect, and was more determined than ever to make my career there. It confirmed an early ambition, for I had joined the Young Conservatives at the age of fourteen.

Meanwhile my passion for politics had been matched by instinctive Tory tribal loyalties. I had lively political ambitions long before 'monetarism' had been invented. In such a state of grace I reached Westminster in November 1961. I was not disappointed. The schoolboy dreams quickly

'Wonderful, dear – you needn't go into the Commons at all if they put it on TV ...' Cartoon by David Langdon, Sunday Mirror, *18 October 1971.*

became reality. The Palace, its procedures, history and personalities were totally fascinating. Immediately I fell in love with my job. It was an affection that has not been dimmed with time. I still get the same sense of elation as I view the Westminster skyline and begin my daily Commons routine.

Since 1961 I have had a varied political career. It has enabled me to appreciate the House of Commons in its many aspects. For much of the time I have been a resolute back-bencher and have enjoyed the freedom that position confers. In the early days I fell in with dubious company, such as Sir Ian Gilmour, MP for Chesham and Amersham. Together with him I celebrated my first 'rebellion' when we abstained on the issue of the deportation of Chief Enahoro. The cause seemed vital at the time, though we were fighting for a little known chieftain from a faraway country. During the Division we repaired to the Smoking Room and toasted our principles whilst our colleagues loyally marched through the Division lobbies. I was later to learn that there were more difficult issues on which to make a stand.

Enjoyment of Parliament must be matched by affection for your constituency. It is no accident that *Hansard* records Members' names alongside

The box is mightier than the word. Cartoon by Vicky, Evening Standard, 6 March 1964.

their constituencies and makes absolutely no reference to party political affiliation. The Oswestry constituency, later renamed North Shropshire, has always been my parliamentary home, and I could not have been luckier in the accident of selection that made me the Member. Shortly after selection, but before adoption for the Oswestry seat, certain rivals circulated the deadly rumour that I was a London journalist foisted upon the constituency by Conservative Central Office. My parents were summoned from their Somerset farm to attend the adoption meeting. They were a living refutation of the slur. However, salvation brought its own danger; my father was such a 'natural' in the Oswestry Smithfield market that I heard farmers say they wished they had 'the guv'nor and not the lad' as candidate.

I have had the good fortune of spending eight years in government as a Cabinet Minister, five of them as Leader of the House of Commons. There can be no doubt that the Whitehall view of Westminster is a very different perspective from that of the back-bencher. Throughout, though, I have maintained the view that Ministers are in the Commons to serve Members rather than the reverse.

During my years as Member of Parliament I have realised the extent to which its many procedures are steeped in tradition. Indeed the traditions and procedures themselves help explain the role of Parliament and its evolution into its present democratic form. Britain's national history is a patchwork. One feature, above all, is striking. Parliament brought about the transfer of government from the Crown to itself. Thereafter there was a process whereby the government, sitting within Parliament, secured its position by organising support through the parliamentary party. Increasingly this process also concentrated power in the Commons rather than the Lords. The widening of the franchise has inevitably made the parliamentary process much more responsive to popular pressures.

Commons procedures, which have to take account of all these developments, have their arcane aspects. These can be bewildering, and I have described many of them in the book. MPs are playing political lawn tennis with all its contemporary gamesmanship, speed and skill; to the public in the galleries, however, the procedures must be more reminiscent of the centuries-old game of real tennis. The media, therefore, have a great obligation to explain how Parliament fulfils its responsibilities. It is essential to explain how the Commons seeks to influence the executive rather than merely to provide the votes the government needs.

The task of relating Westminster to the public today meets a new challenge. In 1988 the House of Commons took an historic step. It authorised an experimental period during which its proceedings should be broadcast on television. On this issue, as on many others, MPs have moved with great caution. Now the first, and probably decisive, step has been taken. Members know that the intrusive eye of television will compel changes in their procedures, as did press reporting in the last century. The prospect of new forms of reporting the Commons is coincidentally matched by the constitutional challenge of European Community membership. Television will provide the public with a ringside seat from which to view both that challenge and Parliament's response.

This book deals with several of the many aspects of the Commons, inevitably in general terms. Part I deals with the history of the Commons as it relates to the buildings and to parliamentary rituals. Part II explains much of the daily routine and procedures in the Chamber. Part III discusses such well-known parliamentary occasions as Budget Day, while Part IV is concerned with the overall running of the Commons ranging from catering to press reporting. Finally, Part V offers a personal description of the MP's working week, concluding with a consideration of some of the questions that parliament now faces.

ACKNOWLEDGEMENTS

I would like to thank Rob Shepherd who has co-operated with me in so much of the research, but who has been spared responsibility for the views or style. I have received unstinted co-operation from so many officials of the House. In thanking the Clerk of the House I would like to thank them all. I am also indebted to the House of Commons librarian, Dr D. Menhennet, and his staff who provided both inspiration and practical assistance in tracing many of the events which feature in this book. I would also like to thank various Members of Parliament who have assisted me with their comments. Throughout I have received inestimable assistance from my wife in all stages of the preparation of this book.

The Houses of Parliament: plan of the principal floor

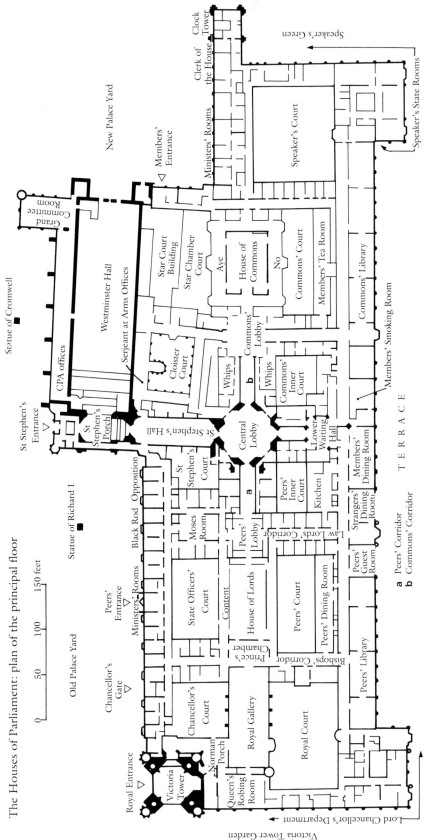

Royal Entrance

Victoria Tower

Queen's Robing Room

Norman Porch

Royal Gallery

Royal Court

Chancellor's Court

Prince's Chamber

State Officers' Court

House of Lords

Content

Peers' Court

Peers' Dining Room

Bishops' Corridor

Peers' Library

Chancellor's Gate

Peers' Entrance

Ministers' Rooms

Black Rod

Opposition

Moses Room

St Stephen's Court

St Stephen's Hall

Central Lobby

Peers' Inner Court

Kitchen

Peers' Lobby

Law Lords' Corridor

Strangers' Dining Room

Peers' Guest Room

Members' Dining Room

Peers' Corridor

Lower Waiting Hall

St Stephen's Entrance

St Stephen's Porch

CPA offices

Westminster Hall

Serjeant at Arms Offices

Cloister Court

Grand Committee Room

Star Court Building

Star Chamber Court

Whips

Aye

House of Commons

No

Commons' Lobby

Whips

Commons' Inner Court

Commons' Court

Members' Tea Room

Commons' Library

Members' Smoking Room

T E R R A C E

Members' Entrance

Ministers' Rooms

Clerk of the House

Clock Tower

Speaker's Court

Speaker's Green

Speaker's State Rooms

New Palace Yard

Statue of Cromwell

Statue of Richard I

Old Palace Yard

Chancellor's Gate

0 50 100 150 feet

Victoria Tower Garden

Lord Chancellor's Department

a Peers' Corridor
b Commons' Corridor

a

b

Press Gallery

H

O

Members' Gallery

Members' Gallery

Strangers' Gallery

Strangers' Gallery

S

C C C

D T D

M

GOVERNMENT

OPPOSITION

L L

X X

Bar of the House

SA

The Chamber of the House of Commons

S Mr Speaker

P Press Galleries

H *Hansard* Reporters

O Government Officials' Box
(advisers to Ministers)

C Clerks of the House

T Table of the House

D Despatch Boxes

X Cross Benches

M Mace

L Lines (over which Members may
not step when speaking from the
front benches)

SA Serjeant at Arms

PART I

Living with History

1 THE PALACE BY THE THAMES

In discussing the Palace of Westminster we must consider both the building and the wide-ranging activity it houses. Of course the work cannot be disentangled from the building. Working in an atmosphere of history does make one aware of continuity, and also aware that the present holds the future in trust. I am sure the college buildings helped my enjoyment of Cambridge. I used to stand and gaze at King's College Chapel with a sensation of respect; and I still do.

When I was elected to the House of Commons in 1961, as at university, I got a thrill and excitement from simply looking at my new place of work. After nearly thirty years of membership I still gaze up at Big Ben, or stand on the terrace contemplating the riverside prospect of the Commons, or look around the high-ceilinged Central Lobby and think how lucky I am. It is not necessarily a comfortable or efficient building in which to work, but if one has to work in a converted palace I will settle for Westminster.

The Palace of Westminster is redolent with history. The oldest part of the building is Westminster Hall. It lies to the left of the usual public access, the St Stephen's entrance. This magnificent building is an oasis of serenity. It has barely escaped the ravages of fire on two recent occasions. In 1834 the firemen saved Westminster Hall although most of the rest of the Palace was gutted. In 1941 the Commons chamber was destroyed by German bombs and only prompt action saved Westminster Hall from serious damage. It is a sad commentary on current times that Westminster Hall has also been the subject of a bomb attack. In June 1974 a bomb exploded in a building adjoining the north-west section of the Hall. Damage was done to this building and the Grand Committee Room but it has now been repaired, and the north-west section today provides a much-needed staff cafeteria.

The bomb outrages of recent years, however, do not compare with the devastation caused by the Irish Fenians. They were conducting a bombing campaign in order to promote the cause of Irish Independence. On Saturday 24 January 1885, they exploded a bomb in the Tower of London, and two at Westminster. PC Cole discovered a bomb in St Stephen's Crypt and carried it almost to St Stephen's Hall before discarding it because of the heat. It exploded, tore a huge gap in the concrete floor, blew out the great south window and injured PC Cole and another constable.

A second explosion quickly followed. Dynamite had been placed just

Winston Churchill: defiance amidst the ruins. The House of Commons was bombed in May 1941, but only the Chamber was destroyed.

inside the chamber near the 'Aye' lobby. The explosion almost completely wrecked the chamber, matching what the German bombers achieved nearly sixty years later. The government front and other benches and the Peers' Gallery were destroyed. The Members' lobby and post office were badly damaged. It being Saturday, there were many visitors in the House but, rushing to the scene of the first explosion, they had left the Commons chamber providentially deserted. The situation had been a whisker from hideous carnage and the bombers were never caught.

The walls of Westminster Hall were built in the reign of William Rufus (1087–1100) and incorporated part of the original palace built by King

Edward the Confessor. Rufus called it the New Hall to distinguish it from the Great Hall of King Edward's palace to the south. Today the names Old and New Palace Yard, describing the areas to the south and north of Westminster Hall, are thought to derive from the days of William Rufus.

Westminster Hall has witnessed major trials, the lying-in-state of monarchs, and proclamations. Many coronation feasts have taken place here. Oliver Cromwell took his oath here as Lord Protector in 1653. After the restoration of King Charles II in 1660, Cromwell's body was exhumed and his head was placed on a pole on the roof where it remained for more than twenty years. Posterity has made rather calmer judgements on the man and his achievements and Cromwell is now commemorated by an impressive statue outside the west wall of Westminster Hall overlooking Parliament Square.

Today Westminster Hall is used only occasionally, and then for ceremonial purposes. In 1953 Queen Elizabeth II gave a coronation feast, in 1959 President de Gaulle addressed Members of both Houses from this building, and in 1988 there was a glittering occasion to mark the tercentenary of the Glorious Revolution of 1688. The monarch received loyal addresses from the House of Commons and the House of Lords, whose members had gathered in the Hall. There were many representatives from Parliaments around the world whose development derives ultimately from the settlement of 1688. It was a glorious reminder that the most successful and enduring of revolutions can be bloodless.

For centuries the Palace of Westminster cradled history and housed the monarch, but it had little contact with the very early and embryonic Commons. Fire, which seems a feature in the history of Parliament, played a crucial role. In 1512, after a fire at Westminster Palace, Henry VIII gave up its use as a royal residence and moved to the nearby Whitehall Palace. In the following decades he made increasing use of the Commons, whose support he needed in his dispute with the Pope. Eventually the MPs were housed in St Stephen's Chapel in the Palace of Westminster. Today the chapel area is called St Stephen's Hall, and it runs from the St Stephen's entrance, used by the public and those queuing for gallery admittance, to the steps leading up to the Central Lobby. St Stephen's Chapel was used for worship by the monarch during the Middle Ages. Courtiers worshipped in the adjacent crypt which is still frequently used by MPs for services and christenings. Use of the chapel was forbidden by a statute of Edward VI in 1547 and it is claimed that the young King, under the influence of the Protector, Somerset, ensured that by 1550 it had become the permanent home of the House of Commons. Hitherto the Commons had sat, infrequently, in either the Chapter House or the Refectory of Westminster Abbey.

The present St Stephen's Hall is 28.9 metres long and 9.1 metres wide.

It closely resembles the old chapel, whose shape probably determined the seating arrangements which continue in the present Commons chamber. The benches face each other as in the choir of a church or cathedral. It was here that the Commons sat from 1547 until the great fire of 1834. Those were three tumultuous centuries of national and political history. Charles I came to this site in person in 1642 to order the arrest of the five members who had defied him. Parliament had passed a 'Grand Remonstrance' criticising the King's role and Charles believed the five members were the ringleaders of such defiance. In turn he was rebuffed by Speaker Lenthall who asserted the independence of the Commons and refused to co-operate with the monarch. In the early 1830s it was in St Stephen's Chapel that the Great Reform Bill was passed, thus launching Britain, albeit tentatively, down the slipway of universal franchise.

The statue of Falkland, Secretary of State to King Charles I in 1642, showing the spur broken by a suffragette in 1908.

Today the visitor proceeds through the security checks at St Stephen's entrance, up the stairs and along the hall towards the Central Lobby. He is probably unaware of treading on the spot that has seen even more parliamentary history than the present Commons debating chamber.

To remind the visitor of the past the walls are lined with the Westminster heroes of the seventeenth and eighteenth centuries. They include Clarendon, the historian and senior minister of Charles II; John Hampden, who died from wounds received when fighting in the Civil War for the parliamentary cause; John Selden, the great seventeenth-century lawyer; and Prime Ministers Walpole, Chatham and Pitt. There are also statues of Edmund Burke, the conservative champion of Parliament, and Charles James Fox, the eloquent and flamboyant radical who opposed William Pitt in the late eighteenth century. These are a collection of statesmen who will match anything the present Members' Lobby can produce. There is also a shred of contemporary history. The statue of Falkland, Secretary of State to King Charles I in 1642, still has a broken spur where a suffragette chained herself to it in 1908 during the campaign for women's suffrage.

As a visitor proceeds along the hall he may see brass stud marks in the floor which show exactly where the Speaker's chair and Commons table once stood. Two brass stud marks in the wall, about nine metres from the western end (furthest from Central Lobby) mark the position where a wall separated the old Lobby from the Chamber. In 1812, while passing through this lobby, the Prime Minister, Spencer Perceval, was shot dead by John Bellingham, a bankrupt who believed that government policies had caused the failure of his business.

Over the period that St Stephen's was used to house the Commons there were a number of building alterations. Sir Christopher Wren added galleries to the Chamber to accommodate 45 Scottish members in 1707, following the Act of Union. In 1800 some walls were cut away to enable the Chamber to be further extended and include the 100 additional members created by Irish union.

The great fire in 1834, which destroyed the chamber and most of the palace, resulted from the overheating of a boiler burning old tally sticks. These were the inland revenue forms of a bygone age. A stick would be notched to indicate that tax had been paid, then split. The tax man kept one half, and the taxpayer the other. Put alongside one another the notches matched, or tallied. This was proof of payment. However, the forerunners of the Inland Revenue were exceedingly reluctant ever to think a case was closed, and by all accounts kept the records for decades, if not generations. In 1834 they were having what Harold Wilson would have called a 'bonfire of controls'. The tally sticks were aged and highly combustible. The workmen wanted to go home, and fed the flames enthusiastically. The boiler blazed and the palace followed. There are many fine pictures in the

Saving Westminster Hall during the Great Fire of 16 October 1834. Painting by G. B. Campion.

Commons today showing the dramatic conflagration and the aftermath of charred ruins. I am sure the revenue has committed many follies, but none worse than this.

From the disaster and ashes, however, there emerged the imposing phoenix of our present House of Commons. In March 1835 a Commons Select Committee was appointed 'to consider and report on such plans as may be most fitting and convenient for the permanent accommodation of the Houses of Parliament'. The Committee decided that the architecture should be either Gothic or Elizabethan. There was a public competition for the design of the new buildings, won by Mr (later Sir) Charles Barry. He used the Gothic style of the Tudor period as being more in harmony with the few remaining old buildings which were to be preserved and blended with the new architecture. Barry was assisted by Augustus Welby Pugin, particularly in matters of detail, such as fittings and furniture. It was an inspired partnership.

In the process of rebuilding, the whole design was recast. The new chamber was built well away from the St Stephen's Chapel that had echoed

St Stephen's Chapel: View
from Speaker's Gallery
after the Fire, 1834.

with the oratory of Burke and Fox. I regret the breaking of that physical
link. The Palace of Westminster site was extended into the river by
reclaiming land and it now covers eight acres. The building was begun in
1840, largely completed by 1860 and finally finished in 1870. The river-
front length of the building is 265.8 metres and the roof line is 21.3 metres
high. There are 100 staircases, 35 lifts, nearly 5 kilometres of passageways,
1100 rooms and 11 open courtyards. Victoria Tower is 98.4 metres high,
the Clock Tower (Big Ben) 96.3 metres high, and Central Tower is 91.4
metres high. On any account it is an impressive building, although its

structure does not easily adapt to the requirements of contemporary parliamentary life.

Over the past decade or so there has been a great attempt to preserve and restore the Barry/Pugin heritage. After leaving the Commons in 1979, the late Sir Robert (Robin) Cooke, formerly Conservative MP for Bristol West, was appointed special adviser to the Secretary of State for the Environment, with special responsibility for the Palace of Westminster. He selflessly devoted the latter years of his too short life to seeing that the Pugin fittings were retrieved and restored. The Leader of the House's room in the Commons is handsomely furnished with Pugin panelling, desk, chairs and clock. For me there is a sombre magnificence about the palace of Barry and Pugin. It is an inspiration to work within its walls.

The building they created contained not only a new Commons but also a new House of Lords. The daily running of the Commons will be described later, so it will be helpful to set out here the broad administration of the Palace of Westminster. As a royal palace, control of the Houses of Parliament was originally vested in the Lord Great Chamberlain as the Queen's representative. In 1965 control of the Commons part of the Palace passed to the Speaker. This covered the northern part, nearest to Westminster Bridge, stretching down to St Stephen's entrance. Control of the Lords part of the Palace, the southern end towards Lambeth Bridge, passed to the Lord Chancellor. The Lord Great Chamberlain retains joint responsibility, with the Speaker and the Lord Chancellor, for the crypt and Westminster Hall.

It is natural enough to think of the Palace simply as a grand Victorian building, constructed with dignity and style. Nonetheless, it is a place to work in as well as look at. The Commons chamber, the terrace, the high-domed Central Lobby, Westminster Hall, all are relatively well known to the public. There is, however, another aspect of the Commons no less vital even if unsung. These are the key services for the working of Parliament.

The Commons could not operate without the post office. The Members have a counter just off the Members' Lobby: there is a post office for public use in the Central Lobby. The first Postmaster was appointed to the Palace of Westminster in 1871. There are sixteen collections a day when the House is sitting, from 6.30 a.m. until 11.00 p.m. There are additional collections at 1.00 a.m. and 3.00 a.m. if the House sits late or through the night. Within the palace itself there are 31 collection boxes, as well as arrangements for collecting mail from parliamentary buildings nearby. The Postmaster estimates that something like 20,000 items are posted daily from the palace when Parliament is sitting.

The House of Commons also has its own barber's shop which is open regularly and is well patronised. No one is quite sure when this amenity was introduced. It certainly existed in 1895 when responsibility for it was transferred from the Kitchen Committee to the Serjeant at Arms. As one might expect it is a traditional barber's shop such as is found in a London men's club. The Commons is a changing place and my money is on a unisex salon before the decade is out.

The House of Commons now has a medical room off the Lower Waiting Hall. This is a development since I have become an MP, and an extremely welcome one. The numbers working in the Palace of Westminster necessitate such a facility for minor ailments. St Thomas's Hospital, at the south side of Westminster Bridge, is on hand for the treatment of more serious accidents. Since 1978, Members have been able to enrol in a Medical Surveillance Scheme and discover through science what they knew intuitively, namely that they lead sedentary, over-indulged and thoroughly unhealthy lives. Mournfully we reflect whether the cure is worse than the disease.

If Guy Fawkes could return to the cellars to perform his mischief, he would discover the House of Commons rifle club and its range. The club was founded in 1916 and is used by members of the Commons and Lords and also by the staff of both Houses. Parliament seems to have a strong desire to put aside the histrionics of political drama and take up the serious business of competitive sport. The Lords and Commons together field a cricket team and a hockey team, have a motor club, and even stage a 'tug-of-war'. And still we need the medical room.

There is a small room located between the Smoking Room and the Dining Room, overlooking the Thames. Traditionally it has been used for chess, which seems to have been the only recreation for which our Victorian forebears made provision. A set of ivory chessmen was presented to the Commons by Arthur Walter, whose family was involved with *The Times* newspaper, commemorating the Westminster and Washington chess match of 1897. Chess is very much a minority pursuit at Westminster. There are no grandmasters, but Julius Silverman, former Labour MP for Birmingham Erdington, was an outstanding player.

The Palace of Westminster offers MPs nearly 5 kilometres of passage-ways and a hundred staircases. Yet some still need exercise. Sir James Spicer, Conservative MP for Dorset West, parachutist and fitness enthusiast, set up a gymnasium in the 1977–8 session. It is situated on the second floor of the Norman Shaw South Building. I have never been there. Among those who supported the venture was Christopher Jones, of the BBC's parliamentary staff and author of an excellent book on Parliament, *The Great Palace*. The gymnasium is independent with its own committee, and membership is also open to civil servants. It is professionally staffed and has a sauna and showers, but no swimming pool or jacuzzi.

The increasing workload of Parliament and the growth of MPs' staff has meant that the Barry accommodation has had to be supplemented by nearby buildings. These house MPs, their staff and also officers of the Commons. They include St Stephen's House, the two Norman Shaw buildings and accommodation at Abbey Gardens, Dean's Yard and Old Palace Yard. There are plans to use Cannon Row, and a major conversion is taking place in Bridge Street, where considerable accommodation is being built behind a carefully preserved street façade. Barry built a fine Gothic palace, but he could not have foreseen the time when 20,000 items of mail were despatched daily from Parliament, when MPs needed a growing support staff to handle the paper, and a gymnasium to add to their exertions.

I have no doubt there are radicals lurking and ready to pounce with suggestions that we reform ourselves utterly and decamp to Milton Keynes or Canary Wharf or, in the name of regional development, to Bootle. I am a Tory to my fingertips. I shall resist the gleaming new office with its gadgets, and any space-age complex of buildings. I stoutly maintain this view because I believe the very floors, walls and ceilings of the House of Commons tell us about its traditions and the sacrifices that have been made for British democracy.

The Crown is offered to William and Mary by Parliament in 1689: engraving after Northcote.

This feeling was particularly strong in 1965 when I attended an impress-ive ceremony in Westminster Hall marking the 700th anniversary of the summoning of Simon de Montfort's parliament at Lewes. It is more relevant, however, to trace the rise of Parliament from the sixteenth century onwards.

The Palace of Westminster illustrates how executive power was initially held in partnership with the crown. By the early eighteenth century that executive power had passed decisively to Parliament. It had been a long and sometimes bloody struggle. The monarchy yielded its authority with varying degrees of reluctance to a Parliament that Henry VIII had hoped would be useful but subordinate in his contest with the Pope. One mile-stone in that struggle was the Glorious Revolution in 1688, when William of Orange and Mary replaced James II. The latter had been suspected of wishing to expand royal power to the detriment of parliament. As a result, Parliament passed the Bill of Rights which, among other things, provided 'that the election of Members of Parliament should be free' and 'that the freedom of speech and debates or proceedings in Parliament ought not to be impeached or questioned in any court or place out of Parliament'.

An exhibition to mark the tercentenary of this occasion was held in June 1988. I was at the Banqueting House, Whitehall, for a moving opening ceremony. It gave Lord Hailsham, a superb parliamentarian with a feel for history, a chance to catalogue the achievements of our rebellious forebears. He dwelt eloquently upon their successes:

> What we are celebrating is actually the birth of modern Britain and its present Constitution. We are celebrating the birth of the twin doctrines of the Sovereignty of Parliament and the Rule of Law upon which all else largely depends. We are celebrating the financial control by Parliament of Government expenditure upon which the power of the Commons depends.

Within a couple of generations the King's government had passed irreversibly from the Court to the Commons. The implications of this are profound for our Parliament and its practices. It means that the executive actually sits in the legislature. There is no separation of powers as in the United States.

The executive sitting in Parliament needs two conditions in order to exercise power. First it must have a majority in Parliament. Secondly it must have an organisation to make the majority effective. There is little similarity between the tightly controlled Cabinet of modern times and the loose grouping of Ministers who sat alongside Robert Walpole in 1721. Walpole, however, is regarded as our first Prime Minister. His associates in administration provided the embryo of modern government.

Robert Walpole, the first Prime Minister, on the left, with Speaker Onslow. Copied from the painting by William Hogarth and Sir James Thornhill.

The early attempts to provide dependable support often rested on loyalties bought with cash. We have moved on from the days of purchasing support which was widely used in the eighteenth century by Henry Pelham, Prime Minister between 1743 and 1754. Today the government Chief Whip, still charmingly called the patronage secretary, has a range of other inducements to secure support for the government. But although much has changed the essentials remain. The government takes collective decisions under the authority of the Prime Minister. It sits within the parliament. It secures the passage of its measures and its general support from group loyalties. That is our parliamentary inheritance, described by the prints and paintings on the walls of the palace.

There is a second important element in the development of our Parliament. It concerns not only the institutions, but also the parliamentarians who came to use them. They inevitably reflected the people entitled to send their fellow-citizens to Westminster. The franchise, or right to vote, was originally narrow and heavily tilted towards the landed and propertied classes. The Reform Bill of 1832, carried at a crucial stage by a majority of one, barely extended the franchise beyond the upper and middle classes. Even so, a pattern had been established for the extension of the voting public. This rested upon defined principles of age, sex and wealth. An important related principle was the right to vote in private, which was secured by the passage of the Ballot Act, 1873.

In the century that followed the electorate was steadily expanded. Landmarks were reached when women over 30 first gained the vote in 1918 and in 1928 received the franchise at 21, the same age as for men. The general voting age was lowered to eighteen in 1969. The first MP to be elected on the younger voting age was Tom King, Conservative victor of the Bridgwater by-election. He was introduced into the House on 17 March 1970. I had a personal interest in the occasion. I was born in Bridgwater. The local grammar school (now a comprehensive) had fired me with a love of history. My early political loyalties were tested as an under-age member of the Bridgwater Young Conservatives.

Those who had fought for the vote had transformed Parliament. The expansion of the franchise over the last hundred years has placed new pressures upon politics and government. The protective role of the state was steadily expanded, and a social role was added to the requirements of foreign affairs and defence. Within the Commons the statues of Lloyd George and Joseph Chamberlain remind us of their part. The overall size of the Cabinet, just above twenty members, has not altered much since the turn of the century, but the number of non-Cabinet ministers has practically doubled to the present level of more than 80. The 'payroll vote', which includes all Ministers and their parliamentary private secretaries, has increased. Functions have changed. The present cabinet contains Secretaries of State for Social Security, Health, Transport, Energy, Employment and Wales which have no counterpart before 1914. The annual budget in 1913 was 12.1 per cent of the gross domestic product; in 1987–8 it was 40.5 per cent.

Practically all our Commons procedures today have their roots in the past. Nonetheless they have been adapted to serve the present. Parliament is continually responding to popular economic and social pressures, and it is impossible to distinguish between the institutions and the new needs they serve. MPs are living with history. That history means that Parliament has an obligation to the past as well as trusteeship for the future. The challenge remains, however, to maintain the House of Commons as a workshop. It must never become a museum.

2 THE SPEAKER'S PROCESSION AND PRAYERS

I still get pleasure in watching the Speaker's Procession. It is led by the Commons Bar doorkeeper who is dressed in knee-breeches and silk stockings and white gloves. As a Crown appointee, he also wears a royal messenger's badge dating from 1755. He is followed by the Serjeant at Arms, carrying the mace. Then follows the Speaker who, in turn, is followed by his train-bearer, his chaplain and his secretary.

The procession, which takes place daily while Parliament is in session, starts shortly after 2.25 p.m. (9.25 a.m. on Fridays) from the Speaker's house – this is within the palace, near Westminster Bridge – and proceeds sedately to the Chamber of the House of Commons, passing through the Central Lobby. It is here that MPs watch the procession with their guests. Members of the public who have tickets to watch Question Time from the public gallery may also be admitted early enough to see the procession. The noise of conversation has been stilled. A path has been cleared for the procession. The advancing footsteps echo, almost like a slow march. The policeman's cry goes up: 'Speaker'; and respect is enjoined by his stentorian cry, 'Hats off, strangers'. I have never seen a man remain 'covered', to use the parliamentary idiom.

Thus begins the parliamentary day. The small group, which moves with such grave deliberation from Speaker's House to the chamber, embodies pageantry and tradition. There is no early evidence for a procession, though the mace even in 1558 had been for centuries the symbol of the House's authority and carried by the Serjeant. By today's fashion the Speaker is dressed in almost theatrical garb. He has a black cloth court suit with linen bands over which he wears a black silk robe and train. His knee-breeches are matched by buckled shoes, and he sports a full-bottomed wig. In fact this dress was worn generally in the Commons until the eighteenth century. It is the MPs whose dress has changed. Although conventions of formal business dress are generally observed, today some men do not even wear ties. It is for the reader to judge whether this constitutes sartorial progress. The pageantry is completed by the Serjeant at Arms wearing black cloth court dress with a sword.

The Serjeant at Arms is an historic post. In the thirteenth century a body of Serjeants was formed to provide a bodyguard for the monarch. The Commons petitioned the Crown for their own Serjeant at Arms and Nicholas Maudit was appointed to the post in 1415. Henry VIII later took away the power of selection from the Commons and for centuries the

Serjeant was a Crown appointment. Disraeli, when Prime Minister, observed in 1875 that the appointment of Serjeant 'is entirely in the gift of Her Majesty'. Since I became an MP in 1961 this particular wheel has turned full circle. In 1962 Harold Macmillan, then Prime Minister, told the Commons that the Sovereign was willing to consult with the Speaker to ensure that future Serjeants had the approval of the House.

The duties of the Serjeant at Arms are described in the House of Commons *Manual of Proceedings in the Public Business*. It states that 'at the time of every Parliament' he is 'to attend upon the Speaker of the House of Commons; but after his appointment he is the servant of the House and may be removed for misconduct'.

Over the centuries the Serjeant has been responsible for carrying out the orders of the House, including making arrests. In 1543 the Serjeant arrested City dignitaries who had ordered the detention of an MP for debt. 'Ferrers' case' established the House's power of arrest without a warrant.

Today the Serjeant's duties are rather more modest. He must ensure the attendance of those who have been summoned to appear before the Commons, for whatever reason. In 1957, for example, John Junor was brought by him to the entrance (the bar) of the Commons chamber. There Junor duly apologised for an article in the *Sunday Express*, of which he was editor, which appeared to be in contempt of the House in criticising petrol allowances given to constituency political parties: this was during the Suez crisis, when petrol rationing was in force. More recently, in 1982, a summons was issued for the leader of the National Union of Mineworkers, Arthur Scargill, to appear before the (Departmental) Select Committee on Energy.

The Serjeant at Arms, usually a retired officer of the armed forces, is also responsible for keeping order within the precincts of the Commons, and so preventing public disturbances. He controls the doorkeepers and some other Commons staff. Thus he now performs a major role in the administration of the Commons, but he still bears his sword to remind us of a rowdier age.

In the Speaker's Procession the Serjeant carries the mace, an object of great symbolic significance, indicating the authority delegated by the Sovereign to the Commons. It features in all major ceremonies, and the symbolism persists in the business of the House. When the Commons conducts general business the mace rests on the table in front of the Speaker. When the House goes into Committee the mace is transferred to two supports below the table. This somewhat puzzling practice has an historical explanation. Centuries ago the House would go into Committee as a means of discussing matters in private, without the Speaker in the chair.

At first the mace was provided by the Serjeant at Arms himself. In 1649

Those reprimanded by the Speaker are required to stand at the Bar of the House. The Bar telescopes into the bench ends. Drawing from the Illustrated London News, *1874.*

the Commons ordered a mace at its own expense, which was produced by Thomas Maundy of London at the cost of £146 11s. 9d. The present mace which dates from 1660 has been in use since 1819. It is thought to have been made up from two maces, and that the orb and cross were added some 25 years later. It measures 1.486 metres in length and is of silver gilt. It is not hallmarked, and bears no inscription, date or maker's mark. Despite this anonymity the mace, through its symbolic daily ritual, is a visible expression of the authority of the Commons. Disrespect for the mace implies contempt for the House. Even so there have been some lapses in parliamentary reverence.

John Beckett, Michael Heseltine and Ron Brown are three MPs in this century who have laid hands on the mace. That apart, they have little in common, by way of either temperament or politics. John Beckett was a youthful Labour MP in 1930, destined to join the British Union of Fascists four years later. He was opposition teller in a division seeking to suspend his fellow Labour MP, Fenner Brockway, for alleged misbehaviour. Beckett stood in front of the table, inches from the mace, for the declaration of the division, and so was well placed for his bold gesture. His action was recorded in Hansard:

> Mr Beckett: Mr Speaker it is a damned disgrace.
> The Hon. Member then seized the mace, and proceeded with it to the Bar; where he was stopped by the Serjeant at Arms who took the mace and replaced it upon the table.

Beckett, having 'seized the mace', was apparently astonished by its comparative lightness – a mere sixteen pounds. He had watched the Serjeant's measured progress in the Speaker's procession, seemingly weighed down by the physical and constitutional burden of this five-foot symbol. It now turned out to be as hollow as the proceedings against which he was protesting. He subsequently explained that he had no clear plan but was prepared to put the mace in a 'porcelain receptacle' in the members' lavatories. Happily the mace was rescued from such a fate and Beckett from such folly.

Michael Heseltine and Ron Brown have both been involved in 'mace incidents' during my Commons lifetime, although I did not witness either occasion. Heseltine's performance occurred after a highly charged debate concerning the nationalisation of the aircraft and ship-building industries in May 1976. Having led the Conservative opposition to the legislation with great vigour, he was angered by the Labour government's suspension of certain Standing Orders to enable the bill to proceed. I had voted but, with a greater sense of duty than theatre, I had returned to my room to sign letters. I missed a show. There was pandemonium and recrimination about the narrow vote. A scratch male voice choir from the Labour benches rendered 'The Red Flag', during which Michael Heseltine held aloft the mace. It was the kind of night best soonest forgotten. Heseltine made a handsome apology next morning and would have done so that evening if procedures had permitted.

In April 1988 Ron Brown, Labour member for Edinburgh Leith, threw the mace on the ground at the end of a 30-minute adjournment debate on supplementary benefit appeals, initiated by another Member, during which he had been present, but had taken no part. As the House adjourned, he left his place, reaching the table before the Serjeant at Arms, raised the mace above his head and dropped it. There must have been an element of calculation, as he normally speaks some distance from the table. He damaged the mace and was suspended for twenty days as well as being held responsible for its repairs.

These incidents demonstrate that the Commons does feel strongly about the symbol of its authority. Whether it feels so strongly about the reality of its authority is another matter.

The chaplain's place in the Speaker's Procession indicates the continuing status of the Church of England in Commons affairs. Sixteenth-century records indicate that prayers, and also a litany, opened the day's sitting. It is said, indeed, that the earliest parliamentary prayer dates from the very end of the fourteenth century. In 1660 the first Speaker's Chaplain was appointed, and the practice has been regularly followed since then. The chaplain is an Anglican, irrespective of the Speaker's own denomination. Speakers Thomas and King were both active Methodists, but they appear to have encountered no problems with this arrangement.

By tradition the Speaker also nominates his chaplain as Rector of St Margaret's Church, Westminster, just opposite the Commons. The Queen makes the appointment. St Margaret's is the Commons' own church, to which MPs accompanied Winston Churchill for a service of thanksgiving after the surrender of Germany in May 1945.

The chaplain opens the daily proceedings of the House, at 2.30 p.m. Monday to Thursday and 9.30 a.m. on Friday, with traditional prayers. I have listened to their cadences over many years and rejoice that they have not yet been modernised by the enthusiasts for Prayer Book reform.

Members attending prayers frequently book their seats by means of a ticket which they can obtain from a member of the staff of the Serjeant at Arms on duty at the door of the Chamber. This is not merely on account of devotion: it enables a member to reserve a seat which is well placed for the debate that will follow prayers. The numbers attending prayers are modest, and certainly well below the capacity of the chamber. Prayers are private and the public and press galleries are open only after prayers have been concluded.

This brief ceremony was shattered on 11 January 1988 when John Hughes, Labour MP for Coventry North East, made a protest concerning the level of public funds for the National Health Service. I was attending prayers and saw the event at first hand. I could find no one who recalled prayers ever being disrupted in this way. The demonstration continued, and the Speaker suspended the sitting to consult his advisers. A vote was taken to suspend John Hughes (which was carried by 152 to 23) and a delayed prayers got under way. The immediate casualty was Question Time which lost half-an-hour as a consequence. The incident, a miserable one in my view, merely encouraged those who argued that parliamentary manners are sharply in decline. I hope not.

Members entering the chamber, for prayers or on any other occasion, have a largely unused and generally unknown benefit in kind. The two doorkeepers flanking the entrance behind the Speaker's chair keep a supply of snuff, paid for from public funds and kept in a box made from fragments of oak which were rescued from the chamber after the German bombing. A plate on the box bears the names of all the head doorkeepers since 1943.

One plate has already been filled up and is now fixed to the doorkeeper's chair at the entrance to the chamber.

Very few MPs currently make use of this 'perk'. No politician has yet been able to do for snuff what Harold Wilson did for the pipe, although it is rumoured that the flamboyant Conservative MP and lawyer Sir Nicholas Fairbairn is trying hard.

The doorkeepers are essential to the smooth running of the Commons. They wear evening dress with black waistcoats and badges of royal messengers. Answering to the Serjeant at Arms, they are responsible for circulating messages around the House, manning division lobby doors, and ringing the division bells. They are universally regarded as great sources of wisdom. Their knowledge of the likely progress of business is widely considered to match even that of the Whips' Office.

3 MR SPEAKER – OFFICE AND MAN

The first day of a new parliament has an excitement all its own. The host of fresh faces makes clear the changes brought about by the recent General Election. So it was on 27 October 1964: following the Labour victory there was both a new House and a change of government. From my recently acquired seat on an opposition bench I looked across at the sea of new faces. One was novel and yet familiar. I realised it belonged to Sir Harry Hylton-Foster, Speaker in the last parliament. Shorn of his wig and trappings he was physically transformed.

Although a Tory, he was now lurking amongst the Labour MPs awaiting his re-appointment as Speaker. Some thought a Labour government would confirm its victory by electing the first Labour Speaker, but wiser counsel prevailed. Labour decided to continue with Sir Harry. The Clerk of the House took charge of affairs. Sir Harry's name was proposed and his praises sung. The vote was acclaimed. I then saw, for the first time, the ceremony of 'dragging the Speaker to the chair'.

Centuries ago the Speakership was an invidious task. It often meant championing the role of the Commons against the monarchy, with imprisonment or even execution as a possible consequence. Such a thankless burden found few willing takers, and the MP selected was often dragged unwillingly to his post. In 1964 only gentle persuasion was needed; but it was a symbolic reminder of the past.

Tradition requires that one of those assisting the Speaker to the chair should be 'father' of the House. This post falls to the MP with the longest unbroken service in the Commons. An MP loses his seniority even if he is absent from the House for only a short time. Churchill, for all his many years in the Commons between 1900 and 1964, became 'father' of the House only in 1959, as he had been defeated and absent from the Commons in the 1930s. I watched Hylton-Foster being escorted to the chair by Arthur Henderson, a veteran Labour MP, and Sir Douglas Glover, Conservative MP for Ormskirk. Today the election of a new Speaker would be presided over by the current 'father', Sir Bernard Braine, a member of the Commons continuously since 1950.

The appointment of a Speaker is a timely reminder of the history of the post, the functions it fulfils, and the personalities who have enriched the office.

Some kind of presiding officer probably existed from the earliest times. From the Tudor period onwards the Speaker had an unenviable but crucial

role in serving both Commons and monarch. Sir Edward Coke, at the
close of the sixteenth century, earned a great reputation in this role. Half
a century later it was clear that the Speaker's loyalties lay increasingly with
the Commons rather than the Crown. The most striking example of this
was when Charles I sought to arrest and impeach the five MPs and Speaker
Lenthall, required to produce the missing members, retorted: 'May it
please Your Majesty, I have neither eyes to see, nor tongue to speak in this
place, but as the House is pleased to direct me, whose servant I am here.'

The views of Speaker Lenthall have been commended by successive
generations of MPs who wish to assert that the Speaker is the protector of

Commons rights, particularly when they clash with the government – the successor to the monarchy. Tony Benn prayed in aid Speaker Lenthall recently. This was during discussion of the restriction of access to certain Commons facilities, on grounds of security, to a research assistant employed by Jeremy Corbyn, the radical Labour MP for Islington North. I will not here argue the merits of that particular case; but that there is a lingering reverence for Lenthall is obvious.

Over the last century and a half Speakers have established for themselves a powerful tradition of impartiality and detachment from party affiliation. In the 1880s the disruptive tactics of the Irish Nationalists made more necessary the effective use of the Speaker's powers. There was also a growing amount of government business, which required some orderly control of the Commons. The adjudication of disputes with the Chair, and some way of bringing business to a conclusion, became matters of central concern. Around this time the Speaker acquired the power to name a Member for serious misbehaviour, leading to his suspension by the House. The power to conclude a debate (closure) and the power to predetermine the time taken on legislation (guillotine) were written into the Commons rules. The modern powers of the Speaker to maintain order and to give effect to the rules for closing a debate were established by the turn of the century.

W. LENTHAL.   Given By His Defcendent John Lenthal Efq. 1803.

Lenthall was Parliament's champion and Speaker from 1640 to 1660. Painting by Henry Paert.

The Speaker, proposed by a senior MP, is elected by the Commons. Contested Speakerships, although not unknown, are rare, and there has been concern about the extent to which the Commons have a real choice in the matter. Many MPs fear it is a 'carve up', with only senior MPs having a voice. Secondly, there has been concern about whether a Speaker should be drawn from among ex-Ministers, or whether he should come from the back-benches. Thirdly, there has been an undercurrent of feeling about whether the Speakership should follow the political colour of the party in office.

The concern about the constitution and procedures for the election of the Speaker was demonstrated with great effect in January 1971. On that occasion the choice of the party leaderships lay between two distinguished former Conservative Ministers, John Boyd-Carpenter and Selwyn Lloyd. The candidature of Selwyn Lloyd was preferred, and he was presented for election. John Pardoe, Liberal MP for North Cornwall, expressed 'a back-bencher's dissatisfaction with the way this election had been handled'. He was trumped by Robin Maxwell-Hyslop, a back-bench Tory expert on procedure. He argued for back-benchers' rights and nominated a senior Labour MP, Geoffrey de Freitas, as Speaker. De Freitas had no warning of this unsought accolade. His demeanour registered both bewilderment and horror. Here was a candidate who would again have to be dragged to the chair. Happily he was spared. Selwyn Lloyd was elected by 294 votes to 55. He proved an excellent Speaker and a good friend to back-benchers. Even so, the back-bench revolt yielded a harvest. The Select Committee on Procedure reviewed the means whereby Speakers were elected; and since that date there has been wider and more effective, albeit informal, consultation between the party leaderships and the back-benches. That is certainly true of the present Speaker, Jack Weatherill, who came to the office having been a senior Whip. He has been outstanding in his resolve to put the Speakership above the politics of the front benches and to preserve the chamber as the focal point of debate.

In past years the Chairman of Ways and Means (Deputy Speaker) frequently succeeded to the Speakership. Recently this has not been the case. Since I have been an MP there have been five Speakers, all save one, Mr Speaker King, having previously held government office. The Speakership has not suffered.

Finally, there has been an undercurrent of feeling about whether the Speaker should be chosen from the majority party. There are no fixed traditions about this. Speaker Clifton Brown, a Conservative, thought the Labour landslide in 1945 would lead to his departure, but he was renewed in office. It was not until 1965 that a Labour Speaker was elected for the first time. It was an historic moment when this occurred. I recall Dr Horace King's simple but moving speech of acceptance, which included the following words:

> I now sever myself completely from all party politics. This is no light matter. No man easily breaks with the political faith which has given the whole of his life purpose and meaning except for the even greater faith that he has in political freedom itself ... My own loyalty henceforth must be to no party, but to Parliament itself ... remember that we are here not because of some merit on our part ... but because free men and free women ... have faith in our free Parliamentary way of life.

Those words retain their vitality and I suspect the Speaker will continue to be chosen without much regard to party affiliation.

The Speaker has key responsibilities in representing the Commons to the outside world. He ranks among commoners after only the Prime Minister and Lord President of the Council in precedence. Inside the Commons he now has the overriding responsibility of maintaining order and interpreting the rules (Standing Orders) of the Commons. This is an immensely difficult task to discharge. The House of Commons is a forum of controversy, where ideas and ambitions are pitted against each other. It is the function of the Speaker, with the aid of Standing Orders, to ensure that the combat proceeds within recognised terms. In particular the Speaker has a responsibility towards minorities, and this does not mean just the main opposition party. Parties often have minorities of their own, whose voices must be heard as well as those of the mainstream party.

The demand for speeches far exceeds the time available. The Speaker keeps a speech book recording the length of every speech made. No member, nursing uncalled star quality speeches, will believe justice has been done, but he would be churlish to deny that it has been attempted. In particular the Speaker must use his own discretion in deciding when to grant urgently requested questions and debates. In these circumstances he must be totally independent of the executive.

As a former Leader of the House I can vouch for the great care the Speaker takes in keeping in touch with the party managers (known as the 'usual channels'). In this he is assisted by the Commons' own administrative corps, the clerks. There are around 60 clerks who are able to advise on all aspects of parliamentary work. These daily behind-the-scenes consultations concern the conduct of business and are at the heart of our democracy. They ensure that the formal political combat is conducted upon an agreed or mutually understood basis.

The Speaker, despite his close involvement with Westminster politics, remains a lonely figure. He cannot be involved in any activities of his political party. He does not even seek the social companionship of members in the dining-room or bars. Speaker King experimented with occasional visits to the dining-room: the innovation did not last. Convention rules that if he stands for parliamentary re-election he must be described as 'Speaker' and not bear a party ticket, although candidates from some opposing parties usually run against him. The remoteness is emphasised by the existence of the Speaker's house, within the Palace, but apart from the Commons. It is here, and on his own ground, that the Speaker is able to entertain and share his problems with those who create them.

I have visited Speaker's House a number of times. The purpose of these visits has evolved with my own changing political fortunes. The first

The assassination by John Bellingham of Spencer Perceval, Prime Minister from 1809 to 1812.

occasion was when Speaker Selwyn Lloyd tried to assuage my resentment that I was being insufficiently called for debate in the early 1970s. It was a classic interview. I was disarmed by reminiscence, worldliness and sherry. As I left he pointed out one of the treasures of his house, the diminutive despatch box that Spencer Perceval carried on the day he was assassinated in the Palace of Westminster, 11 May 1812. He is the only British Prime Minister to have met such a fate. His despatch box not only recalls his untimely death; it is a striking reminder of how few papers burdened office at the outset of the nineteenth century.

No mention of Speaker's House is complete without reference to the huge oil paintings of past Speakers which dominate the walls and silently speak their message of past conflicts, not least those of a hundred years ago when the turbulence of the Irish compelled the Commons to adopt new rules.

Since 1966 the regular showing on television of State Openings of Parliament has made the Speaker a public figure. The magnificent wig and robes and breeches have underlined the ceremonial authority that he symbolises. The Speaker represents the Commons on great occasions, never more memorably than at the wedding of HRH the Prince of Wales and Lady Diana Spencer at St Paul's Cathedral on 29 July 1981. Speaker George Thomas was asked to read the lesson. Those listening all over the world were enthralled by his rich and melodious Welsh accent which declaimed the great nuptial lesson from Corinthians with what *The Times* called 'Welsh lilt and melodrama'. MPs had heard those tones put to sharper use, for Speaker Thomas would brook no insubordination in the Commons.

4 A VIEW FROM THE GALLERY

The world's window on Westminster comes from the galleries that surround and overlook the chamber of the House of Commons. They were a prominent feature of the House built after the fire of 1834 and were given greater significance when the chamber was rebuilt after the wartime bombing. While the dimensions of the chamber remained the same, the galleries were extended to provide an extra 171 seats for reporters and members of the public. As a result of this enlargement there are now 929 seats in all, both in the Chamber itself and in the galleries above; 427 of these are reserved for MPs (in the Chamber and the side galleries), and in the galleries there are 326 seats for Strangers, 161 for press reporters and 15 for officials. 'Strangers' is a rather quaint designation – widely used in the Commons – meaning members of the public, distinguished guests such as ambassadors, and journalists.

The Strangers' Gallery is at the opposite end to the Speaker's chair. It provides an excellent view of the Commons, although the gallery is steeply terraced. The seating consists of benches, with little leg-room. In theatrical terms it is, alas, very much like being in 'the gods' rather than the front row of the circle. The Commons has to provide exceptionally good drama to hold its public once Questions are over.

The side galleries nearest the Strangers' Gallery are reserved for 'Distinguished Visitors' such as ambassadors attending a foreign affairs debate. Most MPs glance occasionally at the public gallery, if only as a distraction from the daily toil. I did so one day, and the years rolled away. There was the American child star of my youth Shirley Temple, now primly seated as a distinguished stranger and diplomat, Mrs Shirley Temple Black.

The peers sit in a gallery consisting of two rows, each with twelve seats, facing the Speaker. They provide a steady audience, particularly on the greater parliamentary occasions. They are mostly Life Peers, having previously served in the Commons. I have no doubt they look down upon our thin performance and recollect their own glorious Commons vintage of the 1950s and 1960s.

The Press Gallery faces the Strangers' Gallery at the opposite end of the chamber. There is a continual flow of reporters, columnists and sketch-writers in and out of the Press Gallery. This general air of activity, albeit informal, lasts until the approach of copy deadlines. The gallery is often deserted from 7 p.m. onwards, but can return to life if there is a late evening vote. The Hansard reporters, who officially record parliamentary

'*They say one of the Lady members got in early and re-arranged the furniture.*'
Cartoon by Lee in the Evening News, *21 October 1937.*

debates, sit at the very front of the Press Gallery, directly above the Speaker's chair. They work in very short shifts, so there is a regular flow of reporters as they alternate between taking their notes and writing up the daily report.

Finally, there are the galleries for MPs on either side of the House. They contain 79 seats for MPs and 12 for officers of the House. MPs may use them at will, and are not expected to sit on the same side as they would in the chamber. On great occasions, such as the Budget, these galleries are

The Ladies' Gallery, 1908: from the Illustrated London News.

packed. I have often used the gallery to watch Members on my own side and note their reaction to the debate.

Tickets for seats in the Strangers' Gallery can be obtained from one's MP, but as each Member is allowed only two tickets approximately every three weeks on a strict rota basis, there is only a modest chance of an MP's being able to satisfy every request. The alternative is simply to turn up at Westminster in the hope of securing a seat in the Strangers' Gallery. Demand far outstrips the accommodation of 326 places, particularly in the summer when so many tourists are visiting London. It may be necessary to queue for an hour or more, especially for the early business of the House. On the other hand it is often possible to walk straight in to the Strangers' Gallery late in the evening, allowing the visitor to view the chamber, although the business will often be technical with only a handful of MPs present.

The great general interest in Westminster is also demonstrated by the large demand for tours of the Palace. When Parliament is sitting, the public can be shown around on the four mornings before the Commons and the Lords begin their daily sitting after lunch. On Fridays tours take place after the House rises at 3.00 until 5.30 p.m. It is also possible to go round on certain days during the recess. People should write to their MPs in order to see if an arranged tour is possible. A limited number of tours is

allowed each day and these tours are generally conducted by guides. The
maximum number allowed in each group is sixteen. The guides follow
a 'line of route' approved by the House of Commons Services Select
Committee, which includes the chambers of both the Lords and the
Commons as well as the lobbies and Westminster Hall. Demand for tours
of the palace is particularly heavy during the summer; they constitute a
superb introduction to the traditions and practices of Westminster and an
education in constitutional history. It is possible to visit the crypt, with its
superb medieval lierne vaulting and fine examples of High Victorian
decoration dating from Barry's rebuilding, but only when accompanied
by a Member and in a party of not more than six.

The galleries have seen occasional dramatic incidents when demonstrators have infiltrated the general public despite the vigilance of the
Commons attendants. These incidents are usually short-lived and quickly
forgotten. There have been the echoing words of a protester as he or she
is bundled away, and sometimes a few pamphlets are scattered over the
gallery rail into the chamber.

Three incidents which I witnessed have remained keenly in my mind.
The most unpleasant took place on 23 July 1970. Anthony Barber, later
Lord Barber, had just started making a ministerial statement on the Euro-
pean Community to an attentive House. Suddenly there was a shouted

*'May I draw the attention of
the House to the deplorable lack
of public interest in our
deliberations . . .' Cartoon by
Vicky in the* Evening
Standard, *6 November 1961.*

protest about policy in Northern Ireland from the gallery. A missile was thrown, and a haze of CS gas quickly developed. Tom Swain, a stalwart ex-miner and Labour MP, vainly tried to stamp upon the gas cartridge. The seconds seemed like days. What else would follow? Would there be an explosion as well as gas? The chamber emptied, some MPs in tears, many spluttering. The streets of Londonderry had come to the inner halls of Westminster. Hansard, prosaic as ever, described the incident as '(Interruption)', and records that the Speaker suspended the House for 25 minutes. The acrid stench of CS gas lingered for some hours. Two men were later charged with firearms offences.

On 6 July 1978 another gallery incident occurred, noteworthy if less sinister. On this occasion Hansard reveals the drama rather better. Tam Dalyell, Labour MP, was speaking on his then favourite topic, Scottish devolution. He was asked to resume his seat by the Speaker. Tam, ever courteous, replied: 'I cannot sit down as I should when you rise, Mr Speaker, because the bench has been soiled by some of the offensive matter that has just been thrown from the Public Gallery.'

The Speaker observed, 'Then perhaps the Hon. Gentleman will sit down a little further along. I am asking unusually for one of the attendants to be allowed into the Chamber while we are sitting to clear up the mess on the floor as well as some of the benches. I am all right here, but I was very anxious for the Hon. Member for Bolsover [Mr Skinner]. He was only just missed.' It was a day to remember. Gallery protesters, including the daughter of the former Maltese Prime Minister Dom Mintoff, had thrown into the chamber bags of manure and straw. The method of the protest rather than its purpose is still remembered. Tam Dalyell and Dennis Skinner survived, and have both flourished.

The third incident reminded me, and many others, that the MPs' galleries are within the chamber and MPs may use them to address their colleagues. In November 1981 James Prior, then Northern Ireland Secretary, made a statement following the tragic assassination of the Revd Robert Bradford, a Unionist MP who had been murdered while working in his constituency. Feelings ran high. In particular Ian Paisley and his two fellow Democratic Unionist MPs felt that security was ineffectual. The Prior statement was interrupted by a chorus of protest by the three MPs in the Members' Gallery. In the chamber we craned our necks and looked up at the trio whose protests reverberated above. Meanwhile Christopher Moncrieff, a Press Association journalist sitting in the adjacent gallery, resourcefully tried to get his scoop. He leaned across the barrier separating the Press Gallery from the Members' Gallery to get his story from Ian Paisley. This evoked further shocked cries of 'Order'. During these exchanges the Serjeant at Arms left the chamber and entered the gallery. The arm of the law was lengthening.

The whole blend of comedy and tragedy, for it was an unhappy occasion, was ended when the Speaker pronounced the three MPs 'guilty of grossly disorderly conduct and of ignoring the authority of the Chair'. They were suspended for five sitting days. Christopher Moncrieff atoned for his enterprise with a letter of apology to the Speaker. Meanwhile his precipitate departure from the Commons had deprived Ian Paisley of his normal security protection. He was nonetheless given a lift from the Palace of Westminster to Heathrow airport in a chauffeur-driven Rolls-Royce. The luck of the Irish?

PART II

The Commons
at Work

5 QUESTION TIME

Prayers over, the day's proceedings begin. On the government front bench sits a Cabinet Minister flanked by his team of junior Ministers. They exchange the occasional word and leaf through their briefing material in the official red-covered ring-folders. Facing them across the Commons table, on the opposition front bench, are their counterparts the 'shadow' Ministers.

The modest number of MPs who have attended prayers are now joined by others who have gathered beyond the closed doors at the end of the Chamber, their level of conversation earning the occasional request for silence from House officials. Half-a-dozen civil servants who have been waiting outside the Chamber behind the Speaker's chair move swiftly to their seats in the official box on the government side of the House. The press and public begin to fill the galleries high above the chamber.

The Commons is about to begin Question Time. This is arguably one of its best-known activities, since it occupies prime time, is widely reported in the press and often makes the early evening radio and television news bulletins. Its somewhat complex purpose is not generally well understood. Some people even believe the main purpose is to elicit information. That is not the case. As with most activities in the Commons we can best understand the present by studying the past.

The precise origins of Question Time are lost in the mists of history. The first recorded parliamentary question was asked in the Lords, prompted by the great financial scandal known as the South Sea Bubble. On 9 February 1721, Earl Cowper questioned the rumour that the chief cashier of the South Sea Company, Robert Knight, had fled the country and been arrested in Brussels. The then Secretary of State, the Earl of Sunderland, gave a factual reply, little realising the convention he was founding.

Questions were long regarded as an exception to the rules of debate. It was not until 1783 that Speaker Cornwall delivered the first recorded ruling on questions in the Commons. He decided that any MP had a right to put a question to a Minister. He also added that the Minister had a right either to answer or not to answer, as he thought proper. All subsequent Speakers have steadfastly refused to be drawn on the way Ministers answer, or avoid answering, questions. The usual practice for a dissatisfied MP is to inform the Speaker that 'in view of the unsatisfactory answer I will seek to raise the matter on the adjournment' – that is, to have it debated at some future date. The point is made, but the threat rarely becomes reality.

The practice of giving Ministers advance notice of questions began in 1833. MPs' questions at first appeared on the daily agenda, or Order Paper, among the motions for debate. They were only listed under a separate heading from 1869.

Questions were traditionally answered before the start of the day's main public business. In 1847 only 129 questions were tabled throughout the entire parliamentary session, an average of one per day. This number increased, particularly after 1880. Then the parliamentary battle sharpened, not least with the Irish Nationalists wanting to use procedure to promote their case for Home Rule. Questions were no longer a sideshow: they had become significant in political and procedural terms.

By 1900, more than 5000 questions a session were being tabled, an average of 41 per day, delaying the main business until, on occasion, as late as 6.00 p.m., so that proceedings could last until later than usual. In 1901 the number of questions put to the Conservative Government seriously impeded its main business and Arthur Balfour, soon to be Prime Minister, imposed a limit on the time allowed for questions. From 1902, the House started meeting at 2 p.m., with questions taken between 2.15 and 2.55. 'Question Time', broadly on the lines we still know it today, had begun.

Balfour also introduced the practice of written answers. These were given when Ministers did not have the time to answer orally during Question Time. Written questions and answers are published in the Official Report (Hansard).

The Commons Order Paper has the questions numerically listed, giving the name of the questioner and the full text of the question. The Speaker calls the name of a back-bench MP. The MP rises and quotes the number of his question, then sits down. A Minister rises and reads a prepared response. Once the Minister has sat down, the MP rises again and asks a supplementary question, advance warning of which need not be given to the Minister.

This is where the fun should begin. *Erskine May*, Parliament's procedural reference work, named after a Commons clerk who first compiled it in 1844, solemnly states the purpose of questions as 'to obtain information or press for action'. Few MPs ask questions without having some idea of the answer. The MP should be able to seize on that answer, whether it reveals unemployment levels in his constituency or local road-building plans, and use it for a well-aimed political riposte which will be recorded in the local media and earn a partisan cheer in the chamber. Question Time has an atmosphere of its own. The occasion provides a chance to judge political horseflesh, in terms of ministerial dexterity or back-bench advocacy.

An attraction of Question Time lies in its brisk pace and its apparent spontaneity. Apart from the initial question and answer, all other exchanges are unscripted. The Speaker usually calls several MPs from alternate sides of the House to put further unscripted supplementaries. On average, it takes between three and four minutes to deal with each question and the supplementaries that follow. Then the Speaker calls the MP whose question is listed next on the Order Paper, and the ritual starts again.

Question Time, like so much of Parliament's work, mingles the mighty with the trivial. Michael Foot once championed this versatility by likening the Commons to an elephant's trunk which could hoist a fallen tree or pick up a pin. His impassioned words still ring in my ears. Certainly the range of Questions supports his thesis.

Questions are mainly directed towards Ministers, but they can also be put to other MPs who speak on behalf of special bodies ranging from the Church Commissioners to the Commons Catering Committee. Parliamentary questions can thus range within the same hour from the government's policy on nuclear defence to the sale of Perrier water in the Commons dining-room. The latter subject earned an ear-splitting reproach from Frank Haynes, a Nottinghamshire Labour MP big in frame, heart and voice. He declaimed: 'I am ashamed and disgusted that we carry foreign waters in this place. What about fighting for Britain? What about the British waters? It is high time that the policy was changed.' The rebuke still echoes in the chamber, although Perrier is still available alongside other brands.

Some of the most modest departments can excite the fiercest passion. The Duchy of Lancaster has few responsibilities of its own. It may be joined with a major ministerial portfolio, particularly when the actual head of the Department sits in the Lords and the Chancellor answers in the Commons. At other times, the duties of the Chancellor of the Duchy beyond the Duchy itself are less onerous. Norman Tebbit, as Chancellor of the Duchy, was also Chairman of the Conservative Party. He was a devotee of the bruising political battle and also a conductor who attracted lightning. He had responsibility for the Duchy's modest and largely agricultural estates in the north of England. Such narrow responsibilities should have meant that the differences between him and his opponents were only a few wisps of straw. Nonetheless, with procedural skill they built these into a veritable brick wall of partisan controversy particularly on 3 March 1986 when Norman Tebbit revealed that his Lancaster duties took only three hours a week.

The news both infuriated and delighted the House and was turned into bitter exchanges tenuously linked to national policies. Norman Tebbit has since left government and the Duchy affairs have now returned to relative calmness.

However, there are strict rules regarding the content of questions. Any question must relate to a matter for which the minister is directly responsible to Parliament. Technically this inhibits questions on the BBC, local authorities and nationalised industries, for which no Minister has formal responsibility. An adroit MP can often side-step this by initially asking the Home Secretary, for example, if he has recently met the chairman of the BBC, and then making his point in a follow-up question. An attempt is made to ensure that every MP is fairly treated when seeking an oral answer from a Minister. From 1909 MPs were limited to a maximum of eight oral questions on the same day. This limit was progressively reduced so that each MP is now restricted to a maximum of eight questions in ten sitting days, and within this period two on any one day, with the proviso that they must not be put to the same Minister. No limit applies to written questions.

An element of fairness is also provided through the quaint procedure known as the '4 o'clock shuffle'. All questions received for future answer are shuffled like a pack of cards. The daily shuffle at four in the afternoon is conducted by the office clerks in the Upper Table Office, which is on the third floor of the Commons, high above the chamber. From time to time it is supervised by the Speaker. MPs are entitled to attend as observers. The questions are duly listed on the Order Paper in the random order determined by the shuffle.

A rota also operates to ensure that all Ministers regularly answer oral questions. Chance used to determine how often Ministers appeared. Questions were called in the chamber according to the random order in which the printer in the parliamentary press chose to list them on the Order Paper. Since the 1940s, questions have been grouped by department. The government and opposition business managers allocate different departments to each day of the week. For example, Foreign Office Ministers traditionally answer oral questions on Wednesdays and the Treasury on Thursdays.

Clearly, the House of Commons has carefully regulated and organised Question Time. It provides opportunities for Minister and back-bencher alike. It is ironic to record that very exceptionally the House has run out of questions. I have witnessed this extraordinary phenomenon on one occasion and revelled in the general embarrassment. It occurred when many Members had still to return from a parliamentary recess and the number of questions was modest. The reason for running out was certainly not on account of succinct exchanges: there simply were not enough questions. MPs had to sit and use the balance of time in subdued conversation before the main business commenced at 3.30 p.m. We consoled ourselves that it was an occasion to remember in wonderment, if not in shame.

Champions of Question Time will claim that it helps the House maintain an investigatory control over the executive. They argue that reputations can still be made and lost in the hour of verbal duelling that opens the parliamentary day. Question Time attracts more MPs into the chamber and more journalists into the Press Gallery than do most debates. In practice, however, the questioning is predictable rather than rigorous. Ministers naturally do not profess to enjoy the ordeal, but it has rarely ruined a career that was otherwise promising.

Occasionally the minister may appear like some stag at bay – straight from a Landseer canvas. Back-benchers snarl on all sides, foe and fair-weather friend alike. On the other hand he is not alone as he grips the despatch box and battles through the noise. Behind him are the ample resources of Whitehall.

Each government department has a Civil Service parliamentary section. This section forwards questions from MPs to the relevant Whitehall officials for draft replies, and collates the answers for ministers. Question Time involves an enormous amount of work for civil servants. Detailed briefing is provided for every conceivable supplementary question. Ministers and their advisers meet beforehand to discuss the draft answers. They devote considerable effort to trying to judge which MPs are likely to ask which supplementaries. Yet often the copious briefing material is of little practical value. Ministers clutch their official folders somewhat as a toddler clasps his teddy bear. The briefs are a much-needed boost to morale. In practice it is virtually impossible to find the right page among the reams of paper while listening to and trying to comprehend the precise point of supplementaries.

The Minister has two bells which are likely to save him from a knock-out in this form of parliamentary fisticuffs. The first is that the Speaker cannot allow particular questions to proceed without limit. He has an obligation to those MPs who are waiting to ask questions on other topics.

Currently about 240 questions are tabled daily, making a total of 50,000 a year. Only 2500 of these are answered orally, the balance receiving a written reply. Ministers only succeed in answering orally the top 15 to 20 questions out of the 70 to 80 on the Order Paper which seek an oral reply.

Indeed, there is a paradox that cannot be easily reconciled. If the Speaker hurries through Question Time in order to cover as many questions as possible, the government is likely to benefit as there are fewer supplementaries to probe the initial reply. If, on the other hand, the Speaker allows time to linger over a question that touches a government weakness, then even fewer MPs will be able to ask their questions. In recent years the convention has rightly been to take fewer questions and allow the more controversial topics to run longer.

The second relief for the Minister at Question Time is the babbling volubility of the questioner. Verbosity is unquestionably one of the seven deadly political sins. Many MPs cannot resist its temptation. The supplementary delivered at length gives the Minister a chance to collect his wits and to select at least the one point he can answer. Candles are lit every night in Whitehall to long-winded supplementaries. No candles are lit for Tam Dalyell. The suave government reply having been delivered to one of his questions, the descending ministerial backside has barely touched the bench before Dalyell's supplementary – a simple 'Why?' – has come and gone.

It would be a mistake to suppose that Question Time is wholly devoted to the Commons cross-examining the executive. Ministers often take the offensive and use the occasion to see that helpful questions are asked which will enable government success to be made public. The Press Gallery, always packed for Question Time, will ensure the wide reporting of the ploy. This end is secured by the 'planted' question. The task of 'planting' is usually undertaken by a minister's parliamentary private secretary. He moves around armed with questions prepared by the department, and usually the prepared answers, seeking and finding friendly accomplices.

Question Time has its charm. It also has its cost. It has been estimated that answering an oral question costs £75 and a written question £45. The total annual cost is over £2 million. Is the money well spent? Question Time is a limited means of holding Ministers to account. Is it any more than a somewhat expensive charade? Question Time is certainly used for personal publicity and making partisan political points. It is questionable whether this is the most effective way of checking the executive and raising individual grievances.

The immediate problem for the reformers is to ensure that if Question Time were abolished, substantially amended or transferred to a different time, it would be replaced by something better. The likelihood is that the departmental select committees will develop an investigating skill superior to that which can be deployed at Question Time. On the other hand, the present arrangements enable MPs, on the pretext of questions, to talk to Fleet Street in time for first edition headlines. They also permit the skilful MP to make his political point instantly topical, even if he was required to table the question a week earlier. Parliament's persistent campaigners make great use of questions. Above all Question Time is the prologue to the part of the parliamentary day when laws are made and issues debated. We get off to a start that is relatively well attended, sometimes boisterous, even noisy. Certainly it is never dull. There could be worse ways of warming up.

6 PRIME MINISTER'S QUESTION TIME

Every Tuesday and Thursday questions are put to the Prime Minister. Regular radio broadcasts since 1978 have greatly increased public interest in the occasion. The House is crowded to capacity: even agnostics have been known to attend prayers in order to get a well-placed seat. Edward Heath is usually there in the front-bench corner seat below the gangway. This is the traditional sunset home for former Prime Ministers. Now he observes the party skirmish which the irreverent call the 'Neil and Maggie Show'. Drama is no stranger to politics.

Prime Minister's Question Time in its present form is a relative new-comer to Westminster. It was first introduced in 1961, when Harold Macmillan was Prime Minister and Hugh Gaitskell Leader of the Opposition. Previously oral questions to the Prime Minister were listed twice a week, but because they had such low priority did not begin until No. 45 on the Order Paper. Subsequent questions were intended to be addressed to him: in practice few were reached. MPs successfully demanded arrangements whereby the Prime Minister would answer questions regularly at the despatch box.

Technically, parliamentary questions must relate to a Minister's direct responsibilities in government, and because particular areas are delegated to the various departments there are very few matters that a Prime Minister must answer for in person. In any case, MPs wanted to question the Prime Minister on all aspects of government policy and avoid the risk that specific questions would be passed to Cabinet colleagues handling the relevant subjects.

Where there is a will there is often a parliamentary way. In the mid-1960s MPs tended to get round this problem by asking the Prime Minister whether a Cabinet Minister's speeches represented government policy. As all members of the Cabinet are assumed to agree with their collective policy, the Prime Minister's predictable reply was 'Yes'. Of course, what MPs really wanted was a peg on which they could hang follow-up questions about policy generally.

The Labour MP Woodrow Wyatt was a great exponent of this technique. Early in 1964 he cited 'the recent speech' by Reginald Maudling, Chancellor of the Exchequer, on the economy. The Prime Minister, Alec Douglas-Home, confirmed that it represented government policy. Sharp exchanges ensued. Economic policy – particularly in an election year – is always controversial. Noise and tempers rose. Speaker Selwyn Lloyd warned the House not to treat the occasion 'as though it were a reception at London airport'. Today this may read like an obscure reprimand, but these were the times when the Beatles were mobbed by hysterical fans whenever they passed through Heathrow. Harold Wilson's Merseyside loyalties were immediately touched. To the Tory's economic pretensions there was now added a further outrage: 'I know that the Prime Minister is even claiming credit for the Beatles ...' From the Conservative benches we admired the verbal footwork – we even laughed – but we knew Alec Douglas-Home could never be accused of Beatlemania.

Today the 'open question' has been so perfected that it can lead to an even wider range of topics than in the 1960s. Current practice is to ask the Prime Minister if she will list her daily engagements. This ingenuous request for diary information accounts for more than 95 per cent of all questions to Mrs Thatcher. A typical reply would be:

> This morning I had meetings with ministerial colleagues and others. In addition to my duties in the House I shall be having further meetings today. This evening I hope to have an audience of Her Majesty the Queen. (Hansard, 19 July 1988)

Many would feel the schedule was heavy enough and the Prime Minister might wisely ease up a little.

When the answer is received the Member can then pose a supplementary question on anything he or she thinks should or should not be in the Prime Minister's diary. She will be expected to find a corner of time for and immediately to comment upon the balance of payments, homelessness, law and order, nuclear disarmament, tariff barriers, the housing benefit of a pensioner in Usk or violence on television. It is a parliamentary quiz game without the cultural urbanity of 'Mastermind' or the jollity of 'Mr and Mrs'.

The focal point in Prime Minister's Question Time is the contest between the two main party leaders. At that moment the chamber becomes more like a meeting of gladiators. The use of the 'open question' permits wide-ranging political comment and can lead to vigorous exchanges between the Prime Minister and the Leader of the Opposition, who has a special role to play. MPs are normally allowed one supplementary question once the Prime Minister has given the initial answer. This rule is now waived for the opposition leader, who may deliver three or more supplementary questions in succession. This is his parliamentary opportunity, twice a week, to score a public triumph. His performance and its reception by his back-bench supporters will be carefully assessed by the Press Gallery. These exchanges between Prime Minister and opposition leader can be a sharp-witted (or bad-tempered) game of political ping-pong. It is never dull.

For all the noise and posturing, it is a serious occasion for the leadership of the parties.

Occasionally the Prime Minister is absent and a deputy has to handle questions in her stead. When I was Leader of the House between 1982 and 1987, this was part of my duties – an immense privilege but also a daunting one: the office boy in the boss's chair. It gave me an insight into the complex arrangements that precede Prime Minister's Question Time as well as the experience of answering in a crowded and excited House.

Preparation for questions started with the delivery of two large folders on the preceding evening. These usually arrived too late for much work before my evening engagements, but early enough to blunt my appetite for dinner. One folder would list the individual questioners (invariably asking open questions), with details concerning employment and industrial and social investment in their constituencies. In fact this information was of modest use when dealing with open questions. Most members wanted to stride the national or world stage. The second folder, much more indigestible, would carry a legion of statistics to demonstrate the health of the economy, together with a brief on about ten topics of current concern. The statistical section of the folder was continually up-dated for each Question Time, and the selected topics were constantly revised. I read them feverishly.

The next morning an early meeting was held involving a small group of civil servants and political advisers, including my parliamentary private secretary, Richard Page. The task of a PPS cannot easily be defined. It varies according to personalities. Richard Page was invaluable in judging the parliamentary situation and what specific issues were likely to arise from open questions. Ian Gow, once a ubiquitous and attentive PPS to Margaret Thatcher, informed himself so well on Members' opinions that he was known, affectionately, as 'supergrass'.

The morning meeting was crucial. The newspapers had been studied for topics likely to be raised by questioners. I would ask the civil servants to provide additional material in the light of this. At about twelve noon a further meeting was held to up-date all the information and decide what summary sheets of facts I would take into the chamber. This became a working lunch, and on the basis that the condemned man should always eat heartily I treated myself to smoked salmon sandwiches.

I chose to enter the chamber well ahead of the magic hour of 3.15 p.m. so that I could gauge the atmosphere. Then the Speaker called my first question. The apprehension of waiting was over, the exhilaration of battle had begun. The briefing was of modest value. Statistics rarely elevate an argument. In any case there was a dilemma. In the hubbub you could keep your head down, study your brief and barely hear a word. Alternatively you could lean backwards and hear the exchanges from the amplifier concealed at head level in the bench. I preferred the latter course. At 3.30 my six or seven questions had been dealt with. I consoled myself that even Harold Macmillan, one of the most accomplished performers, had confessed to feeling physically ill before questions. I was in good company.

Occasionally Parliament has a bad conscience about the noise and frequent bad manners that accompany questions addressed to the Prime Minister. It is well known that Mrs Thatcher will answer specific questions more generously than her predecessors. But parliament prefers the spontaneity and occasional drama that open questions produce. It is also true that politicians generally enjoy a personal clash between the party leaders. We have always personalised the party conflict: Thatcher and Kinnock, in this respect, are in the tradition of Gladstone and Disraeli. Moreover, the Prime Minister, by convention, does not give evidence to a select committee. It is therefore particularly important that Parliament's chance to question the government leader in the chamber should not be undermined by trivia and knockabout comedy.

7 MINISTERIAL STATEMENTS AND PRIVATE NOTICE QUESTIONS

Much of Parliament's business is about fundamental long-term issues. Should Britain have nuclear weapons? Should the railways be publicly owned? Nonetheless, Parliament also has the capacity to move speedily from the philosophic to the specific. At 3.30 p.m. a Minister is frequently called by the Speaker to make a major statement of immediate impact. This happens so suddenly that it is not even shown on the Order Paper. Similarly, an MP is often allowed to ask an unscheduled question, called a private notice question (PNQ), requiring an instant ministerial answer that day at 3.30 p.m. These are not rare incidents. In the 1987–8 session there were more than 90 ministerial statements and 39 PNQs. Together they averaged three occasions a week.

The scene is easy to picture. The House knows that something is afoot. Since 1 p.m. the closed-circuit television annunciators have been proclaiming that after advertised questions there will be statements or PNQs on given topics. There are 813 of these machines placed strategically throughout the Commons. They carry news of current business or, before the House sits at 2.30 p.m., of business not printed in the daily agenda. In the course of a debate they show the subject being debated, the name of the speaker, the time when he began speaking and the current time. They are also equipped with a persistent bell that summons MPs from Doomsday whenever there is a division. Members normally have one in their rooms, but there is also a friendly Commons policeman who stalks the corridors and bawls 'Division' for those who do not rely upon modern technology. In this instance, however, the annunciators merely warn of impending business.

Meanwhile, Whitehall has been busy preparing the ministerial statement. Usually its content is no surprise for the department. For example, the statement made on 14 January 1988 outlining proposed government policy on television was the outcome of long preparation. The day for its delivery was carefully chosen to enable the case to be presented effectively and not be overshadowed by other political events. There would have been private briefings of the media beforehand so that 'informed comment' could be offered within minutes of the matter being disclosed to the Commons. This convention of confidential pre-release to the media is often resented by MPs, but it is difficult to see how it could be otherwise. The public needs the information shortly after it has been given to parliament. It is also true that a statement of some delicacy may be strategically timed so that outside events will be likely to distract attention from it.

The ministerial statement is normally made available, by courtesy of the Minister, to the opposition and sometimes to spokesmen of the smaller parties at about 3 p.m. – half-an-hour before its planned delivery. This puts a premium on the nimble wits of the opposition. The House does not like long statements, but inevitably some topics defy brevity. For example, in November a Treasury Minister may need to take twenty minutes to make a statement on public spending.

Ministerial statements are followed by a range of questions from all sides of the House. These can last up to 45 minutes. The Speaker normally calls questions from all parties and shades of opinion. Frequently these exchanges show the Commons in a mood that goes much wider than party.

In July 1988 Kenneth Clarke, then Minister of Trade and Industry, made statements on two successive days concerning the proposed sale of the Rover Group to British Aerospace and the involvement of the European Commission. He was assailed from all sides. Many did not like the prospect of Rover's passing into private hands; some doubted the logic of merging a motor manufacturer with an aircraft company; and others questioned the propriety of the European Commission in seeking to influence a British government decision. Parliament may nurture adversarial politics, but on this occasion the conflict went beyond political loyalty.

In such circumstances as these a Minister is heavily dependent upon his departmental briefing. As with normal questions, he will be equipped with a defence against every possible criticism the civil servants can anticipate. The chances are that the volume of briefing will defy its speedy assimilation. A ministerial statement is often a major political challenge. There are those who respond by tossing their briefs aside, like Scottish Secretary Malcolm Rifkind, and then seem to operate without civil servants if not without hands. They are much envied by the House.

The private notice question operates by a different route from the ministerial statement, but its consequences are much the same. Any MP can apply to the Speaker for permission to ask an oral question for answer that day. The device is often used by the opposition front bench to secure a statement *not* willed by the minister. Governments thus prefer PNQs to be something of a rarity. Happily, Speaker Weatherill has returned to traditional practice and has allowed on average four times as many PNQs as his predecessor.

As with the ministerial statement, there is a frenzy of background activity. An MP must notify the Speaker before noon (10 a.m. on Fridays) that he has a question he wishes to put. There is a strong convention that this request must be made in confidence. The Speaker's office then informs the relevant department that the Minister might be called upon to answer

RIGHT: St Stephen's Hall, the site of the old Chamber before the great fire of 1834. It now leads from St Stephen's Entrance to the Central Lobby.

BELOW: *Sir Thomas More refusing to grant Wolsey a subsidy in 1523*, a mural by Vivien Forbes (1927) in St Stephen's Hall. Thomas More was perhaps the most distinguished Speaker in the Commons' long history.

ABOVE: Westminster Hall depicted in 1819: the only part of the old Commons that survived the fire of 1834.

OPPOSITE ABOVE: Charles James Fox by Anton Hickel. Fox, a distinguished radical, formidable orator and life-long opponent of William Pitt, addresses the House.

RIGHT: *Baron Lionel de Rothschild being presented to the House of Commons*, painting by Henry Barraud. The custom of introducing a new member by two sponsors persists.

BELOW: The House of Commons viewed from Old Palace Yard, 1854. Anon.

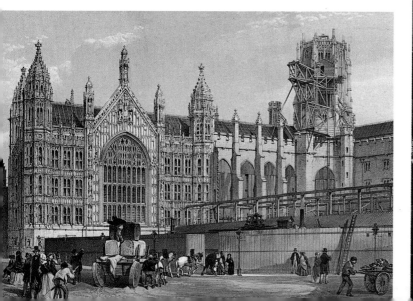

ABOVE: St Stephen's Crypt is used by MPs for services and christenings. This watercolour was painted by E. M. Barry (son of Charles Barry) in 1863.

LEFT: *Leo Amery MP speaking in the debate on defence on 7 May 1940*, by John Worsley c. 1947. The painting shows the debate which led to Prime Minister Neville Chamberlain's resignation and his replacement by Winston Churchill.

BELOW: *Introduction of Lady Astor as the first woman member of the House of Commons* (1919) by Charles Sims. Nancy Astor, the first woman MP to take her seat in the Commons, was introduced by David Lloyd George (right) and A. J. Balfour (left).

The State Opening of Parliament by Queen Victoria. The ceremony has barely altered since then. Painting by Joseph Nash, c. 1860

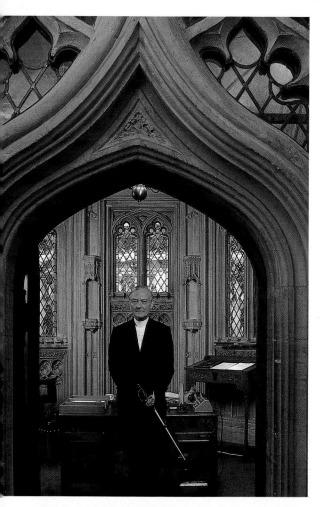

ABOVE: Black Rod carrying the Lord Chamberlain's Great Mace.

LEFT: Serjeant at Arms.

BELOW: The Members' Dining Room, where the political parties sit at separate tables.

BELOW: One of the Committee rooms where the House of Commons considers detailed legislation and holds private party meetings.

RIGHT: The Library: less of a gentlemen's club, more of a work-place.

FOOT: The Members' Tea Room, scene of much informal debate.

The House of Commons by June Mendoza (1986–87) portrays a crowded House; nonetheless there was insufficient room to include all the Members.

'The other picture' by A. T. Festing, which was commissioned on behalf of those members not included in the official Mendoza painting. It shows different aspects of the Commons at work.

a question that afternoon. There is then frantic departmental preparation while a full brief is prepared for dealing with the question and the Minister's diary is cleared to enable him to attend the Commons at 3.30 p.m.

The Speaker decides whether or not to grant the question at his daily meeting at noon which involves the Speaker's Secretary, the Clerk of the House, the Clerk Assistant and the Principal Clerk of the Table Office and any other clerk whose presence may be required.

It is easy to understand why Ministers are anxious and often annoyed at the uncertainty and work that PNQs involve. Nevertheless, they are a vital facility for back-benchers. PNQs are permitted over a range of topics from the specific to the general. For example, MPs are usually entitled to ask about accidents in their constituencies. On 26 April 1988, Bruce Grocott, Labour MP for the Wrekin, raised the matter of a fire the day before at the Central Ordnance storage depot at Donnington, within his constituency. On the other hand, a PNQ can easily match a ministerial statement in its general significance, as was the case on 7 March 1988, when George Robertson, Labour Foreign Affairs spokesman, taxed the Foreign Secretary on the shooting in Gibraltar of IRA members by soldiers of the SAS.

Ministerial statements and PNQs very properly occupy an early spot in the Commons agenda. The presentation of government policy should begin with the Commons and not at some high-powered press conference in Lancaster House. On the other hand, it may be argued that the quite reasonable demands of government public relations cannot always accommodate the procedures of parliament, particularly when an issue involves many private interests and public bodies.

It is an inherently unsatisfactory situation, and perhaps it can never be totally resolved. The most potent reform would be to enable more effective media presentation of these events which dominate a vital part of the parliamentary day.

8 STANDING ORDER
NUMBER TWENTY

On the morning of 27 June 1988, the government released the trade figures for the previous calendar month. They showed a record deficit of £1.2 billion. The news was topical and contentious. Selected MPs were at once summoned to radio and television studios to air their reactions. Yet what could be said in Parliament? The agenda had been fixed and announced the previous week. The next occasion for questions to the Department of Trade and Industry was on Wednesday 13 July, by Westminster standards well into the future. The situation challenged the ingenuity of MPs who wanted a speedy response to this situation. Parliament's rules (Standing Orders) provided the means, the Bolsover constituency provided the man.

Once Questions had been concluded at 3.31 p.m., Dennis Skinner, government gadfly and acute parliamentarian, rose to his feet. He sits on the front bench below the gangway, the recognised home of the awkward squad. Generations of the disrespectful have sat there, impervious to patronage and essential to the vitality of parliament. I was happily 'in my place' and able to observe the Skinner performance at first hand. The charge was formulated in the somewhat stilted language demanded by the rules: 'I beg to ask leave to move the Adjournment of the House under Standing Order No. 20 for the purpose of discussing a specific and important matter that should have urgent consideration.' In the world outside Parliament I cannot think of anything more improbable than Dennis Skinner 'begging to ask leave' of anyone.

The ritual opening dispensed with, the member for Bolsover proceeded vigorously. He had three minutes in which to make his argument. This should always be devoted to the case for urgency, not used to dwell upon the political and economic infamy that has produced the 'specific and important matter' in question. The time limit will be sternly enforced, but no one can easily say when advocacy for a debate becomes a discussion of politics rather than timing. We awaited three minutes of vintage Skinner denunciation of the government and were not disappointed. 'The truth is that the figures show ... that the country is bleeding to death ... While the Prime Minister is consistently preaching prudence to others, she is presiding over a pawnshop economy.' The three-minute fusillade over, the Speaker confirmed our fears: 'I regret that I do not consider the matter he has raised is appropriate for discussion under Standing Order No. 20.' The Speaker's discretion is total; he does not have to give any reasons. We knew there would be plenty of opportunities to discuss Britain's economic and trade policy in the time ahead. Dennis Skinner, however, had used the announcement of the May trade deficit to launch a solo assault on the government. It was nimble footwork.

To understand today's procedures we must again look back to the last century. It was not until the 1880s that Commons business came increasingly under the control of party managers. Their task was to bring more order into the conduct of parliamentary affairs, and to make them more predictable. Consequently there was much less scope for emergency debates on the initiative of back-bench MPs. The pendulum had swung to the government side and it became overwhelmingly weighted in its favour during this century. Throughout the 1940s, a decade of turmoil, the Commons had only four emergency debates. In the 1950s there were only eight. These included one moved by Tony Benn on 27 March 1952, alleging that the government had deposed Seretse Khama as chief of the Bamangwato tribe in Bechuanaland.

Urgency is clearly in the eye of the beholder. From the Cabinet room it seemed that problems were likely to be worsened by instant parliamentary debate and public government response. The Commons thought otherwise. Over the years it became clear that the House lacked effective provision for debating emergencies and issues of sudden concern.

Reform eventually came in 1967, masterminded by the Leader of the House, Richard Crossman, a colourful Labour intellectual, and my first parliamentary opponent when I vainly ventured into his Coventry stronghold in 1959. One of his many Commons procedural changes was to relax the rigid rules that had previously governed emergency debates. Henceforth the Speaker had discretion in deciding the justification for an emergency debate. From the government's viewpoint the greater role of the Speaker was balanced by the decision that an emergency debate should not be held until 3.30 p.m. on the day after it had been granted unless the matter was extremely urgent, when the debate could be held at 7 o'clock on the same day. These arrangements are written into the rules of the Commons and appear under Standing Order No. 20, the popular name given to an emergency debate.

The circumstances of an application for an emergency debate are illustrated in the unsuccessful bid by Dennis Skinner on the occasion of the trade figures. An MP is required to give the Speaker advance notice of the intention to raise the matter, but it will come as a surprise to other members as it will not have appeared on the annunciators that show the business of the House. In practice, an MP wishing to seek a debate under SO No. 20 is always allowed to have his three minutes' worth; possibly because there is a strict time limit. A consequence is that the three-minute spot, in mid- to late afternoon before a crowded Press Gallery, enables the MP almost at will to command a good audience for a lively topic. Thus many

'Taking a Division in the House of Commons – the Tellers at the Table.' The procedure has barely changed since this drawing of 1881.

SO No. 20s are sought not so much with a view to compelling a three-hour debate the next day, but rather to make a succinct political point with no danger of a ministerial riposte. It may not make the *Guardian*, but it could just manage the *Wrexham Leader*.

On the relatively rare occasions when an SO No. 20 application does lead to a debate, the urgency of the matter is beyond question. The SO No. 20 debates granted since the 1983 General Election have covered such matters as the police operations connected with the coal-miners' dispute, the publication of classified information relating to the future of Westland plc, and the AWACS airborne early warning system.

On these occasions, following the application, the Speaker, implying his own consent, asks: 'Does the Hon. Member have leave of the House for an emergency debate?' Those in the chamber supporting the application are asked to stand up. As long as 40 or more MPs rise, the debate is granted. If less than 40 but more than ten stand the decision whether to proceed with the emergency debate is then decided by a division of the House. This procedure rests heavily upon Members being in the chamber. Inevitably the Speaker must give some hint of his expected reaction so that the business managers can arrange for members to be present.

On average about three or four SO No. 20 debates are granted annually. These are only a fraction of the applications sought. Following the Crossman reforms there were 20 applications a session, by the 1970s the figure was 30, and by the 1980s it was around 70. In truth SO No. 20 applications have become as much a means of back-bench advocacy as a method of promoting emergency debate. Parliament has its own way of using its procedures to serve its intentions.

The SO No. 20-inspired debates perform an important role, even though they are few in number. One significant development is that those now granted tend increasingly to be in response to front-bench requests. Since 1983 seven of the eight debates granted have been as a consequence of front-bench applications. The eighth applicant was an opposition whip.

It is as though the front benches have colonised the procedure while the back-benches have used it for other purposes. This can place the Speaker in a difficult position. There may be a highly contentious and immediate issue, where the government would like a few days to redefine its policy. The opposition, by contrast, wants an immediate debate. This was the case in April 1988 when new Social Security regulations were introduced. Some Conservatives resented the Speaker's decision to grant a debate. I wrote on 13 May in the weekly *House Magazine* which circulates at Westminster:

> One recent issue has symbolised the difficulties for the Speaker. It concerns the granting of a Standing Order No. 20 debate on Social Security. The debate was sought immediately upon the Commons return from the Easter Recess. The demand was instant, and the terms of SO No. 20 meant the debate also would be speedy.
>
> Charles Kennedy and I, visiting a North Sea oil rig, were frustrated and inconvenienced observers of the process. Even so, the Speaker was absolutely right. No one with a shred of social sensitivity can doubt that the issue was causing distress to our constituents. No one knows how the topic would have obtruded upon the business of the House had an SO No. 20 debate not been provided. The action of the Speaker secured an early opportunity for debate and a safety valve for a situation where passions ran high.

It was a vigorous and well argued debate. Within days the government policy had been adjusted.

I clearly recollect the SO No. 20 debate on the United States invasion of Grenada. It is open knowledge that this action was undertaken without consulting the British government, and with an exchange of information that was more formal than fraternal. The unease within government was not calmed by the knowledge that an SO No. 20 was being sought. If it was granted the Foreign Secretary, Sir Geoffrey Howe, would be forced to face the Commons sooner than he would have liked. The sequence was swift. The United States invasion took place on 25 October 1983. Denis Healey, Labour MP for Leeds East, successfully applied for an SO No. 20 on the same day and the debate took place on the next day. Parliament had spoken, and who can doubt that the occasion justified the speed?

The debates provided by SO No. 20 always take place on the motion or proposal 'that this House do now adjourn'. If carried it means that business is instantly concluded for the remainder of the day. This sounds rather archaic but it really is an extremely useful procedure. The adjournment motion cannot be altered, and so neither government nor opposition can hi-jack it with an amendment designed to rally their supporters. Secondly, if it is carried it means only a modest change. The business that has been lost can usually be fitted into the week's remaining programme.

In the debate the arguments and the voices count as well as the vote. In May 1940 Neville Chamberlain answered a two-day debate on the adjournment on the conduct of the war. He won by 281 votes to 200, but next day he resigned. Winning was not enough, given his normal majority and the temper of the debate. In its own way and by its own procedures the House had pronounced, for itself and the nation.

The SO No. 20 procedures are well understood in the House. They must, however, be confusing for the public. It may seem unfair that the private member using the SO No. 20 procedure can put a case with no government reply. Many feel that Skinner on trade needs to be matched by a junior Minister, for political balance if not for entertainment. Secondly, the Speaker refuses 95 per cent of the applications. There he stands, in full-bottomed wig and braid, seemingly indifferent to anguish and suffering. His dilemma was sharply underlined on 11 February 1988 when Joan Walley, the Labour MP for Stoke-on-Trent North, sought a debate on 'the urgent need for Claire Wise, from Kidsgrove, to be admitted to the Birmingham children's hospital for open-heart surgery as a matter of urgency'. The public will not easily understand the Speaker's decision to reject the application, but MPs knowing parliamentary procedures and how to use them will appreciate his restrained judgements.

9 GESTURE POLITICS:
BILLS, MOTIONS AND PETITIONS

The politics of action are well understood. Laws are made. Taxes are raised. Executive government proceeds. And yet politics is more than this. Enoch Powell once observed that for a politician 'words are his deeds'. It is hardly surprising then, that much of Parliament's time is used in debating and advocacy. Parliament seeks to create the climate of popular opinion as well as responding to it. Methods of opinion-forming are rooted in the past, and not easily understood by the layman. Three such techniques are the ten-minute-rule bill, early day motions, and the declining practice of petitions.

What could have persuaded government whips to organise an all-night vigil of MPs outside the Public Bill Office? The answer concerns the shrewd way the Scots Labour MP Dennis Canavan spotted a chance to upstage the Chancellor of the Exchequer on Budget Day in 1985. It was a hilarious use of the ten-minute-rule bill.

In 1950 the Commons rejected Labour government advice by the close margin of 235 votes to 229 and restored to individual MPs the right to initiate legislation. The House decided that no private member's bill could be debated during the first seven weeks of a parliamentary session. Thereafter bills could be introduced on two days a week, Tuesday and Wednesday. Only one private member's bill may be moved each day. The speech introducing the bill should not exceed ten minutes and may not be interrupted. The time limitation has created the popular terminology 'ten-minute-rule bill'. The bill may be opposed by a speech, also not exceeding ten minutes, and there may be a division, that is, members may vote by trooping through the 'Ayes' and 'Noes' lobbies.

The privilege of a ten-minute-rule bill is available to all back-bench MPs, who number roughly between 500 and 550. The actual occasions when a bill could be moved amount to rather less than 60 a year. There is potentially a great excess of demand over supply. No attempt is made to ration, as with parliamentary questions, or to ballot, as with private members' motions for debate. The right to use a ten-minute-rule bill is allocated on the day on a 'first come first served' basis. So great is the pressure of demand on supply that a Member normally has to give the maximum three weeks' notice that he wishes to use the procedure on the allotted day, and he must be first in the queue outside the Public Bill Office. The demand is so great that back-benchers often camp all night outside the office. In this way Dennis Canavan was awarded a ten-minute-rule bill on Budget Day. In subsequent years the government Whips organised an all-night posse of Conservative MPs to ensure that the Budget Day spot went to a member who, by the simple ruse of not moving his bill, gave the Chancellor a clear run.

Dennis Canavan rose to present his bill on 19 March 1985. In a crowded House he made the most of his opportunity. Many members were genuinely angry with his tactics. They felt he was abusing the spirit of ten-minute-rule bills and damaging the traditions of Budget Day. Other MPs were amused by the modest diversion. They enjoyed the prospect of the Treasury bench being up-ended by such a piece of impudence.

Canavan opened his speech by stating the objects of his bill: 'that leave be given to bring in a Bill to make the Chancellor of the Exchequer more accountable to Parliament in budgetary matters and to monitor his economic performances; and for connected purposes'. He then observed, 'I am pleased to see such a good attendance for the First Reading of my Bill.' The following ten minutes were pure irony. There was the paradox of a crowded House and the tradition that a ten-minute-rule bill should not be interrupted. Canavan argued from a stoutly left-wing standpoint '. . . the Chancellor is getting away with economic murder. The British economy has been reduced to a shambles by an incompetent Chancellor, who has the brass neck to tell us to pull in our belts while he seems to become plumper and smugger.' The verbal assault concluded: 'He [the Chancellor] should be made redundant, and my Bill will make provision for that.' Canavan only occasionally touched upon the purported aim of making the Chancellor more accountable to parliament. The speech, while in order, strained patience as a partisan tirade delivered to a crowded House that could not answer back. None the less, Canavan had made his point. He was not interested in fashioning law: he wanted a platform for his economic arguments.

Sir Michael Shaw, Conservative MP for Scarborough, opposed the Bill with a dry comment concerning Canavan's 'most excessive way of drawing [his] virtues to the attention of the Committee of Selection so as to sit on the Finance Bill Committee'. The Finance Bill Committee sits many long hours debating the details of the Budget in the early summer months. It is a penance, not a reward. The House gave Canavan permission to introduce his bill. His attack on the Chancellor was opposed by only four Tory MPs. Disillusion with Nigel Lawson? The answer is simpler. Packed like sardines to hear the Budget, no Conservative wanted to go to the division lobbies and forfeit his or her seat. Nothing was heard of Canavan's bill thereafter. He never served on the Finance Bill Committee. The Chancellor of the Exchequer, despite the delay, still got massive media coverage. In Westminster terms it was a happy ending for all concerned.

The Canavan episode is an untypical exploitation of the ten-minute-rule, but it demonstrates how it can be used by an MP. More frequent is the situation where a largely uncontentious proposal is made and not opposed in the House. Two recent examples have been the Smoke Nuisance (Domestic Sources) Bill introduced by Mrs Gillian Shephard, Conservative MP for Norfolk South West, and the Horses, Ponies, and Donkeys Bill introduced by David Amess, Conservative MP for Basildon. Neither of these bills proceeded any further, but they assisted members campaigning on these issues, and the Protection Against Cruel Tethering Bill met some of David Amess's points.

On very rare occasions a ten-minute-rule bill does make some further progress. The vote on a bill is usually a free one – that is, MPs are not subject to the guidance of the party managers (Whips). Further progress, however, depends upon the bills being uncontroversial and having the tacit support of the government. Few bills meet these criteria: at Westminster controversy sprouts like a weed. In recent years the Solvent Abuse (Scotland) Act 1983, concerning glue sniffing, and the Rent (Amendment) Act 1985, a narrow tenancy issue, have started the ten-minute course and become law.

Campaigning members may also reveal their plans for a bill without having to use the ten-minute-rule procedure. Standing Order No. 58 permits a member to table a bill and make known its existence, without the formality of a ten-minute debate. This provision has existed since 1852.

In May 1988 that well-known radical Tony Benn, MP for Chesterfield, used this device to publicise his campaign 'to disestablish the Church of England'. The Bill's supporters included such well-known church activists as Bernie Grant and Tony Banks, two of London's Labour MPs. A modest sense of history will remind us that the established status of the English church was bought with much blood and conflict over the hundred or so years after the Reformation. It seemed doubtful that this could be reversed by the use of a private members' bill introduced under Standing Order No. 58, but Tony Benn, as ever, has a keen nose for publicity.

Signing Early Day Motions is another means whereby MPs make their voices known. Each day the agenda (Order Book) carries a list of the motions which have been submitted to the Commons clerks the previous day, or of additional names recently attached to motions already submitted. It is helpful to understand how the practice has evolved.

In the last century the Commons was largely dominated by private members rather than by the government. MPs often announced in the chamber that they intended to raise topics for debate. In those distant days the Commons had a modest number of gladiators and a large number of non-speaking spectators, whose silence would not provoke adverse constituency comment. This situation changed from the 1880s onwards when a great deal of parliamentary time was taken over by the government.

MPs were encouraged to inform the clerks of their intention to raise matters for Commons debate. Since the government now controlled the time available, this was an exercise of hope rather than expectation.

The present form of seeking a debate by means of an early day motion (EDM) was established in the 1940s. A member seeking an EDM sets out a proposition and states a point of view which he would like debated in the near future. This means of expressing opinion, for there was little chance of debate, grew during World War Two. There were only 21 EDMs in the 1939–40 session. Within four years the number had quadrupled. Since then the number has expanded substantially as MPs have used this technique to express their views and, they hope, to influence others. During the 1950s there were about 100 EDMs annually, but this increased to 700 in the early 1980s. The 1000 mark was passed in the 1983–4 session, and the total currently stands well above that.

A member seeking to submit an EDM can obtain a specially printed form from the Table Office. A motion can be submitted for publication with only the author's name attached, but most MPs prefer to collect at least five co-signatories since these names will be published on subsequent days when other MPs add their names to the motion. Awareness of the motion is secured by its publication in the Notices of Motions attached to the Order Paper.

In my parliamentary youth I signed EDMs. Indeed I kept the adventurous company of my fellow-Conservatives Humphry Berkeley, then MP for Lancaster, and Julian Critchley, now MP for Aldershot, and signed one on the Yemen – not a Shropshire topic. Since then the explosion in the number of EDMs has devalued them. I have decided it is better to sign none rather than to pick and choose. For example, I have a warm regard for West Indian cricketers, but do not feel moved to use the parliamentary agenda to congratulate them on their 30 years' unbeaten record at Lord's.

The highest-ever number of signatories was in 1964 for a Manchester MP Sir Robert Cary's EDM on War Disability pensions for limbless ex-servicemen. More recently John Marek, Labour MP for Wrexham, secured more than 370 signatories for his EDM on Commercial Whaling. I have no doubt that back-bench EDMs, so long established, are here to stay. Nevertheless, I can hardly recall an occasion when one has been debated.

Petitions have a long and honourable history, which is hardly belied by their present farcical parliamentary role. The right to petition the monarch, and later parliament, goes back to Magna Carta in 1215. In 1571 a Commons Committee for Motions of Griefs and Petitions was appointed to deal with grievances addressed to the Commons. From the reign of Charles I, with the upsurge in the importance of parliament, petitioning became a major means of airing grievances. The Bill of Rights in 1689 restated this principle:

... it is the right of the subjects to petition the King, and all commitments and prosecutions for such petitioning are illegal.

Over the centuries petitioning became less a matter of personal grievance
and more related to public policy. The nineteenth-century Chartist petitions calling for democratic parliamentary reform are examples of this

The petition bag, as depicted in 1882.

trend. The volume of petitions led Parliament to establish in 1842 what are now the general rules governing their presentation.

The public may obtain rules for submitting petitions direct from the Clerk of Public Petitions, Journal Office, House of Commons. The petition, once collected, must be given to an MP. It may be sent to the House of Commons post free, provided it does not weigh more than 2 lbs. Petitions may be formally presented by an MP, in the chamber, before the adjournment debate from Monday to Thursday and immediately after prayers on a Friday morning. An MP may present a petition informally at any time when the House is sitting by putting it in a dark green bag which hangs at the back of the Speaker's chair and looks as if it could have been salvaged from Epsom Downs after a bookie has cut and run.

In effect there are no practical consequences from modern petitions. They are sent to a Minister, who generally gives a reply as he would to a letter. The petition and reply are published as supplements to Parliament's daily record – 'Votes and Proceedings'.

Controversy is not easily laid to rest in Parliament. It is the timing of petitions rather than their substance that is now contentious. From Monday to Thursday they are presented just before the adjournment debate, when the House's main business is over. On Fridays, however, petitions are heard just after prayers and before the day's business begins. Friday is usually devoted to private members' business. Such business is not protected by the authority of the Whips or the mutual understanding of party managers. Procedural marksmen can use all their skills to delay contentious matter. Such an occasion arose in the 1984–5 session, when Andrew Bowden, Conservative MP for Brighton, Kempton, tried to secure more time for Enoch Powell's Unborn Children (Protection) Bill. Over twenty petitions were presented, ranging from the M11 Link Road to Ambulance Services in Gwynedd. Although each member may say only a few words in presenting the petition, the number of petitions ensured that the ritual lasted well over an hour, and contributed to Andrew Bowden's motion having insufficient time to permit a vote.

It is a commentary on petitions that they are now remembered for what they prevent rather than for what they advocate. They no longer retain even a shadow of their past importance. Even so the concept of the public's being able to petition Parliament directly still lingers. I have been requested once by constituents to deliver a petition. I duly popped it in the Speaker's bag. There the matter ended.

Ten-minute-rule Bills, Early Day Motions, and Petitions are examples of opinion-forming methods, and of the interplay of relations between public, parliament and executive. It is noteworthy that the most effective form of gesture politics, the ten-minute-rule bill, keeps its early afternoon position, while petitions have been edged into parliamentary darkness.

10 PRIVATE MEMBERS' BILLS AND MOTIONS; PRIVATE BILLS

Friday is a day apart in the Commons. Many members are in their constituencies and the chamber is usually thinly attended. It was quite otherwise on 6 May 1988, the day on which David Alton's private member's bill to limit abortion was to be debated further. The chamber was crowded and passions ran high. The time allowed for the debate was taken up with a succession of points of order (see Glossary). The day ended in a defeat for David Alton, the Liberal MP for Liverpool, Mossley Hill, whose bill was lost for the session. The strategy triggered off another round of recrimination about the use and abuse of private members' bills.

The parliamentary fuse that exploded that Friday had been lit at the beginning of the session on 2 July 1987. A Commons committee room was packed with MPs. The Chairman of Ways and Means, or Deputy Speaker, presided over the ballot to select which MPs might be permitted to bring forward their own legislation. Little is known about the origins of the ballot, but lottery is a frequent feature of the Commons when demand exceeds supply – as it always does on these occasions. All MPs not holding ministerial posts are eligible to enter the ballot for a private member's bill, and about 200 had handed in slips. The Chairman of Ways and Means will draw only twenty names. Moreover, the time allotted for private members' legislation is governed by Standing Orders, and it is likely that less than half the names drawn in the ballot will be successful in getting a bill made law because of the limited time available.

The task of negotiating a private member's bill through the Commons is formidable. It takes time, trouble and money to draft the bill and get support for it. There is now some help from public funds, and the ten MPs drawn highest may claim up to £200 expenses for drafting their bills.

I have never entered the ballot for private members' bills. There are many other aspects of parliamentary life which I enjoy more. In addition, it would involve a conflict with my commitments on a Friday in Shropshire.

There is one significant constraint on private members' legislation: an MP cannot introduce a bill the main object of which is to create a charge on the public purse. Otherwise the field is clear for every lobbyist and reformer. Successful MPs are inundated with requests that they should take up bills that have been prepared by special interest groups. David Alton's Abortion (Amendment) Bill, for example, rested heavily upon the work of the Society for the Protection of the Unborn Child (SPUC) and related groups. They were tireless in campaigning in the country as well as lobbying within the Commons.

MPs lucky in the ballot have three broad options. They may introduce a modest and uncontroversial measure. Secondly, they may choose a controversial topic but where there is the likelihood of all-party support. Finally, the member may go for a major measure which has no chance of reaching the statute book without government support. Each option is worth considering as they illustrate the infinite variety of Westminster life.

The most likely source of a ready-made modest measure is Whitehall. Every government department has a ready supply of small but useful proposals, known as 'hand-outs', that will block or round off a legal anomaly. The Ministry supplies the member with a prepared bill, and no drafting is necessary. There will be no likelihood of opposition in the House to such a mild and worthy bill. It is all very routine, and while the procedure is hardly heroic it does provide limited but helpful reform. The MP concerned will have his name on an Act even if not in the history books. Many MPs accept the Whips' encouragement to enter the ballot in order to undertake this chore.

Austin Mitchell, the Labour MP for Great Grimsby, tried to bring in much more ambitious legislation in 1983–4. His Home Buyers Bill, which had the encouragement of the Consumers Association, sought to deal with the solicitors' conveyancing monopoly. The bill did not become law, but encouraged subsequent government legislation on the matter. MPs are rightly proud of the interest groups who have campaigned for and been consulted on their bills. In 1972 Greville Janner QC, the Labour MP for Leicester West, gained a prize for novelty. He brought in a bill to install alarm devices in homes for the elderly as a result of consulting teenage schoolchildren in his constituency.

Finally there are the major measures that would never make law without the normal time limits on private members' bills being set aside. Sidney Silverman, the late Labour MP, piloted a bill in 1965 to abolish hanging, but needed considerable government time for the purpose. The same was true for the bill of former Liberal leader David Steel which in 1967 provided a legal framework for abortion. Other Members trying for a private members' legislative 'big bang' have been less successful. Richard Shepherd, Conservative MP for Aldridge Brownhills, tried to reform the Official Secrets Act and got a hostile government three-line Whip for his pains. Such whipping was unknown for a Friday, which is normally devoted to private members' business.

The time allocated for private members' bills is strictly limited by the rules of the House. Every MP knows that he must have either general goodwill or else government assistance if he is to complete his private bill. This can be very frustrating for the supporters of a bill. Frequently they feel that its merits are so self-evident that the government should adopt or provide time for the bill. This view was sharply expressed when David Alton's Abortion (Amendment) Bill was becalmed. Since private members' time is known to be limited it is a legitimate ploy by opponents to take account of that factor, as happened in Alton's case. It shows misunderstanding to describe their tactics as 'cheating'.

However, experience may compel Parliament to reconsider its procedures. I doubt if the original authors of the procedure now governing private members' legislation intended that it should guarantee success only for minor measures prepared by government departments. Furthermore, the private member's initiative is often valuable in raising a 'conscience' issue where government has felt reluctant to promote its own legislation backed by a party vote. The death penalty, abortion, and homosexual law reform are examples of such topics. The key to any reform is parliamentary time. It can unlock the constraints – even occasional absurdities – that now exist.

Another treasured possession of the back-bencher is private members' motions. These share, with private members' legislation, the overall time allotted to back-benchers. A session will usually contain 16 to 18 such debates, often of three hours, and initiated by a back-bench Member. These are not a part of the legislative process, but are intended to air Members' concerns.

Periodically a ballot is held for these debates. A Member gives his name to one of the Commons clerks who enters it into a book and assigns it a number. At the end of Question Time the Speaker announces the ballot. A clerk at the Table of the House selects a number from a box which he then reads out. The Speaker calls from the ballot book the Member's name. He calls three names for the period allocated to the debate. The first name effectively has the full use of the time. The calling ceremony is the occasion for low-grade banter: three names in succession from the same party earns the limp joke 'House'.

The topics chosen for debate can range from issues of national controversy to matters of constituency and regional interest. On 12 December 1986, Robert Hayward, Conservative MP for Kingswood, debated the defence industry. Later in the same session Peter Lilley, the Conservative Member for St Albans, debated a more narrow subject: gypsy caravan sites in the green belt. It may have had less *gravitas* than the defence motion, but that was more than compensated for by the passion that both gypsies and the green belt generate.

While the debates are much appreciated by MPs they are usually low-key in tone and seldom end in a vote. Westminster always provides its exceptions. Tam Dalyell, Labour MP for Linlithgow and no respecter of front-benchers, announced that he would use his balloted motion to debate the Prime Minister's Office. The content of his speech was unlikely to be deferential, and many Conservatives felt that it was abusing the conventions of private members' motions to exploit the occasion to attack the Prime Minister. Passions ran high. Dalyell's motion was never reached as the day's business, on Friday 6 June 1986, was lost because the previous day's debate on the Channel Tunnel ran through the night and into the next day. It was a case of Tam Dalyell, no mean procedural expert, being outpaced (or out-talked) by his Conservative opponents.

Finally there are private bills, which must be sharply distinguished from private *members'* bills. A private bill originally related to a person or organisation that sought rights and powers beyond those permitted by public acts or the common law. Occasionally a bill has been promoted by the government of such a character, and this is known as a hybrid bill.

Private bills were invaluable in the last century in giving commercial companies the legal authority necessary to build the network of railways. Victorian individualism did not hesitate to grant these powers that overrode private property rights. The tradition has been maintained: British Rail chose the private bill procedure to gain permission for a high-speed rail link between the Channel Tunnel and its London terminus. Today those seeking powers of private legislation are often local authorities or public utilities, as well as private companies. Private bills can also be brought by individuals – such as couples wishing to marry who fall outside the legal criteria of permitted relationships.

The whole private bill procedure is under review. At present the promoters of a private bill must make their plans widely known. They are encouraged wherever possible to accommodate any opposition to their original proposals. Copies of the bill have to be available to MPs and all others with a direct interest. Petitions for bills are to be presented to the Commons by late November. There then follows a process of examination to see that all notices have been only given to those who may be adversely affected, after which the bill comes to the Commons (or the Lords). Thereafter attempts are made to reconcile the promoters of the bill and those who object. In that case the bill proceeds through its subsequent stages without hindrance.

If, on the other hand, there are still objectors, they will have primed MPs to shout 'object' when the second reading is called. A debate must then be arranged. These debates are normally the subject of vigorous whipping; but this is undertaken by supporters of the bill not by the party managers.

No one can doubt the usefulness of much of the legislation provided by this process. The Dartmoor Commons Act of 1986 was designed to check over-grazing of the moors. The Birmingham City Council Act 1985 allowed motor racing on public roads in Birmingham. Monte Carlo without the sunshine. The legislation is significant. In the three sessions 1986–8 there were 142 such bills altogether. Their organisation and execution lie in the hands of the Chairman of Ways and Means or Deputy Speaker.

The private bill procedure allows the maximum opportunity for a promoter of a bill to come to an agreement with his opponents. If opposition does persist there is the chance for the bill to be debated and decided without traditional party conflict. The procedures are complex, but where major planning decisions are undertaken, they are infinitely speedier than the normal inquiry and appeal procedures. This consideration has provoked a strong all-party demand that the procedures should be reviewed. The outcome will not be a technical debate. It will touch the heart of public controversy on planning and environmental issues.

11 MAKING THE LAW – RULE AND DIVIDE

Kenneth Baker's name is called by the Speaker and he says, in respect of the Education (Reform) Bill, 'I beg to move that the Bill be now read a Second Time.' This comes as no news to the House. The proposals to bring about major educational changes were mooted in the General Election. This debate in December 1987 means a late start for a large and complex bill which is certain to be closely analysed by the educational establishment in the House of Lords. At last the second reading is now launched.

The term 'Second Reading' invites comment upon the 'First Reading'. This is the occasion when the bill is first presented. A dummy copy is placed upon the table in front of the Speaker's chair, consisting of a single sheet of paper which contains the title and a short description of the bill and a list of the Ministers sponsoring it. Just before main business the Speaker calls the name of the Secretary of State presenting the bill. The Clerk of the House reads its short title, and a government whip names a notional day for its second reading. This quaint and speedy process is known as the First Reading and serves as the House's order for the Stationery Office to print the bill.

With most bills the second reading takes up a full day. It is the first item of business (or Order of the Day) after time given for questions, government statements, requests for emergency debates, and so on. There should be a general debate lasting from around 4 p.m. until 10 p.m. The rules allow the discussion to be generally related to the subject of the bill, and not merely to its specific contents. In the second reading of the Education (Reform) Bill, Kenneth Baker and his Labour 'shadow' counterpart Jack Straw are well-matched adversaries. They speak easily in the House of Commons and can raise the volume of controversy without recourse to deafening partisanship.

Whatever his debating skills, a Minister will read the speech carefully prepared by his civil servants. He is permitted what are euphemistically called 'copious notes'. The department takes no chances: even if the speech does not contain all that is desired, it will certainly contain nothing that is departmentally undesirable. Although this rarely produces parliamentary eloquence, one glorious exception was Michael Foot. For years from the back-benches he had enhanced the Commons with radical protests delivered with passion and without notes. Could departmental officials cage the nightingale? In February 1974, as Secretary of State for Employment, he provided the answer. He still spoke mainly without notes, merely turning to them at some really crucial stage of the argument when the record would have to be beyond question.

Kenneth Baker meanwhile argues the case for his bill. He speaks for 37 minutes and is interrupted seven times. Jack Straw's speech lasts 34 minutes. To anguished MPs listening, and even more to those awaiting a chance to speak, it all sounds much longer. The main speeches having been delivered, the debate proceeds.

Membership of the Privy Council, awarded for life to Members of the Cabinet and some other senior government Ministers and politicians, carries the privilege that, by convention, Privy Councillors are called to speak ahead of mere mortal MPs. A wise Privy Councillor speaks rarely and briefly. Today Edward Heath speaks for twenty minutes. The Speaker would like ordinary back-benchers to take no more than ten. But we are off to a spirited start. In the 1970s Edward Heath was served loyally by Kenneth Baker as a parliamentary private secretary. Generosity, however, does not blunt Heath's judgement. He sharply attacks the general direction of the bill and the modest time (one day) allowed for the debate. This sets the tone for a lively debate.

Even with a measure as important as the Education (Reform) Bill there are counter-attractions for MPs. Letters must be signed, party committees attended, visitors seen, as well as much else. The second reading audience drops sharply after Edward Heath has spoken. After a while those remaining are Members still hopeful of being called to speak.

Altogether, nineteen members speak from the back-benches, including the Social and Liberal Democrat Paddy Ashdown. He was then education spokesman but subsequently became party leader. The broad provisions of the bill include the introduction of a national curriculum, the enablement of maintained or state schools to obtain their finance from central rather than local government, and schools having responsibility for their own budgets.

As with so many second reading debates the welcome, even from government benches, is qualified. The House expresses an independence and liveliness not reflected in the predictable voting majorities. At 9.10 p.m. the wind-up speeches begin. Derek Fatchett, MP for Leeds Central, speaks for Labour and is answered by the Tory Minister, Mrs Angela Rumbold. Thereafter the vote is taken.

At this stage a number of other votes may be taken. If the bill gives rise to expenditure it needs a 'money resolution' which will authorise this. An immediate and limited debate can take place if the resolution is opposed, as it was in the case of the Education (Reform) Bill.

Sometimes, if a bill is of great constitutional significance, the next stage involves consideration by the full House of Commons rather than by a numerically limited standing committee. Often, however, the opposition will press for a bill's committee stage to be considered by the entire House merely to demonstrate how unacceptable they consider the measure. The Education (Reform) Bill, for all its importance, did not have its committee stage taken by the full House of Commons. Rather it was sent to a standing committee, where its fortunes depended upon detailed analysis. This is no casual process where the outcome can be guaranteed by spaniel-like political loyalty. (The procedure is considered further in Chapter 12.)

There was comment and some Conservative anxiety that the Education (Reform) Bill was introduced as late as 1 December. This raises the technical but vitally important issue of how and when bills which have been announced in the Queen's speech are presented to parliament. There are also the departmental aspects of preparing a bill and securing its place in the legislative programme. At the outset it is necessary to assess what will be the opinion of those most likely to be affected by the proposed changes.

In the case of the Education (Reform) Bill those consulted obviously included the teaching unions and the local authorities. The imminence of a General Election in the early summer of 1987 hurried the process of consultation and decision. The education reform plans became an election manifesto commitment. It was a political judgement that the bill should be presented to the first session of the new parliament. This was an exceptionally tight timetable. Consultation was taking place when the intention to proceed with the Bill was announced in the Queen's Speech. Secondly there was the problem that barely adequate time was available to the parliamentary draftsmen, who cast the policy into legal form.

These were the pressures that led to the delayed second reading. Essentially they derived from a decision to include the proposals in an election manifesto and to include the subsequent bill in the first session of parliament. In some ways it was an unsatisfactory situation. It demonstrated that politics is often the pursuit of the second-best but most realistic option. But whatever the difficulties in the preparation of a bill its passage is reasonably assured once it reaches the Commons. In the 1983–7 Parliament one bill, on Sunday Trading, was defeated at second reading – a rare event.

The final hurdle to be negotiated at second reading is the division. Some bills are given an unopposed second reading. The opposition may vote against a bill outright or they may use the technique of a 'reasoned amendment' which registers qualified disapproval. A recent example has been the second reading of the School Boards (Scotland) Bill, when Labour made it clear that it was the government's general educational policy rather than the specific provisions of the measure which offended.

The division itself is another process rooted in tradition. The prime purpose of a division is to count and record the number of votes so that a proposition may be carried or defeated, and so that the votes of individual members can be made public. There is a powerful British tradition that the electors should know how their members have voted. This is a crucial aspect of modern parliamentary democracy, although it involves archaic forms.

Originally MPs were probably counted as they sat. When the Commons moved into St Stephen's Chapel in 1547 the practice developed of members either remaining in the chamber or going out into the anteroom or lobby to register their respective views. Names of Members voting began to be recorded only a century and a half later, and then only sporadically and often unofficially. A Select Committee in 1835 established the present procedures. It suggested that the House should be cleared entirely on every division. It also recommended that there should be separate lobbies for the 'Ayes' and the 'Noes', with four MPs to act as tellers and four clerks to record the votes. It was also suggested that the tellers should stand in front of the table and announce the results, and that the totals of the votes cast should be included in the parliamentary records. The rebuilding of the chamber after the fire of 1834 enabled the construction of the two lobbies and the voting arrangements then put in hand still persist.

There is something dramatic about the actual voting procedure. If the bill is contentious the debate will have concluded in some excitement. In this atmosphere the Speaker states that 'The question is that the bill be read a second time'. Supporters shout 'Aye', opponents retort 'No'. The Speaker then commands 'Clear the Lobbies'. We file away into our respective lobbies to register our votes.

Meanwhile Members will have appeared from throughout the House in answer to the calling of a division which is flashed on the annunciators and by the insistent ringing of bells. The bells are linked to many places adjacent to the Commons termed 'within the Division Bell'. These include Whitehall departments, Lockets Restaurant in Marsham Street, and such establishments as St Stephen's Tavern, the Red Lion, Methuselah's Brasserie and St Stephen's Club in Queen Anne's Gate.

The Speaker calls out, 'Lock the doors', referring to the entrances to the division lobbies. This is done with great expedition by officials of the House. I have seen near-injury in the scuffle to get through the closing doors. The doors are locked no sooner than eight minutes after a division is called. This means a division can take up to fifteen minutes. Very occasionally a small group of MPs has called frequent divisions as a procedural tactic, as happened over the Report Stage of the Firearms (Amendment) Bill in May 1988. Opponents of the bill were able to call a succession of divisions which would have protracted the business considerably. In these circumstances the Speaker is empowered to rule that a division has been 'unnecessarily claimed', and will ask MPs in the Chamber

'Late for Division': from the
Illustrated London News,
1 February 1908.

Saluting the tellers, 1908: hats
were frequently worn before
the First World War.

Division Barrier and Lobby: Members recording their votes in 1882.

to stand to show whether they support or oppose his ruling, and record the number in the minority.

The division lobbies provide a political world of their own as MPs amble through gossiping to each other. The lobby is an excellent place to meet other MPs and to exchange views. The voting lobbies in 1988 provided me with a welcome opportunity to meet Shropshire MPs and co-ordinate views and actions on local hospital closure proposals.

In 1972 I frequently voted in the Labour lobby. I was opposed to Britain joining the European Community and to the prices and incomes policies of Edward Heath. I made a startling discovery. In the Labour lobby members smoked. For Conservatives such behaviour would have been socially unacceptable. I am a strict non-smoker, but my political convictions ensured that for a time I continued to vote more frequently with Labour than any other Conservative.

Members register their votes with clerks who sit at desks armed with large alphabetical lists of MPs' names. They then pass through a pair of open doors which are flanked by two MPs representing 'Aye' and 'No' who act as tellers.

Centuries ago members of the public occasionally mingled with MPs and cast illicit votes. In 1771 a Thomas Hunt of Dartmouth Street was discovered doing so and confessed it was not the first time he had voted in divisions. He was let off with a Speaker's warning. Also at this time, some MPs would send their servants to vote as their proxy. To counter this the convention was established that MPs would clearly state their names to the clerk and walk through with their heads held high. This exhortation is now observed by the MP inclining or nodding his head. In theory this makes his impersonation more difficult. Enoch Powell characteristically held to the old convention of holding his head high and enunciating his name most clearly.

When the votes have been counted the tellers return to the chamber. They line up just beyond the table which is in front of the Speaker, and which divides the two front benches, with the teller for the majority to the Speaker's left, on the opposition side. They bow to the Speaker, advance, and then the teller standing near the opposition despatch box announces the numbers. The Speaker is given the card bearing the voting figures which he then repeats and announces, 'The Ayes (or Noes) have it.'

This rather stately minuet often proceeds in an atmosphere of mounting tension. This could be on account of the decision itself or the extent to which a majority has been qualified by abstentions or cross-voting, that is, voting against party affiliation. It produces a sense of climax which most MPs appreciate. The Education (Reform) Bill may have many hours of unsung work ahead in its committee stage, but when the second reading vote is called the whole process is momentarily touched with drama.

12 STANDING COMMITTEES AND THIRD READING

I was elected to the House of Commons in November 1961 and almost immediately I was selected to serve on the Standing Committee on the Transport Bill, which was to provide the framework for Dr Beeching's reorganisation of the railways. It was a protracted learning curve. Even now my ears still ring with the railway sentiments of two Labour MPs, long since departed from the Commons, Archie Manuel and Charlie Mapp. They rivalled each other for the length of their speeches. I was under a novice's obligatory vow of silence throughout the committee's $91\frac{1}{2}$ hours of business.

Mid-way through this ordeal by silence the Conservative members of the committee were given a consolation lunch by the Transport Minister, Ernest Marples, in his own home, where we were exhorted to give our support with thought rather than tongue. This I continued to do. My neighbour Sir Robert Grant-Ferris, MP for Nantwich, a great sailor, broke ranks and talked about inland waterways. Grant-Ferris had a commanding presence, and he evoked the spectre of the Grand Fleet even on the subject of the Erewash Canal and inland waterways in general. 'Come on Nelson', was the good-natured encouragement from the Labour benches. It was the only time I smiled.

This was my inglorious and bewildering introduction to the world of standing committees. Over the years I lost my innocence and gained my voice. I began to appreciate just how important the standing committee is in the process of parliament. Some years later, in 1972, I served on the Standing Committee that dealt with the development of Concorde, the Concorde Aircraft Bill. The experience was quite different from the Transport Bill. It was a smaller committee. The opposition were not seeking to prolong the passage of the bill. I was a lone Tory voice opposing Concorde, having acquired my prejudices from *The Economist* and its aviation correspondent Mary Goldring. Indeed I soon found I was the bill's only real opponent.

I spoke from a seat in the committee adjacent to the public benches. Thus I had close at hand Richard Wiggs, the director of 'Anti-Concorde'. He was an enthusiastic environmentalist with a comprehensive knowledge of the Concorde project. As the debate proceeded, clause by clause, he passed me the latest and most relevant facts and figures. I had the doubtful pleasure of being a mere David against the Goliath of Michael Heseltine and his cohort of Ministry advisers. Richard Wiggs and I fought with vigour; we were voted into oblivion. Nonetheless I never felt as well briefed subsequently, even as a Treasury Minister, as I did on this back-bench occasion.

My two examples of standing committee work demonstrate how varied it can be. The work lies at the heart of legislation. After the second reading most bills are sent to a committee for detailed consideration. This work is usually known as being done 'upstairs'. This is because there are a number of large, high-ceilinged rooms on the Westminster first floor (known as the committee floor) which accommodate the committees that consider bills. A standing committee room is rather like a miniature House of Commons. At one end is the chairman, who is also an MP. He has powers similar to those of the Speaker and will be flanked by clerks and officials. The room itself has benches and movable leather chairs. Government members sit to the chairman's right, opposition members to his left. The committee normally meets from 10.30 a.m. to 1.00 p.m. on Tuesday and Thursday

The Burial of Harold by F. R. Pickersgill (1846) hangs in Committee Room 14.

mornings, although it can meet in the afternoons and evenings depending upon the nature of the bill and the speed with which it is required. It is an immensely informal atmosphere. As the debates proceed a carpet of discarded papers accumulates as MPs both attend to the bill and deal with their post.

A bill is usually examined clause by clause. All the amendments selected by the chair are subject to debate, and, at the end of this process, often the clause itself. Members of the committee may speak more than once to an amendment, as I learned only too well from my early experience with the Transport Bill. Members may not stray far from the committee room, since divisions are called with only a modest gap of time before the vote is taken. Committee work can become very onerous for MPs if they are serving on a highly controversial bill where the debates become very lengthy. In effect they become prisoners of the committee room and cannot attend other business in the House.

It is perhaps not generally realized that members of the public, including schoolchildren, may attend standing committees simply by turning up at the House and requesting admission to the public benches. These are within yards of the committee benches, and often a more intimate and livelier impression of parliamentary work is gained from the committee than from the chamber.

Those serving on a standing committee will have been chosen by a Committee of Selection which is a group of MPs appointed by the House. It chooses a standing committee with a government majority roughly reflecting the balance of voting in the Commons. Some MPs tell the Committee of Selection they would like to serve; more accept service with the stoicism of conscripts. It is hard work, occasionally it can be enjoyable, but it is essential. The heroes of standing committees are largely unsung. Could greater public interest rescue them from oblivion and government supporters from silence?

Once a bill has completed its committee stage it is 'reported' back to the House. The report stage follows when the House has an opportunity to consider and debate the bill once more. Often during a standing committee a Minister will use the prospect of a report stage to promise that changes to the bill will be made at that time, although no immediate amendments can be devised. A standing committee usually has between 18 and 40 members, and the defection of two or three government members can cause defeat. The influence of the Whips is far greater at report stage, when the whole House can vote and many will not be familiar with the issues. In this situation any committee-stage rebels are likely to be outvoted.

The report stage of a bill is followed by a Third Reading. Strictly, debate on the third reading must be related solely to the contents of the bill and not to the subject generally, as at second reading. It is hardly surprising that the proceedings are peremptory and of little public note. There have been exceptions, and one was the Third Reading of the Race Relations Bill on 7 July 1968.

The second reading some weeks earlier had been preceded by a speech outside parliament by Enoch Powell, setting out his fears concerning large-scale immigration and securing his dismissal from the shadow Cabinet. The Tory party was divided and passions ran high. The debate opened with a seemingly casual comment from the Speaker: 'I have not selected the amendment.' The amendment to the third reading had been moved by Powell supporters in exactly the same terms as the one moved by Edward Heath and the opposition front bench to the second reading. To the spectator it must have seemed like musical chairs, to the participants it was a wilful demonstration intended to show that the Conservative leadership was more liberal over immigration than it cared to admit. When the division on the third reading was called, 46 Conservatives and Unionists, including Enoch Powell, rebelled by voting for exactly the same amendment as the party had supported on second reading. The Commons floor was littered with gauntlets. This certainly had been no normal third reading.

The circumstances of the committee stage of a bill – many amendments and no restraint on frequency and length of speeches – mean that the opposition have ample opportunities to delay the measure. Thus it can upset a whole session's programme as the passage of all bills is interrelated. Normally the government and opposition will agree informally on the time needed for a bill. There is still plenty of debate, but the virtue of nocturnal activity is discounted. There are a few occasions when a bill is so controversial that progress is slow and the government provides a timetable for phasing and ending debate at pre-determined times – the 'guillotine'. Examples of its use in recent years have been the Social Security Bill in the 1985–6 session and the Abolition of Domestic Rates (Scotland) Bill in 1986–7, which introduced the new community charge.

Most guillotines are preceded by Polyfilla verbiage from opponents that has little merit in content or delivery. All members of the standing committee are released from their misery by the guillotine. Indeed I have moved guillotine motions, as Leader of the House, when the sense of release was evident on all sides of the House.

One oratorical memory will live as long as there are MPs to walk the committee floor. It reflects the resistance to the Telecommunications Bill, intended to place telecommunications under private ownership, in 1983. John Golding, the Labour MP for Newcastle under Lyme, moved an amendment at 5.35 a.m. on 3 November. He proceeded with a speech, punctuated only by the adjournment of the committee, that lasted until

The Guillotine, as portrayed by John Jensen in the Sunday Telegraph, *19 May 1968.*

the early hours of 9 November. It had lasted 9 hours and 45 minutes. It was a speech of skill and stamina, and probably could not be repeated as a result of rule changes. Both the Golding speech and the Telecommunications Bill were nonetheless great parliamentary events. It is just possible they will aid those who argue that all standing committee stages should either be subject to an informal and agreed timetable or else one provided for by the rules of the House. Many argue for this change and the debate continues. Golding's speech, meanwhile, remains a record.

13 THE WHIPS: SHEEPDOGS NOT SCORPIONS

The Whips Office has a misleadingly sinister name. In fact it is primarily concerned with managing affairs so that parliamentary business can be done, not with coercion or the trampling underfoot of tender consciences. Parliamentary organisation relates to the practices of the Commons.

George Canning, the nineteenth-century Tory Prime Minister, said that the function of a Whip was 'to make a House, keep a House, and cheer the Minister'. These admirable qualities of organisation and support are not easily found. Disraeli judged that the office of Chief Whip required 'consummate knowledge of human nature, the most amiable flexibility, and complete self control'. The standards are daunting.

An explanation of the Whip's function must first distinguish between message and men. The term 'Whip' is applied to both. Today's message takes the form of a weekly communication which sets out the Commons business for the week, notices of party political meetings, and finally a sheet with 'all-party' notices. It is a brisk and business-like document, packed with information and carrying very little commentary. Each item of Commons business is underlined: two or three lines indicate the importance of being present to support the party vote. A one-line whip usually means that a vote is not expected. The general form of the Whip concerning parliamentary business has remained substantially unchanged since the last century. The inclusion of party and 'all-party' information has developed steadily since World War One.

If the message has remained rather peremptory and austere in form, more than enough colour has been provided by the politicians who have played the Whip's role. The term 'Whip' is derived from the hunting field, where whippers-in have the responsibility for keeping hounds from straying from the pack. Whipping, in the sense of organising friends or the like-minded, was being practised before the Civil War. Messages sent to the friends of James I in the House of 1621 were underscored as many as six times.

There is evidence of the increasing organisation of votes in the eighteenth century. At this time parliamentary seats, election votes and official positions were purchased. The government used public funds to secure Members' attendance and support. The senior government Whips still carry titles which remind us of their former link with the Treasury. The government Chief Whip is Parliamentary Secretary to the Treasury (sometimes known as Patronage Secretary). Five Whips are appointed as Lords Com-

missioners to the Treasury, and three Whips have titles related to the Royal Household: Treasurer, Comptroller and Vice Chamberlain. The substance has changed, but the old form is quaintly preserved.

A striking example of change is the method of summoning support. A royal Whip was issued on 21 September 1675 on King Charles II's behalf. It read:

The Unionist Whips photographed on the Terrace in 1899. The term 'Unionist' referred to Conservatives and those Liberals who deserted Gladstone over the issue of Irish Home Rule.

> Sir J. Williamson to a Member of Parliament. The King being firmly resolved that Parliament shall meet 13 Oct, that you may not be surprised with any contrary reports, nor be detained by the business of the sessions, which unhappily is near that time, has commanded me to give you this notice, and to desire you will not fail to be here at or before the time appointed, and I desire you will let me know as soon as you come to town, that I may acquaint the King how his commands to me have been executed.

Throughout the eighteenth century there were numerous factions within each of the two major parties, the Whigs and the Tories. The exhortations to attend the Commons and vote were generally issued on behalf of those factions, which thereafter grouped themselves to support an administration. These exhortations to attend were, in effect, letters sent to rally 'friends'. On 23 October 1753, towards the end of his career as Prime Minister, a typical letter was sent by Henry Pelham at the start of a parliament.

Sir,

The meeting of the Parliament being fixed for the 15th day of next month, when it is expected to enter upon the publick business, I take the liberty to acquaint you, that your early attendance there will be very agreeable to your friends, and particularly, Sir, to your

most obedient, humble servant,
H. Pelham

Sometimes these letters were not sent direct to Members but to the leaders of factions. The Duke of Newcastle was often at the centre of such organisations. His letter to Lord Sandwich brought a response which indicated that there was already an awkward squad in the eighteenth century. The modern Whip would understand.

I have the honour of your Grace's commands, which I shall immediately obey by desiring all the gentlemen (except one) to appear at the Cockpit the day before the meeting of Parliament, and I should imagine they will very readily follow my advice.
As to my cousin, Mr Montagu, I much fear he never will (as he never yet has) give his countenance to any administration.

The organisation of friends, or whipping, had improved considerably by the early nineteenth century, but it was still a relatively secret activity. Sir Robert Peel, later Conservative Prime Minister, wrote to the Duke of Richmond on 26 May 1813: 'Holmes was extremely active in managing our friends [on the Catholic Emancipation Bill] and did it without any appearance of being employed by any part of the Government.' William Holmes became a key figure in the history of Whips. During his time whipping became a well-recognised and eventually an open practice. His long public career spanned nearly 30 years as an MP with a period in office as Treasurer of the Ordnance. The *Dictionary of National Biography* summarises the significance of his career. 'For thirty years "Billy Holmes" was the adroit and dexterous whip of the Tory Party, and his great knowledge of the tastes, wishes, idiosyncrasies, family connections of all members on the Tory side of the House made him a most skilful dispenser of patronage and party manager.'

Today's Whips Offices carry forward a tradition established by Holmes. Over the past century that tradition has further reflected the growth of party organisation in response to a much larger electorate, and the enormous increase in the volume of government business.

Whips are paid when their party is in government (as are the Opposition Chief Whip, the Opposition Deputy Chief Whip, and one other Whip) but both Conservative and Labour parliamentary Whips follow the same general practice. There is, however, one major difference. The Labour Chief Whip and his deputy are elected by the parliamentary party. The Conservative Chief Whip is a key appointment made personally by the Conservative leader. It is assumed that effective party management needs complete accord between leader and Chief Whip. The rest of the Whips are chosen on the same basis as junior ministers, although the views of existing Whips are taken into account when adding to their number.

The main purpose of the Whips Office is to have a comprehensive knowledge of what is happening in the Commons. Whips not only transmit the wishes of government to the parliamentary party, they also act as sounding-boards for back-bench opinion. They evaluate and report back to Ministers how policies are being received, what issues are likely to be difficult, and what members of the government are shining or fading on account of their ministerial performances. The Whips are also assessing the performance and worth of back-benchers, and their judgement ensures the initial promotion prospects of those likely to ascend the government ladder. It is the Whips Office, not Ministers, who choose parliamentary private secretaries.

There is, of course, a disciplinary aspect to the work. This is usually carried out in a spirit of regret, even if occasionally accompanied by anger; no penalties are imposed. If a member is in genuine disagreement with his government there is little the Whips Office can do. It is a sensible courtesy for a dissident MP to inform the Whip of his intended vote. The Chief Whip is expected to be able to tell the party leader what will be the size of the majority; and he can reasonably expect to be informed by those intending to buck the party vote. Occasionally a ministerial wind-up of a debate may be so brilliant or appalling that it will bring last-minute conversions. Even so, Westminster generally agrees with Clemenceau's dictum: 'A speech may often change my mind: but my vote, never.'

In the 1970 parliament I had a formidable record of voting against the Conservative government. I opposed three-line Whips on British membership of the European Community and on the Conservative prices and incomes policy. For good measure I also opposed the local government 'reform' which created the artificial county of Avon substantially at the expense of my native county of Somerset. Throughout all this I maintained good and courteous relations with the Chief Whip, Francis Pym. I never received even the faintest hint of reproach. On the other hand if I had missed votes because of being in Honolulu, perhaps, without notification – albeit with loyalty unbounded – the story could have been different. The immediate consequence would be a Whip's note blending enquiry with implied reproach. Julian Critchley, Conservative MP for Aldershot and seasoned traveller, has announced his intention of keeping his collection of these notes for eventual publication.

The Conservative Whips Office performs its role of collecting and disseminating information from a set of rooms strategically situated off the Members' lobby. Similar facilities exist for Labour. There are fourteen Conservative Whips. The Chief Whip attends the Cabinet each week, but is not formally a member of it.

There is a daily meeting of Whips between 2.30 and 3.30 p.m. This meeting enables a thorough check to be made of the day's business, and to ensure that individual Whips have been assigned to tasks such as manning the front bench. The front benches, government and opposition, will always have a Whip in attendance no matter whether the business is major or modest. There is also a weekly Whips' meeting on Wednesday mornings. This is largely concerned with choosing the business for the following week, which will subsequently be confirmed with the opposition and made known to the House the next day (see Chapter 14).

The work of the Whips can be divided broadly between territorial and subject responsibilities. Twelve Whips have 'areas' and are in direct contact with MPs who represent constituencies within, say, the West Midlands or the Western Area. An MP will often be contacted by his area Whip to ascertain his views on such delicate issues as Sunday trading. The MP may make the first move and inform his area Whip of his views, unprompted, while there is time to influence decisions.

Subject responsibility involves both legislation and political party committees. Whips are generally assigned to a government department for this purpose. Thus the Transport Whip would normally sit on the standing committee of any bill sponsored by the Transport Secretary. He would also attend the weekly meeting of the party back-bench committee on Transport. The same Whip, of course, would also have an area role, meanwhile taking his turn in round-the-clock manning of the front bench. A Whip's work is never done.

The Government and Opposition Whips Offices have a close working relationship. There is a fraternity between Whips. Together they provide the 'usual channels' which develop a network of common knowledge and understanding that enables parliament to work without the need for detailed and elaborate Standing Orders. This relationship is crucial in respect of 'pairing'. A Member and his 'pair' agree to be absent from voting on occasions to their mutual convenience. The arrangement is not

admissible where a three-line Whip applies. A Member often finds an opponent who will agree to 'pair' so they need not necessarily be in the House when there is no voting, or only voting on minor matters. It is also possible to get permission from the 'pairing' whip to be absent from voting to honour engagements outside the House. The 'pairing' Whips from the two main parties work together, comparing their books so there can be no misunderstanding or subsequent accusations of broken faith. It demonstrates a reality that should discomfit those who so easily accuse Westminster of practising adversarial politics.

One member of the Whips Office, the Comptroller to Her Majesty's Household, has the task of sending a hand-written letter to the Queen on each day's Commons proceedings. Whips are not expected to speak but at various stages in the parliamentary day they utter phrases such as 'I beg to move', or 'I beg to move that the question be now put' or 'Tomorrow, Sir'.

The Conservative Whips Office is undeniably a male club. The Whips room is suitably untidy, almost to the point of disorganisation. Amid the papers strewn around I could swear I have seen the *Sporting Life*. To date, such casualness has never been challenged by a Conservative woman Whip. On the other hand Labour have boasted no fewer than five women Whips.

The 'Parliamentary Pairing Season' a century ago.

The Whips Office is an excellent nursery for ministerial office. Nigel Lawson, a pugnacious debater, exceptionally had dispensation to be a speaking Whip. He and his fellow Whip Cecil Parkinson both became Cabinet Ministers. Without doubt, however, the most distinguished Conservative ex-Chief Whip is Edward Heath, the only one to become Prime Minister. As Chief Whip he had the difficult task of taking the Conservatives into Suez and then nursing them out again. With Macmillan he takes much credit for the post-Suez recovery leading to the 1959 General Election victory. When I came to the Commons in 1961 he was confident and business-like in his approach to the European Community. These managerial qualities secured his election to the Conservative leadership in 1965. Events since then are well known. Today he sits defiantly in the Commons, determined to fight for a long-held faith which he believes will outlive current fashion.

The other distinguished ex-Chief Whip I recall is the late John Silkin, Labour MP for Deptford. There was an acrimonious debate on the committee or report stage of some bill. I was bouncing up and down, imploring to be called. The Chair was indifferent. My anxiety to speak increased. Suddenly, to my fury, John Silkin moved to close the debate. I bellowed 'Reichstag' and a few other epithets and stormed out of the chamber. So great was my temper that I had forgotten to stay and vote against the Silkin closure motion.

Years later, as Leader of the House, I met John Silkin frequently as he was my shadow. I cannot recall a pleasanter or more tolerant working opponent. I never completely forgave him for that closure, but he always assured me that it was not personal. Chief Whips are ever disarming.

14 FIXING THE AGENDA

Thursday is the climax of the parliamentary week. After the duel at Prime Minister's Questions the Leader of the Opposition turns to a more manageable task: 'Can the Leader of the House tell us next week's business?' The Leader of the House reads out the following week's business, itemised like a laundry list, day by day and subject by subject. The Leader of the Opposition should have no difficulty with his supplementary questions. He probably knows the business from the behind-the-scenes discussions the previous evening. Nonetheless he will ask a number of questions, usually complaining about the issues not yet being debated. The Leader of the House responds, affecting some puzzlement and pain at the opposition's response. He promises liberally that 'these matters can be considered through the usual channels'.

An observer may find this all rather bewildering. The quiet promise to 'consider matters' further is in such sharp contrast to the aggression of Prime Minister's Question Time. What are the 'usual channels' that seemingly flow without turbulence? Parliament wears an adversarial mask. The Commons is properly seized with occasional anger and indignation. Overwhelmingly, however, it operates by means of conciliation and adjustment. This is seen most effectively in the arrangement of next week's business. This process eventually includes the sessional programme and the passing of the measures contained in the Queen's Speech.

Securing broad agreement over the conduct of business is the job of the Whips Offices of the various political parties. These are the 'usual channels'. The principle that governs them is the realistic judgement that one day an election will reverse their fortunes. Government Whips possessing power always remember that one day they will be in opposition. Opposition Whips, tempted by irresponsibility, also know that one day they will bear the responsibility of office. The combination of hope and fear produces self-discipline. Power is never absolute at Westminster.

The two Whips Offices are in constant touch. They assess each other's tactics and objectives, but there is little desire to fight for unconditional surrender. Handbag-swinging is strictly for the Chamber.

One civil servant plays a key role in this process of continual judgement. He is the Principal Private Secretary to the government Chief Whip. Although he is on the payroll of the Cabinet Office, he is as likely to be found in the company of opposition spokesmen as that of government ministers. He must rival Henry Kissinger's skill in shuttle diplomacy, as he seeks to narrow differences and dovetail the agenda.

This task of preparing for 'next week' starts not later than Monday – allowing three clear days for soundings and making deals. Many factors have to be taken into account. Constituency distance and travel are very real factors for many MPs. Good sense therefore argues that Northern Ireland business should not be taken on a Monday, or Scottish business on a Thursday evening. A well-judged programme takes account of this. Occasionally debates are timed to suit the legitimate travel plans of opposition spokesmen. Debates have to be arranged taking account of the government legislative programme and the requirements of European Community meetings.

The draft week's programme will almost certainly meet some unforeseen difficulties, and not only on major items. Eventually an agreed outline programme should be available in time for the Shadow Cabinet meeting on Wednesday evening. If there are any problems outstanding they must be speedily resolved. The Cabinet meets on Thursday morning and it is essential that it should be informed of the proposed agenda. There is a powerful convention that the Cabinet does not amend or set aside 'next week's business'. Occasionally this is breached, but generally in response to last-minute situations.

From time to time there is failure to agree on the agenda. Shuttle diplomacy has been tried valiantly, but failed. The Leader of the House then 'imposes' the government's proposals. There are dire threats about relations breaking down, but the threat soon passes. The two Whips Offices are both dependent on the success of the parliamentary system.

For five enjoyable years from 1982 to 1987 I was Leader of the House of Commons. As a departmental Cabinet Minister I had had, necessarily, to spend much time in Whitehall. Now I was back in the Westminster world I loved. I soon discovered that 3.30 p.m. on Thursday afternoon meant more than informing the House of the content of next week's business.

The initial exchanges over, a forest of members then shot up. Every one had views on more subjects and more debate. Cynically, I wondered if we could arrange a special night shift for such enthusiasts.

In truth most of them were nursing in question form a speech they had been unable to deliver during the week. I crouched on the front bench as though I were in a dug-out being bombarded by questions on every conceivable topic. On 22 January 1987 they ranged through elderly police widows, the failure of the water system in London, and abuse of diplomatic immunity. In all I had to field 23 questions. The barrage lasted just short of half-an-hour. The Speaker did not call a truce. I was not released until the last back-bencher had raked the Treasury bench with a final burst of

*The Leader of the House's
room in the Commons, used
while the House is sitting.*

Sten-gun fire. I had survived. Triumphantly – or only mildly bloodied –
I would bow to the Speaker, and retire to the Leader's Commons office
to be revived with tea. There was a speedy inquest on the occasion with
my private office and my parliamentary private secretary. My answers
were analysed, and where I had given commitments, work was put in
hand to fulfil them by referring specific topics to the relevant Minister.

The Speaker was very wise to allow business questions to run an
unimpeded course. It was a safety valve, and appreciated by MPs who
wanted to put something on the record but had not been called to make
a speech. Some members made a speciality of using this opportunity. One
such was Peter Bruinvels, a Conservative MP for Leicester in the 1983–7
parliament. Every week he asked questions that were robustly partisan and
intensely parochial. After a while I felt I had earned the freedom of
Leicester. One week Bruinvels and his Labour sparring partner Greville
Janner QC, aided by Derek Spencer, Conservative MP for Leicester South,
took me through the issues of Leicester unemployment three times over.
They may not have devastated Hansard, but they earned respect and notice
in the *Leicester Mercury*.

As Leader of the Commons I wish I could have awarded Oscars for performances at next week's business. Surely John Stokes, High Tory MP for Halesowen and Stourbridge, would have earned his statuette when he referred to St George's Day and called for a debate on England 'in view of the amount of time and money that we spend discussing the affairs of other countries within the United Kingdom'.

The Leader of the House is sustained by two traditions. One is ancient and distinguished, the other fairly recent and decidedly professional. Latterly, the Leader of the House has acquired a major responsibility for the passage of legislation. The 1945 post-war Labour Government was committed to a massive King's Speech. In these circumstances Attlee appointed Herbert Morrison to the post. He master-minded the legislation and was also a powerful organiser of the party machine. Between 1945 and 1951 Morrison established the modern role of Commons Leader. Thereafter the post was rarely combined with any other departmental responsibility.

This development replaced the old-style post of Leader of the House. Formerly the volume of government business was so modest that Commons leadership was a prestigious part-time task. It could be undertaken by the Prime Minister if he was in the Commons and by a senior Commons Cabinet Member if the Prime Minister was in the Lords. Neville Chamberlain was the last person to be both Prime Minister and Leader of the House.

The Leader works from a split site. In the morning he has a superb room on the first floor of the Privy Council Office in Whitehall, which was rebuilt by the Duke of Dorset in 1730–40. It is an imposing room with an ornamental plaster ceiling, white marble mantelpiece and a huge bay window. The pictures were chosen by Norman St John Stevas (now Lord St John of Fawsley) who was Leader of the House from 1979 to 1981. I was content to live with them, but I shared with Michael Foot, also a former Leader of the House, a strong antipathy towards a huge portrait of James II. I worked with my back to it.

The room is central for all the Whitehall and Downing Street meetings the Leader has to undertake. Like a travelling troupe, at lunchtime the Commons Leader and his modest private office transfer themselves and their papers to rooms in the House of Commons. This is essential because of his responsibilities once the House is sitting. That room, too, illustrates Commons history. A painting of Wilberforce proclaims the great parliamentary struggle against slavery. Also evocative is a huge oil canvas 230 cm wide and 140 cm high depicting 'The First House of Commons Steeplechase in 1889'. We have retained much of our tradition and symbols, but alas the Commons steeplechase is now as much lost in the past as the medieval exchequer tally sticks. (Today I believe there are only two MPs

who have been amateur National Hunt jockeys. One is Nicholas Budgen, MP for Wolverhampton South West and an eloquent advocate of sound money economics. The second is Henry Bellingham, Conservative MP for King's Lynn.) Finally a bust of Disraeli is a reminder that he led the Commons when Derby was Prime Minister in the Lords. His main task, of course, was Chancellor of the Exchequer. Possibly no politician in the last century was more skilled, charming or subtle. He represents a very different tradition from the brutal party management practised by Morrison. A modern Commons Leader is inspired by both examples.

The First House of Commons Steeplechase, 1889. *This picture hangs in the Leader of the House's room near the Chamber. I sat beneath it for five years.*

15 THE ADJOURNMENT DEBATE AND 'WHO GOES HOME?'

The vote at 10 p.m. concludes the debate on a government bill. Summoned by division bells, MPs appear in the chamber from every nook of the House. The vote proceeds and the result is announced. There is good-natured banter and members then stampede for the doors, and for their cars or taxis. Within minutes the chamber has become deserted.

The government Whip rises and intones, 'Mr Speaker I beg to move, that this House do now adjourn.' The Speaker then calls the MP who has been awarded the 'adjournment debate'. A junior Minister sits alone. Often the Minister, the government Whip and the Member are a mere trio who conduct these parliamentary vespers. There will be a debate with no vote and which lasts for half-an-hour equally divided between Minister and Member.

This, however, is no anti-climax. It is a valuable parliamentary occasion, allowing MPs to raise specific issues with the Minister responsible. Originally any Member could move at any time that the House should adjourn its business and so scupper other arrangements for the day. It was the Irish MPs who used this technique to obstruct government business. As a consequence a Standing Order was passed in 1882 to restrict the use of the tactic. By 1945 the present arrangements for the adjournment debate were evolved. A major factor was an extension of adjournment debates in World War Two as a compensation for much less general debating time.

The present rules allow for a debate of half-an-hour at the end of each day. The Speaker chooses the member and topic for one day a week – Thursday – but otherwise it is determined by ballot. An MP wishing to take part in the ballot must give prior notification to the Speaker, who then presides over this parliamentary lottery on alternate Thursday mornings, when debates for the next fortnight will be decided.

MPs are entitled to nominate any subject for which there is ministerial responsibility, but most tend to choose domestic and constituency interests. This means that there is a ministerial short straw. Some junior Minister will have to be on call throughout the evening until government business has been concluded, after which the adjournment debate begins. Sir George Young has the unenviable record. His work in the Health and Social Security and Environment departments between 1979 and 1986 required him to answer no less than 134 adjournment debates.

The subjects that are debated in this daily postscript vary enormously. During a fortnight the ten debates could produce issues including dumping

of American waste in Warrington, trunk roads serving Bradford, the Department of Trade and Industry's handling of an insider trading case, the treatment of an inmate who had died in Barlinnie Prison, and police resources in Leicestershire.

Some members cannot seek an adjournment debate by reason of their office, namely Ministers and the Speaker and his deputies. A former deputy Speaker, Sir Robert Grant-Ferris, asked me in December 1973 to take an adjournment debate on his behalf. I was given a closely argued and typed draft on the recreation area at Hough in South Cheshire. I then discovered how eerie the occasion could be as I stumbled through my lines before an empty House and a Public Gallery graced only by my dinner guest, ironically an actress. One member who could be guaranteed to maintain the same voice and demeanour as always was Ian Paisley. To him an adjournment debate, a crowded House or the Martyrs Memorial Church merited and received the same rich voice, powerful delivery and uncompromising message.

The normal convention of the MP and the Minister equally dividing the half-hour available can be breached by prior arrangement. This was done with the debate on the Leicester police initiated by Michael Latham, the Conservative MP for Rutland and Melton. He agreed to share his debate with six other Leicestershire MPs. Latham limited his remarks to five minutes and the others spoke very briefly, thus allowing the Home Office Minister the normal fifteen minutes to reply. Some argue that this may be a harbinger of future developments.

Obviously, the subject-matter of late evening adjournment debates is appealing to provincial media. The conventional form of the debate is, nonetheless, daunting – a lonely dialogue between a sole Member and a Minister separated by acres of green leather benches. A mini-debate about a local topic with half-a-dozen extremely short speeches would be a much livelier prospect. The adjournment debate, already the product of reform, could be poised for further change.

There are also other occasions when the House has guaranteed time for wide-ranging debates. These include the three-hour debates which take place before the decision is taken for the standard parliamentary holidays, namely Christmas, Easter, Whitsun and Summer. There is also a debate that takes place on the day the House adjourns for these holidays, running usually from 9.30 a.m. until 3.30 p.m. On these occasions topics may be debated for approximately 30 minutes. Finally there is the debate which follows the Consolidated Fund Bill. The last-mentioned is a planned all-night marathon which does not end until nine o'clock in the morning. In addition the government occasionally initiates debates on major topics on the adjournment formula since it enables a general debate. This can be controversial, because the adjournment motion is not amendable – we go home or we do not. There are circumstances where the opposition would like to express qualified disagreement by an amendment which could hook some government dissidents. In these circumstances the choice of either an amendable motion or the adjournment motion is a matter of political tactics. In making their decision Ministers will wish to avoid any procedural banana skins.

There are no such problems about the general debates that are related to the impending holiday or recess, and to the Consolidated Fund. Usually they are debates where members have given notice of the subjects they wish to raise and where the timing and the duration of the debate are known and published. The time allocated means that several MPs can speak on the topic as well as allowing a government reply. The three-hour

'Just a wet cloth over the back benchers and a bit o' polish on the Junior Ministers, this morning, girls. Not time for much when they 'as all-night sittings.' Cartoon by Lee in the Evening News, *12 March 1951.*

debate which precedes the decision to take a holiday (rarely challenged) is completely open. Back-benchers will speak on any topic and the Leader of the House, in answering the debate, will be required to show omniscience on issues ranging from ward renovations at the cottage hospital in Ludlow to the threatened destruction of the Amazonian rain forest. Equipped with Whitehall briefs and the generosity of the House, he survives.

Over a tenth of Commons time is devoted to back-bench adjournment debates. This is an indicator of how valuable they are for the MP who wants to raise local matters that previously he has championed in correspondence and private visits to Whitehall. The adjournment technique is also available to the Member who is campaigning on a national issue. Jeff Rooker, Labour MP for Perry Barr, did this on 28 June 1988 in respect of the British prisoners-of-war murdered at Wormhoudt in Belgium in May 1940. Of course we are dazzled by the great Commons law-making events – the Queen's Speech and the Budget – but the House has another and equally important role. It is the parliamentary 'talking shop', where MPs speak out on a wide range of issues. Those who despise it do not understand Parliament.

One Commons ritual is never heard by the public. When business is over and the chair has been vacated, the Speaker tells the Serjeant and the Serjeant tells the doorkeeper, who repeats the information, 'Usual time tomorrow'. This quaint custom dates from the early days when there were no fixed hours for meetings of the House and when, because printing was slow and copies scarce, MPs were given a spoken reminder of the time of meeting.

As each day's business ends the Commons police bellow, 'Who goes home?' It is an impressive performance that would match any town crier. As the echoes die away the laggard MP drifts off, and the assiduous Minister

'Who goes home?' Illustrated London News, *1 February 1908.*

closes his red box of ministerial papers and contacts his driver. For a few hours Westminster sleeps.

The phrase 'Who Goes Home?' originates from the days when the streets around Westminster were unsafe. Doorkeepers would then organise groups of MPs going in the same direction so that they could leave the Palace of Westminster together. They might hire a link boy to guide them through the dark, cobbled streets with a flaming torch. Some MPs, and not just law-and-order politicians, wonder if the lawless wheel is not turning full circle. In 1987 Metropolitan Police District 'A', which covers the Westminster area, recorded 329 crimes of violence against the person, including 125 muggings.

Today MPs do not leave in groups. They mostly go home by private car, and members of the government in ministerial cars. Occasionally MPs use public transport, but a larger number gather 'under the canopy' at the Members' entrance in New Palace Yard. From here a button operates a flashing light and bell situated on the corner of Bridge Street and Parliament Square which summon taxis. There is a rule that Members awaiting taxis have precedence over journalists and other non-members. Although MPs usually seek the best possible relations with the press, I have always observed that they strictly assert their privileges in the queue. Often the waiting seems endless. Eventually the taxi arrives and the relief is then tempered by the robust advice proffered by the driver on crime and transport.

The most distinguished method of departure is the bicycle. Jack Dormand, former Labour MP for Easington and chairman of the Labour back-benchers' committee, used to swathe himself in luminous strips and cycle home. Jock Bruce Gardyne, former Tory MP and Treasury Minister, now Lord Bruce Gardyne, had a very old-fashioned bicycle which I swear had seen better days at university. Sir George Young, Conservative MP for Ealing and former Minister, would easily qualify for the Westminster yellow jersey. His angular figure and somewhat sporting bicycle enable him to shoot from New Palace Yard into Parliament Square. The police would have held back the traffic had he been in his ministerial or private motor car: as a cyclist he and his insurers are on their own. I once had a bicycle which I bought at a street market. Cycling to the Commons was healthy, but I decided I would be laid low by over-exertion or by a continental juggernaut. I left the aged machine in the cycle rack in the colonnades alongside New Palace Yard. After years rather than months it was towed away.

PART III

Parliamentary Occasions

16 STATE OPENING TO PROROGATION

It is thirty years since the State Opening of Parliament was first shown on television. However superb the spectacle, it does illustrate some of the pitfalls in presenting Parliament to the public. It always has to be patiently explained that the Queen is reading a speech which has been prepared by her Ministers and in no sense conveys her own feelings.

As with most parliamentary ceremonial it is difficult to date its origins. Before 1512 parliaments were opened in the Painted Chamber. This room was at the far end of the Lords where the throne is now situated, and it was demolished in 1847. The current practice of opening Parliament from the House of Lords, where the Queen makes her speech from the throne, began after 1536.

The State Opening usually takes place in November, at 11 a.m. It is a magnificent occasion – the peers and peeresses resplendent in ermine robes, the peers' wives looking on in full evening dress and tiaras. While the ceremony of the Queen's arrival and procession to the throne is taking place in the Lords, the Commons is crowded and expectant. A handful of Members wear morning dress. They all await a summons to hear the speech from the throne. Meanwhile, in the Lords, at the Queen's command the Lord Chamberlain, a royal official, raises his wand. This is the signal for the Gentleman Usher of the Black Rod to proceed and summon the House of Commons.

Black Rod leaves the Lords, crosses the Central Lobby, and passes through the Members' Lobby towards the door of the Commons chamber. As he approaches, the door is slammed shut in his face by the Serjeant at Arms. This custom dates from earlier times, when the Commons feared being interrupted by a royal messenger. Black Rod is acting in that capacity. Slamming the door demonstrates the right of the Commons to secure their deliberations against all comers.

Black Rod raps three times on the door of the Commons with the ebony stick which is his symbol of office. It is surmounted by a golden lion rampant and has a gold sovereign embedded in it. Years of this treatment has damaged one of the panels of the door to the chamber. The door is then opened, and as Black Rod advances an usher precedes him to the bar of the House and cries 'Black Rod'. Black Rod continues slowly to the table in front of the Speaker, bowing as he does so. He then delivers the royal message: 'The Queen commands the honourable House to attend Her Majesty immediately in the House of Peers.' Black Rod escorts the

Entry to the Commons Chamber used by Black Rod at the State Opening of Parliament. The statues of Churchill and Lloyd George flank the bomb-damaged archway.

Speaker, who is wearing his state robes and accompanied by the members of his daily procession, to the House of Lords. They are followed by the Commons, walking two by two, led by the Prime Minister and the Leader of the Opposition. As members emerge from the chamber the television cameras film them walking towards the House of Lords. It is very informal. Viewers can see those who will do fierce battle in the forthcoming session casually chatting.

The Members of the Commons cease their babble of conversation as they stand at the far end from the throne. There is precious little space to accommodate the front-bench MPs, let alone all the others, and so there is something of a scrum. Ministers look suitably thoughtful, even occasionally surprised, as they hear read aloud the words they have collectively composed. Once the Queen has completed her speech she leaves, and the Speaker and Members return to the Commons.

The Leader of the House has a walk-on role in the ceremony before the speech is read and stands close to the throne while the speech is being delivered. In that capacity I had a chance on one occasion in the 1980s to appreciate the formidable qualities of the Earl Marshal of England, the Duke of Norfolk, who is effectively in charge of ceremonies. Participants were summoned for a non-dress rehearsal in the late afternoon preceding the opening. An attractive young woman, rumoured to be from the Lord Chancellor's office, was the surrogate royalty. Her consort also came from somewhere in Whitehall. We were put through our paces. The Earl Marshal had a distinguished military background and a blend of firmness and charm that got us more or less in order. The ceremony always went astonishingly well on the day.

Two ceremonies take place on the eve of the State Opening; one is traditional, the other more recent. First the Yeomen of the Guard (Beefeaters) search the cellars of the Palace of Westminster, a custom they have followed every year since the Gunpowder Plot of 1605, when Guy Fawkes and his fellow conspirators tried to blow up parliament. Secondly, at 10 Downing Street there will be a great dinner for all members of the government. The meal is preceded by drinks, and there comes a dramatic moment when silence is called and the text of the Queen's Speech is read. Ministers then proceed to their tables. The occasion is obligatory for Ministers and recently a charge has been made to help balance the account.

The modern Queen's Speech, setting out the government's proposals, derives from medieval times. Then the Lord Chancellor made an address explaining why parliament had been summoned. This rarely concerned a desire for new laws, except when Henry VIII wanted statutes to authorise his reforms of the Church. Today's Queen's Speech is a different matter. The extension of the franchise and growing public responsibility for social welfare has added to both public spending and the range of legislation. The Queen's Speech reflects this demand for new law-making.

There are a number of factors which contribute to this voracious legislative appetite. There are election manifesto commitments and Whitehall's requests for new laws, often to meet public pressure. Laws are also needed to fulfil international obligations. The task of assessing and listing ministerial requests for legislation is undertaken by a committee dominated by the government's business managers. The ever-watchful Treasury also attends.

As Leader of the House I sat on this committee, usually under the chairmanship of Lord Whitelaw, then Lord President of the Council and Leader of the House of Lords. Ministers would be interviewed and would champion the merits of their proposed bills with great intensity. It was expected of them, not least by their senior civil servants. Eventually a recommended list of bills was put to the Cabinet. The list allowed for the Cabinet to add possibly one or two bills. The room for manoeuvre is limited. There is a physical limit to the number of bills that can be piloted through parliament, which is already working longer hours than any other in Western Europe. Then there is the additional problem of how the work of the Lords and the Commons could be related, so that one chamber is not over-burdened while the other is underloaded.

The result is a complex plan showing when bills would be introduced, and in which House, what time should be allotted to each bill and when they could expect Royal Assent. The plan I saw looked like a critical path analysis chart. The reality was not quite so scientific. Slide rules were not the only basis of our work. The personality of Lord Whitelaw helped, for in dealing with colleagues he had a worldly charm and the negotiating stamina of a Borders cattle-dealer.

Once the Cabinet has authorised the number of bills for the new session, the text of the Queen's Speech can be compiled. This proves to be a daunting task. The document is not likely to be lively, and certainly not designed to give wanton offence. On the other hand it need not compete in style with the London telephone directory. It is the ritual references that are so leaden-footed. In 1986 the speech avowed: 'My government will play a constructive role in the Commonwealth and the United Nations.' Then there were changes and in 1987 the anodyne sentiments were replaced by, 'They [my government] will play their full part in the United Nations and the Commonwealth. They will seek peaceful and lasting solutions to the most difficult international problems.' Lord Hailsham was given the task of trying to give life to this listless and stilted prose. He made valiant efforts and only those who saw the original drafts know with what success he toiled. Even so, neither Milton nor Shakespeare seems to have had much hand in proclaiming our foreign policy. It is some consolation to know that this problem is by no means recent. Sir Robert Saunders (later Lord Bayford and a Conservative Cabinet Minister) noted in his diary on Monday 21 February 1910, 'King's Speech shortest and most ungrammatical on record.'

The procedure for closing a session of parliament is a marked contrast to the glittering ceremonial of the State Opening. A session, which usually lasts about a year, is ended by the ceremony of prorogation, an exercise of the Royal Prerogative which prorogues, or suspends, the parliament until a specified date. The procedure can be undertaken by the monarch, but since the last century the Lords Commissioners, or Whips, have requested the Commons to attend the Lords for the ceremony.

This is now accompanied by the giving of Royal Assent to the outstanding bills of the session. The Speaker and MPs crowd at the bar of the House as they do for the Queen's Speech at the opening of a session, but the difference is striking. There are no peeresses, no tiaras, and not much ermine. The public galleries have a scattering of spectators. A modest number of peers attend the ceremony with a matching lack of MPs. The list of bills receiving royal assent are read out one by one. A Clerk standing at the far end from the Lord Chancellor intones, '*La Reine le veult*': 'The Queen wills it'. Native tongues such as Welsh or Gaelic may now be used for oath-taking, but Norman French has retained its usage at this fixed and vital stage when the weeks and months of Commons debate are confirmed into law. Throughout this proceeding the Lord Chancellor is flanked by Lords Commissioners wearing red robes and ermine and large black hats.

Once the Royal Assent has been given, the Lord Chancellor reads to his fellow peers and those MPs present a review of the session's work. This, like the Queen's Speech, will be from a text confirmed by the Cabinet. The Speaker, followed by the MPs, then leaves the Lords and returns to the Commons, where he reads the speech reviewing the session, presumably for the benefit of those MPs who have not just heard it in the Lords. Quite often the Speaker stays and shakes hands with members as they file out. For a few days Westminster is in abeyance; but shortly the sparkling ceremonial of the Queen's Speech sets a new session in train.

The Commons, having listened to the Queen's Speech in the Lords, begin their own proceedings at 2.30 p.m. or thereabouts. They will have assessed the Queen's Speech over lunch. There is a festive air during the preliminaries; there are formal motions to be agreed, including such matters as disqualifications from sitting as an MP, policing of the House, and publication of Commons votes and proceedings.

Then the Clerk of the House rises from his seat at the table and reads the title, 'Outlawries Bill'. No Member comes forward to present the bill, it has never been printed, and it is not intended the bill should progress any further. This ritual affirms the Commons' law-making independence. In 1604 the House resolved 'that the first day of sitting in every parliament, some one bill and no more receiveth a first reading for form's sake'. In giving a first reading to the Outlawries Bill the Commons is granting precedence to an item of their choice, not to any measure contained in the Queen's Speech. Today it seems to be more a demonstration of form than of substance; but the ritual maintains the memory of the origins of parliamentary independence.

These formalities completed, the House turns to the main business. This is a six-day debate on the contents of the Queen's Speech. There is, however, another preliminary. Two government back-benchers will open the debate by moving a motion expressing loyal sentiments to the monarch: the Loyal Address.

It is a privilege to be chosen to move and second the loyal address. The choice involves attempts to balance youth and age, the party's regional strength, rising stars and seasoned Privy Councillors. Geoffrey Rippon, former Conservative MP for Hexham and Cabinet Minister, gained the accolade both as a rising star and as a respected ex-member of the Cabinet. Traditionally civilian movers of the address wore court dress and service MPs wore uniform, but this was discontinued at the onset of World War Two. The loyal address is not usually the occasion for barbed politics. There is plenty of that to come. The House will be packed – awaiting the clash between the Prime Minister and the Leader of the Opposition. Movers are generally obliged to make a scenic tour of the constituency supplemented by an industrial guide. Steve Norris, former Conservative MP for Oxford East and now MP for Epping Forest, seconded the address in 1986 and vouchsafed he had been advised to 'keep it light, keep it uncontroversial; but whatever you do, for goodness' sake, keep it short'.

I have heard many speeches moving the loyal address. One still lingers. It was given by Charles Curran, Conservative MP for Uxbridge in Middlesex, in 1963. Curran had a lean frame and a gravelly voice. Sir Alec Douglas-Home, who had just become Prime Minister, had to listen to only a few guide-book references to Uxbridge. These were followed by a hilarious and pointed speech comparing him with Lord Bute, an eighteenth-century Prime Minister who had inspired the contempt of John Wilkes, the Radical MP for Middlesex. Home and Bute shared almost everything: a Scottish earldom, the Order of the Thistle and an Eton education. The House loved every second of it, and it lasted eighteen minutes. None enjoyed it more than Douglas-Home.

I very much regret that I was not elected to the House soon enough to hear Maurice Macmillan move the address on 1 November 1960, when his father was Prime Minister. This was a unique occasion, although a number of sons have served with fathers who were Prime Ministers. Maurice Macmillan's speech was traditional, even including the name of the building society associated with his Halifax constituency. Harold Macmillan, responding, acknowledged the family connection. 'I confess that I was a good deal more nervous than he seemed to be while he was speaking, but that is only fair, for, from earliest youth, children suffer acute embarrassment about what their parents may say.' The occasion is shown in an excellent painting by Alfred R. Thompson, a copy of which hangs in the Commons corridor behind the Speaker's chair.

Once the loyal address formalities are over a general debate begins. It is started by the Leader of the Opposition, after which the Prime Minister speaks. The gladiatorial contest between these political titans is rare and significant. They are seldom pitted in debate otherwise during the session. The twice-weekly clash at Prime Minister's Question Time is a contrived alternative.

The debate on the Queen's Speech is partly general and partly structured around topics normally chosen by the opposition. They usually follow a set routine, taking account of the areas where the opposition wish to mount a political offensive and force a vote. Politics, however, usually produce their own tales of the unexpected, as happened in March 1974. The General Election had produced a narrow Labour lead over the Conservatives, but no overall majority. The Conservatives, under the leadership of Edward Heath, moved an amendment to the Queen's Speech intended to unite Conservatives and Liberals. Many Conservative MPs were apprehensive of the implications of such co-operation. In the lobby I met Ronald Bell, the Conservative MP for South Buckingham who died in 1982. 'Ted's trying to get his piano back into Number 10,' he snapped – clearly not a man in favour of furniture removals. There were furious backstage pressures. In the country the political mood was that Harold

Wilson should be given a chance, rather than be brought down within weeks by a hasty Conservative–Liberal combination.

There was a public and somewhat inglorious back-track. At the last minute the Conservatives sought to withdraw their amendment to the Queen's Speech, and the debate concluded with an overwhelming government majority. Conservatives, meanwhile, had been summoned from all corners to vote. At six o'clock that morning Julian Critchley had been in Atlanta, Georgia, and he made an unplanned Atlantic crossing for a vote that never was. Loyalty should not be subjected to such strains. Some believe it permanently impaired his affection for the Whips' Office.

Mercifully, debates on the Queen's Speech generally have a great air of predictability and the Leader of the House's winding up of the debate has the kind of noisy and sympathetic reception usually associated with the last night of the Proms.

A Parliament usually lasts for several sessions. Today the law states that Parliament must be dissolved after no more than five years, although between 1715 and 1911 Parliaments were permitted to last as long as seven years. There have been two exceptions to this restriction. Both world wars resulted in the extension of Parliament's lifetime until main hostilities had been concluded. Parliament is dissolved by the Royal Prerogative, and a Royal Proclamation is issued on the advice of the Privy Council.

Parliament was dissolved in person by Charles II in 1681, and by the Prince Regent in 1818. Thereafter it has invariably been dissolved by proclamation. The long-standing practice is for the monarch to grant a dissolution on the request of the Prime Minister, and that has certainly been the case for the years I have served in the Commons. Autumn elections are frequently favoured by British politicians, so Parliament is usually dissolved during the summer recess. There is then much less ceremony than that associated with the prorogation of a session.

The parliamentary year, or session, normally begins in November with the Queen's Speech. It lasts until the end of July with a Christmas break of two or three weeks. There are also two breaks of around ten days each at Easter and the late Spring Bank Holiday. The House has a long summer recess until mid-October, and the 'spill-over' period enables outstanding legislative business to be dealt with. The session is prorogued at the end of October and a new session is summoned within the week. It is a hard and demanding routine.

Political and Commons life is so unpredictable that the government's business managers have never liked to commit themselves to fixed recess dates. There is understandable pressure for a fixed timetable, but as Leader of the House I knew enough of July business difficulties to make me wary of such plans. Many Scots MPs, having regard for their earlier school holidays, would like the House to rise at the end of June and return in mid-

September. That would, incidentally, enable MPs to excuse themselves honourably from the Party Conferences. They would cheerfully sacrifice their seaside hotels and their standing ovations.

The House has not always sat at these periods. In the seventeenth and early eighteenth centuries the Commons would assemble in November and sit until spring, even as late as May, enabling Members to avoid the stench of the polluted Thames outside their windows in hot weather. In the nineteenth century the pre-Christmas session was abandoned, and the rising date was extended, eventually reaching August. A typical session in the late nineteenth century began with a Queen's Speech in February. There was an Easter recess of a week or so, and a further week or ten days at Whitsun. Parliament would sit at least until mid-August, the long recess lasting until early February. It is ironic that when the landed interests dominated the Commons there was no question of rising in time for the start of grouse shooting on 12 August.

One parliamentary custom, alas, has disappeared. In the nineteenth century the Commons often adjourned on Derby Day when this did not fall in the Whitsun recess. The last time this occurred was in 1891. In the following year the motion to adjourn on Derby Day was defeated. When the day arrived, however, there was a very ill-attended House and a count was called at 4 p.m. which showed there were insufficient members present to form a quorum. (The count was discontinued some years ago.) Today the Commons does not sit on the May Day Bank Holiday. It is a dubious compensation for Derby Day and I cannot believe that even Neil Kinnock would call it progress.

In years of exceptional controversy Parliament would sit well into the summer. As the heat rose, how tempers must have shortened. Even today July is a bad month for civilised political business. The hours in July are lengthy because government business must be concluded before the long recess. Members are cooped up in the Commons like fretful chickens, and they have little to do but consider their own discomfort and the shortcomings of their leaders. When my judgement and temper are next affected by July 'fever' I will remember 1909. In that session the Lloyd George 'people's budget' kept the Commons at work right through the summer. There must have been a shortage of Edwardian courtesy at Westminster. In 1928–9 the Commons reverted to the pre-Christmas start of the session and the King's Speech was delivered on 6 November 1928. The pattern has been maintained ever since. The Scots are still awaiting a reform that will enable them to spend summer holidays with their children.

Whatever may be the quality of Westminster's work, there is no question but that the hours are long and relatively arduous. The average length of a session in recent decades has been between 160 and 170 days. The length of each sitting day is around nine hours. To this must be added the considerable time that MPs spend in their constituencies. Much of the constituency work is related to social welfare. Many MPs, including me, would argue it was one of the more satisfying aspects of the job, but it is time-consuming, particularly so for the representatives of large rural constituencies.

Ministers have to work at their departmental desks during the mornings. This has always frustrated ambitions to recast the parliamentary day. And yet I feel change must come, perhaps giving greater scope to committees. As a consequence the House would generally sit for shorter hours, but would still retain a crucial role in debate and legislation. One day these changes will come and I hope I shall be around to welcome them. Meanwhile it is worth noting how the hours of Westminster generally compare with other Western parliaments. No precise comparison is possible because of the federal structure and committee work of some parliaments. The Commons, however, in daily hours and weeks per year is one of the hardest-working.

I do not make the comparisons out of any sense of discontent. Of course we depart to the nightly cry of 'Who goes home?' with some sense of weariness, but there has been the stimulus of controversy, the fascination of being at the heart of affairs, and the Westminster friendships that transcend political party. We go home; but we will return cheerfully, next morning, next session, and we hope next Parliament.

After the election campaign comes the count. My first parliamentary contest was in Coventry East against the sitting Member Richard Crossman. I expected to lose and I was not disappointed. My next campaign, in 1961, was a by-election in Oswestry and I have been in Parliament ever since, having fought eight subsequent General Elections. I still go to the count with anxieties, although I am now used to the routine. The votes counted, the returning officer declares the victor. Once more I make my pilgrimage to Westminster, regretting how little I shall see of Shropshire in future after the last few weeks of full-time campaigning.

Ahead lie the formalities of being introduced to the new Parliament. This inevitably involves tradition. The Clerk of the House of Commons receives a Return Book of the names of the Members elected to serve in the Parliament. This document is provided by the Clerk of the Crown in Chancery, head of the permanent staff of the Crown Office which is a responsibility of the Lord Chancellor. The Crown Office issues writs for elections to returning officers, and receives from them a 'return' to each writ. The Crown Office records in a book the name of the Member properly returned. Erskine May states: 'This book is sufficient evidence of the return of a Member.'

The first day of a new Parliament is full of excitement. Old hands, reelected, are joined by the novices. They crowd the benches. The Speaker, having been elected, proceeds to the Lords to receive royal approval for his election. On his return to the Commons the Speaker takes the oath, followed by the rest of the House. The government front bench are generally the first to be sworn in followed by the opposition front bench, the other Privy Councillors, and then other MPs, bench by bench. The oath reads: 'I [name] do swear that I will be faithful and bear true allegiance to Her Majesty Queen Elizabeth, her heirs and successors, according to law, so help me God', and it is taken with the New or Old Testament held aloft.

Administering the oath has created its own problems. The government despatch box contains a range of Bibles designed to meet most religious tastes. There is the Authorised Version of the New Testament, a Hebrew Old Testament for Jewish members, and Bibles in Welsh and Gaelic. As yet there is no Qur'ān.

In the last century there was great controversy over how a non-Christian should take the oath. It centred on Charles Bradlaugh, atheist, freethinker and Radical MP for Northampton. He had done much to secure the passage of the Evidence Amendment Acts 1869 and 1870, under which it was possible to make affirmation in the courts of law instead of taking the oath. He argued he was entitled to affirm, rather than take the oath, as a new member of the Commons, and at the start of the 1880 Parliament he gave notice to Mr Speaker Brand of his intention to do so. A select committee ruled against Bradlaugh. In the light of this he decided not to press ahead with his original decision, but to take the oath after all. At the same time he wrote to *The Times* declaring the oath's words 'are to me sounds conveying no clear and definitive meaning'. It was what my sergeant-major would have called 'dumb insolence'. Bradlaugh tried to take the oath but was interrupted by MPs allegedly outraged by his cynicism.

After further consideration by a select committee, Bradlaugh was committed to the Clock Tower which is part of Big Ben. The prison room was in the lower part of the tower and Bradlaugh was its last prisoner. (It is now used as a staff rest room.) Notwithstanding or because of this Bradlaugh was constantly re-elected despite being excluded from the House each time. The whole episode, which now seems bizarre, engendered the fiercest controversy. The Prime Minister, Gladstone, was tar-

Arrest of Bradlaugh in the House of Commons, 1880. Soon afterwards he became the last Member to be imprisoned in the Clock Tower.

nished by his irresolute handling of the episode and Lord Randolph Churchill, a major Tory figure, added to his own reputation by his staunch opposition to Bradlaugh's acceptance. Eventually Mr Speaker Peel, in 1886, decided to allow Bradlaugh to take the oath, and forbade any MP to question his decision. Eventually atheists were allowed to affirm by the Oaths Act of 1888.

Once the member has sworn, or affirmed, he signs his name on a parchment folded into the shape of a book, headed by the oath or affirmation. This ceremony takes place at the large table in front of the Speaker by the government front bench. Finally the Member is introduced to the Speaker, and is thus authorised to take part in the parliamentary rough and tumble that will begin a few days later with the Queen's Speech. Most

The new House of Commons: Members sign the Roll of Parliament, 1880. The custom remains unchanged to this day.

MPs disappear for that short break and write endless thank-you letters to constituents who have helped their election success. A handful, however, with the returning officer's winning words still in their ears, take flight to the sun for post-election therapy. I have enviously watched them arrive, bronzed and alert, to take the oath just minutes ahead of the Queen's Speech debate.

A different procedure takes place when Members are introduced after a by-election. Having fought the Oswestry by-election in November 1961, I was introduced on 14 November. I was sponsored by the Chief Whip, Martin (later Lord) Redmayne and, at my request, Sir Gerald Wills, then MP for Bridgwater. I was born in Bridgwater, and there had become an underage Young Conservative and a precocious political zealot. Sir Gerald had been patience itself in tolerating these enthusiasms. On sponsoring day he kindly entertained my parents and me to lunch. They had come up from their Somerset farm for the occasion. Afterwards I was given a quick rehearsal for the impending ceremony. My introduction took place after Question Time and before the commencement of the main business. We waited at the far end of the chamber opposite the Speaker. I fidgeted nervously while I endured private notice questions about relations with the Republic of South Africa and about the East Goodwin Lightship.

The Speaker's chair seemed like a distant mirage. Then Speaker Hylton-Foster's command was given: 'Members desiring to take their seats will be pleased to come to the Table.' With my sponsors I advanced six paces and bowed. Another six paces, a bow. I had made it. There was a scatter of cheers. I went to the government side of the table and gave the clerk my certificate, issued by the Public Bill Office, showing that I had been duly elected. I took the oath, as remains my practice, and signed the roll. I was then presented to the Speaker. In my nervousness I cannot recall a word that was said.

Over the years there have been many dramatic by-election introductions. Often they derive from the notoriety of the by-election itself. No such victor can equal Nancy Astor for sponsors. She was the first woman MP to take her seat at Westminster. Following her by-election victory for the Sutton division of Plymouth in November 1919 she was introduced by David Lloyd George, then Prime Minister, and Arthur Balfour, who had been Prime Minister fifteen years earlier. The occasion is still remembered in the Commons by the picture which hangs in the Centre Curtain Corridor.

Since I have been a member I have often watched the ceremony of new members 'desirous of taking their seats', with particular interest if I have assisted in the by-election. It is the occasion to lend some moral and vocal support to the newcomer. If the seat has changed party allegiance the newcomer will be subject to a good-natured commentary of 'not for long' and 'make the most of it'. Some remarks are a good deal more pointed. Hansard, out of discretion or deafness, reports nothing. The Commons initiation ceremony remains one of the least daunting of all such ceremonies.

The by-election victory I remember best was that of Gwynfor Evans, who won Carmarthen as a Plaid Cymru candidate in July 1966. There had been speculation as to how he would take the oath. Some judged he would make the occasion into an opportunity for extolling the Welsh language. We were not deprived of our anticipated drama, although it took an unexpected form. Gwynfor Evans was then the sole Plaid member, and he was sponsored by two Labour MPs from the government benches. This is the practice where a member does not have party colleagues available. When Gwynfor Evans reached the clerk there was absolute silence. The widespread view was that we should hear 'Yr wyf yn addo trwy gymorth y Goruchuf . . .' It was not to be. Gwynfor had a superb speaking voice. Its pitch and intonation were perfect. He enunciated the cadences of the oath in impeccable English. It made many of us sound like murderers of our mother tongue.

We relaxed – in some puzzlement, but to general relief. No one wanted a latter-day Bradlaugh. The next move, however, lay with Gwynfor Evans. Clearly he possessed a feel for Commons tactics even before he had put a foot within the place. He slipped past the Speaker and into a Commons seat, and appealed: 'On a point of order, Mr Speaker. May I have leave of the House to take the oath now in the Welsh language?' The Speaker had been alerted to the intended question but it was news to most. There then followed an impromptu and animated debate. It showed much sympathy for Gwynfor Evans, but he was tentatively offered the stones of a committee rather than the bread of action. The exchanges were rounded off by the cryptic comment of Sir Harmar Nicholls, then Tory MP for Peterborough, now Lord Harmar-Nicholls: 'Are we to assume, after all, that the Hon. Member for Carmarthen has made his maiden speech?'

The episode had a happy ending. Although no committee was summoned to pronounce on the subject, the three Plaid Cymru MPs elected in the February 1974 election were allowed to swear in Welsh as well as in English.

Some members secure election to Westminster with no intention of taking their seats. They have been in the Sinn Fein tradition of Irish republicanism. Their commitment to a united Ireland has led them to reject any association with the constitutional forms of the United Kingdom. That is why the first woman elected to the House of Commons was never sworn and never took her seat. Countess Constance Markievicz was of Anglo-Irish Protestant origins and had married a Polish Count. A devoted nationalist, she had been involved in the Dublin Easter Rising of 1916 and was the successful Sinn Fein candidate for the St Patrick's division of Dublin in the 1918 General Election.

A spiritual successor of Countess Markievicz is the Provisional Sinn Fein MP for Belfast West, Gerry Adams. He was first elected in 1983 but has still not taken his seat. This will doubtless come as no surprise to those who have elected him, since he exemplifies in the manner of the Provisional Sinn Fein the irreconcilable clash of loyalties between a united Ireland and the United Kingdom. Cynics may wonder what is the pay entitlement of an MP who, though elected, does not attend Westminster. A Member's salary is payable from the moment he is sworn, backdated to the day of polling or for six months, whichever period is the shorter, until he is no longer a Member of Parliament. Sinn Fein, however, wholly rejects the institutions of the British Parliament, including the pay cheque.

One member has made parliamentary history in my lifetime by his determination to remain in the Commons. Tony Benn's early and brilliant dedication to politics was always under the shadow of a hereditary peerage. He overcame the disability with patience and tenacity. In the process he irked Tory traditionalists who felt that, if providence had provided a silver spoon, why whimper for a plastic pusher? The episode, nonetheless, has a part in the story of Westminster elections. Anthony Wedgwood Benn was first elected for Bristol South East in 1950. His father, Viscount Stansgate, died in 1960. Tony Benn, on becoming a peer, was obliged to resign his seat. He promptly muddied the constitutional waters by standing in the by-election he had created, receiving more votes than any other candidate. The Speaker informed the House on 31 July 1961 that he had heard from the judges appointed to try the Election Petition, brought by the Conservative candidate among others, that Tony Benn had not been duly elected, and that his Conservative runner-up, Malcolm James St Clair, 'was duly elected at the aforesaid by-election'.

I arrived as a new MP shortly thereafter. It was clearly an absurd situation. Malcolm St Clair conducted himself with great dignity throughout the period, but understandably did not take an active role in the House. Meanwhile Parliament was forced to look at a situation which obliged Tony Benn to give up the Commons when the voters were perfectly happy that he should stay. Parliament resolved the situation by passing the Peerage Act, 1963, which allowed heirs to renounce their hereditary titles and so remain in the Commons if they so wished. The Act also provided for renunciation by those already sitting in the Lords. The upshot was that the Lords lost a Viscount Stansgate and the Commons gained a Sir Alec Douglas-Home (formerly the Earl of Home). Who says there is no fairness in politics?

The great quest for membership of the Commons remains powerful.

Since 1974 more than 2000 candidates have stood at every General Election for (currently) 650 seats. This is more than double the figure at the turn of the century, when there were rather more seats. Much of the difference can be explained by the emergence of the Liberals and their successors as comprehensive national campaigners from the 1960s onwards. In addition there is immense pressure to be accepted on the candidates list of the main parties.

There is also an exotic fringe of persistent candidates including David Screaming (Lord) Sutch, of the Monster Raving Loony Party, and the late Commander Bill Boakes, who first stood in Walthamstow in 1951 and subsequently stood and lost his deposit a further 25 times. Boakes pursued a harmless retirement pastime; but evening classes in home decoration would have been less expensive. Each candidate must now put up a deposit of £500, which is forfeited if he or she fails to attract a minimum of five per cent of the votes cast (excluding spoilt or rejected ballot papers). A rash of reluctant servicemen took to the hustings in by-elections during the 1960s because standing for parliament was held not to be consistent with membership of the regular armed services. Resignation from the forces was required, and cheerfully accepted. A lost deposit was considerably cheaper than buying oneself out of the colours.

On a happier note, Fitzroy Maclean, a respected Conservative member between 1941 and 1974, used Westminster to enter the forces rather than to escape them, since in wartime MPs can be serving members of the armed forces. In 1939 Maclean was in the diplomatic service, and his post was classed a reserved occupation. In his book *Eastern Approaches* he tells how he achieved his objective. 'I want to go into politics,' he told Sir Alexander Cadogan, the Foreign Office supremo. 'In that case, you will have to leave the Service.' He speedily joined the army, and quickly validated his action by becoming Conservative MP for Lancaster in a by-election in October 1941.

Some MPs do not stay the full parliamentary course. Some become members of the European Commission, others take up senior business or trade union posts. Some are elevated to the world of television. Technically MPs cannot retire voluntarily. Their seats can only be vacated as a result of death, elevation to the peerage, dissolution of a Parliament, expulsion or legal disqualification.

A resolution of the House of 2 March 1624 stated that MPs having been 'duly chosen' could not 'relinquish' their position. The ban on resigning probably dates from the time when serving in Parliament was often regarded as an onerous obligation. Resignation would have enabled reluctant MPs to quit all too easily. A way had to be found to enable them to make their exit.

Nowadays an MP wishing to resign applies for an 'office of profit' under the Crown. This custom derives from the late seventeenth century, when it was considered that an MP could not properly scrutinise the actions of the Crown if he was a salaried employee of the monarch.

The Crown used to have many sinecure offices. They have long since disappeared but two have been retained solely as purely nominal 'offices of profit', neither of them actually bringing any profit or salary: Crown Steward Bailiff of the Chiltern Hundreds, and Steward or Bailiff of the Manor of Northstead. The Chiltern Hundreds was first used as a means of resigning in 1751 by John Pitt, who wanted to switch from the Wareham seat to stand for Dorchester. The Manor of Northstead was first used for a parliamentary resignation in 1844.

'Applying for the Chiltern Hundreds' is now the colloquial Westminster term for an MP's resignation. An MP wishing to retire from the Commons applies to the Chancellor of the Exchequer for one of the two offices. On receipt of an MP's application a warrant of appointment is signed by the Chancellor of the Exchequer for one of the two offices. On the day this is signed, a letter is sent to the Member, omitting 'MP' after his name, informing him that he has been appointed to the office. Letters of notification are also sent to the offices of the Speaker and the government and opposition Whips. As soon as practical the appointment is gazetted in the London Gazette. This daily publication, technically a newspaper, is devoted to government announcements and notices, notices by other public bodies such as local authorities, and legal notices concerning such matters as insolvencies. It is also the practice of the Treasury to issue a brief press notice.

After the bustle and drama of election to the Commons, departure is an anti-climax relying upon archaic procedures. MPs depart on tiptoe, whatever the affluence or grandeur of their post-Westminster careers.

19 MAIDEN SPEECH AND PERSONAL STATEMENT

Once elected and sworn, a new Member has an early and difficult decision to make. When should he make his maiden speech? It is an important judgement. There are no second chances. A defeated member who is subsequently re-elected is casually referred to as a 're-tread'. His first speech on his return to the House has little significance.

There are a number of conventions which make a member's first speech so important. First, he is likely to be called early in the debate, however important the subject and however many speakers there are. It is almost as if he were made Privy Councillor for a day, a short-lived inversion of status, rather like officers serving the men's Christmas breakfast. Secondly, it is an occasion of provincial and even national press interest. Some, like John Davies, a well-known oil industry executive, and Frank Cousins, General Secretary of the Transport and General Workers' Union, were elected to the House already possessing considerable public reputations. Most MPs, however, are relatively unknown. The maiden speech is their chance to make a mark. Finally, there will be interest within the House in how a maiden speaker shines. The performance will be analysed leisurely in the smoking room where the inner judgement may belie outward effusiveness. The duty Whip sitting in the chamber will have noted content, style and general reaction. A maiden speech should not be undertaken lightly or wantonly, as my own experience testifies.

I arrived at the Commons in 1961, aged 31 and generally unprepared for parliamentary life. After leaving university I had worked for a Birmingham-based engineering company, and latterly for the Economist Intelligence Unit. Ideally I should have been a little older and with rather more worldly experience. In politics, however, you jump on the carousel whenever it passes. I reached Westminster delighted but diffident and spent the first few days sitting on the benches at the rear of the chamber, which are technically outside the debating area. Gradually I became acclimatised and moved to the furthest back-bench on the government side. It was as though I wished to be as inconspicuous as possible. I then began my long apprenticeship of silence as a prelude to my maiden speech. Meanwhile I broke my Trappist practice by going to private party meetings where I aired my views on such matters as standard quantities for farm products.

Even allowing for a genuine shyness, I cannot imagine why my maiden speech was deferred so long. The 1961–2 session was a period of great political liveliness. Selwyn Lloyd, then Chancellor of the Exchequer, was struggling with a rough-and-ready pay policy. R. A. Butler, at the Home Office, had to contend with a fractious House of Commons over controls on Commonwealth immigration. Edward Heath was locked in negotiations to secure British membership of the European Community. Domestic politics were in flux with the startling Liberal by-election victory at Orpington on 14 March 1962. As the months rolled by my reticence seemed positively perverse. I was sharply reprimanded by 'Crossbencher' in the *Sunday Express*.

Eventually the waiting ended. I delivered my speech on 26 July 1962, almost nine months after I had been sworn in. The occasion was a debate mounted by Hugh Gaitskell and the Labour opposition on a vote of no confidence against the government after the 'night of the long knives',

'The nervous new member makes his maiden speech.' Cartoon by Lee in the Evening News, *1 July 1938.*

when Macmillan had dismissed over a third of the Cabinet, no less than seven Ministers. It was an unprecedented reshuffle taken in response to growing political difficulties since the budget of spring 1961. The victims included the Chancellor of the Exchequer, Selwyn Lloyd. Like many, I feared his departure would lead to lax public spending. Others were struck by the politics of such an upheaval. Gerald Nabarro, a colourful Tory back-bencher, snorted, 'I feel I have been living in an abattoir', while Jeremy Thorpe, the future Liberal leader, gibed: 'Greater love hath no man than this – that he lay down his friends for his life.'

I informed the Speaker several days before that I would like to speak in the debate called by the opposition. Whether or not I had been awaiting a 'great occasion', I had certainly got one. The House was packed. The debate was opened, effectively, by Labour's leader Hugh Gaitskell. Macmillan countered. Then Emmanuel Shinwell, at that date a Labour veteran aged 77, delivered a passionate oration – exactly the kind of speech that is impossible to follow. I stood up, mouth dry and my heart pounding. 'Mr John Biffen,' the Speaker called. From the furthest back-bench I broke my nine months' silence.

The speech was eighteen minutes long. The conventional criteria of a maiden speech require paying respect to one's predecessor, praising one's constituency and avoiding undue controversy, thus inciting no interruption. My speech broadly fulfilled the requirements. I began with a warm tribute to my predecessor, Sir David Ormsby Gore (later Lord Harlech), whose departure as ambassador to Washington had brought about the by-election. My Labour opponent had been Brian Walden, later to become a Labour MP and subsequently a television pundit. I had to confess that 'I was described as indistinguishable from the Labour candidate by the *Sunday Express*, but worse was to follow because the *Guardian* referred to me as an impeccable Liberal.' (These observations have been made from time to time throughout my parliamentary career.) My point of deviation, however, was in the content of the speech. It offered restrained but unmistakable support for the deposed Selwyn Lloyd and his economic policies. The point was not lost on the succeeding speaker, Jo Grimond, the Liberal leader. By convention he was expected to praise my speech and he was kindness itself, but observed, 'I discovered some rather oblique shafts at his own government, as well as at the opposition.'

My speech over, I sank back on the bench with total relief. I had not realised the pitfalls of speaking from the furthest back-bench. The acoustics are not ideal, and my nervously delivered words were only just audible. The Hansard writers, happily, produced a text which matched my recollection and modest notes. I stayed for several successive speakers and felt the inevitable sense of anti-climax. Then Geoffrey Johnson Smith, Tory MP and later a Minister, seized my elbow, 'Come on, John, you need a drink.' I did; and a meal. I still remember his kindness. I returned for the speeches concluding the debate, voted, and then went home. My parliamentary career had begun in earnest.

MPs receive congratulatory notes after their maiden speeches; it is one of the many kindnesses in the Commons which soften the harshness of politics. The custom should, however, be regarded as a gesture: every adjective should not be assessed at face value. The notes I particularly liked were those stating what Members had heard other people say. My Shropshire neighbour, the Conservative MP Jasper More, wrote: 'Nigel Birch said to me, "One of the best maiden speeches I have ever heard". Many congratulations.' That was an accolade. If I had made my mark with Nigel Birch, a former Treasury Minister and possessor of one of the sharpest tongues in the Commons, then I must have made clear my position as a 'sound money Tory'.

The maiden speech convention concerning absence of controversy and lack of interruption is not of long standing. It does not seem to have operated before World War One. One of my predecessors was the Hon. William C. Bridgeman, MP for Oswestry from 1906 to 1929. He made his maiden speech on 22 February 1906, following Hilaire Belloc who interrupted his literary career with a spell in parliament. He made no mention of his predecessor or of the Oswestry constituency, but commented trenchantly on the highly contentious issue of Chinese contract labour in South Africa. His speech was not heard in silence. This excerpt is from a series of exchanges with Winston Churchill, then a Liberal.

> Mr Bridgeman: That leads me to another question. I should like to know when the telegram was sent.
> Mr Churchill: Long before the Hon. Gentleman made his speech.
> Mr Bridgeman said that answer showed the telegram had only just been sent.

It is difficult to relate the vigour of the speech to current practice. In this instance the present Commons is more sedate and less noisy than its forebears.

The most famous maiden speech was delivered by Disraeli on 7 December 1837. He was later to become Prime Minister, but never has a distinguished political career started so inauspiciously. The speech was in a debate concerning an alleged campaign to present petitions against the return of Irish MPs. It was convoluted, with a surfeit of classical allusions even for that age, and it was very long. It was certainly not a success. Hansard concludes his speech with: 'The impatience of the House would not allow the Hon. Member to finish his speech, and during the greater part of the time when the Hon. Member was on his legs, he was so much interrupted that it was impossible to hear what the Hon. Member said.' The Speaker and the House would certainly not allow such rowdy spectator behaviour today.

The most impressive maiden speech I ever heard was made by Bernadette Devlin (later Bernadette McAliskey). She had won a by-election in Mid-Ulster for the Independent Unity Party in April 1969, at a time when the Northern Irish difficulties were intensifying. On 22 April she was introduced to the House. Her reputation as a political firebrand preceded her: and she fulfilled it. The day before her twenty-second birthday she sat like a sullen pixie on the opposition benches close to the Liberals. At the first opportunity she rose to make her maiden speech. The opening sentence was in character: 'I understand that in making my maiden speech on the day of my arrival in Parliament and in making it on a controversial issue I flaunt the unwritten traditions of the House, but I think that the situation of my people merits the flaunting of such traditions.' The speech, which lasted 24 minutes, combined an assault on the British for their involvement in Ireland and upon the Unionists for their loyalties to the British, delivered with the utmost fluency and passion. It was not interrupted. She drew genuine applause from Members, for style if not for content. The next speaker was the Liberal leader Jeremy Thorpe, who spoke of her 'quality of courage'. After a short and exotic career, Bernadette McAliskey left the Commons in February 1974.

A most striking maiden speech was delivered on 5 February 1960 by the recent General Election victor at Finchley, Margaret Thatcher. This took the unusual form of introducing a private member's bill, the Public Bodies (Admission of the Press to Meetings) Bill. It showed enterprise and

'Westminster doesn't seem to have improved her image!' Bernadette Devlin delivered a stormy maiden speech on her first day at Westminster and never looked back. Cartoon by Emmwood, Daily Mail, 14 August 1969.

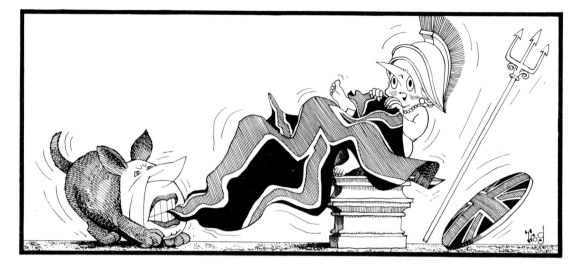

Ex-Prime Minister Edward Heath worries away at Margaret Thatcher's new persona.

political acumen to use the status of a maiden speech to introduce legislation helpful to the press. Mrs Thatcher began her 27-minute speech in characteristic fashion: 'This is a maiden speech, but I know that the constituency of Finchley which I have the honour to represent would not wish me to do other than come straight to the point, and address myself to the matter before the House.' There were no traditional references to her predecessor, and no constituency travelogue along the Northern Line to Golders Green.

Personal Statements share with maiden speeches the convention that they are not interrupted. Thus they are normally cleared with the Speaker for controversial content, so that he may be satisfied that they will not trade upon the accustomed silence. Personal statements are relatively rare. Often they clear up some ambiguity or misunderstanding that stands in Hansard and must be formally corrected. They are usually made after questions and before the beginning of general business. This is when the Commons is still relatively well attended.

Occasionally personal statements follow a major political event such as a resignation. This was so when three Ministers, Aneurin Bevan, Harold Wilson and John Freeman, all resigned from the Attlee government in April 1951 following the decision to take powers imposing charges for NHS dentures and spectacles.

Aneurin Bevan made his personal statement on 23 April 1951. It was a memorable occasion. The departure of three Ministers further weakened an ailing government. Bevan opened his remarks by stating: 'It is one of the immemorial courtesies of the House of Commons that when a Minister has felt it necessary to resign his office, he is provided with an opportunity of stating his reasons to the House.' He then ranged widely in a personal statement that lasted around twenty minutes. It questioned the whole basis of the government's economic and defence policies in response to the Korean War. He observed tartly: 'It is clear from the Budget that the Chancellor of the Exchequer has abandoned any hope of restraining inflation.' The rift between Bevan and Gaitskell that was to dog Labour in the 1950s was being dramatically trailered on the Commons floor. When Bevan sat down a Conservative asked if the government would now announce the date of the General Election. In fact it was only six months away.

I witnessed the short and sad personal statement by George Brown on 18 March 1968. George Brown had a low tolerance threshold with opponents, particularly if they came from the Labour Party. Tired and frustrated, he decided to leave the government, not so much because of government policies but on account of his Prime Minister's style. He informed Harold Wilson that 'It is, in short, the way this government is run and the manner in which we reach our decisions ... I regard this general issue as much more fundamental than any particular item of policy.'

Such feelings have been known before, but the matter is usually resolved discreetly: only as a last resort is resignation pressed. There was nothing discreet on this occasion. George Brown had already aired his misfortunes in the Members' Tea Room. I was there and felt I was intruding upon family grief. He declaimed his complaints to any who cared to listen – no party was excluded. The novelty of the situation overlaid the deep sadness of the occasion. George Brown had energy and talent that balanced his other qualities. The statement in the House seemed like cold hash after the richness of the Tea Room. The tragedy was complete. The man who was Foreign Secretary and deputy Labour leader had effectively written himself out of politics.

I was in the Chamber when a tragic personal statement was made by John Profumo, the War Secretary, on 22 March 1963. He was a gifted man who paid heavily for lapses in discretion and judgement. His statement was made on a Friday morning. The previous evening, in an all-night general debate, three Labour MPs had linked Profumo with Miss Christine Keeler and a trial at the Central Criminal Court. This allegation matched rumours that had been commonplace at Westminster over previous days, particularly among journalists. I watched John Profumo as he vindicated his conduct in measured but decisive tones. 'Mr Speaker, I have made this personal statement because of what was said in the House last evening by the three Hon. Members, and which, of course, was protected by Privilege. I shall not hesitate to issue writs for libel and slander if scandalous allegations are made or repeated outside the House.' The statement was heard in total silence. There were no questions and no interruptions. Its conclusion was greeted with a murmur of relief and approval from the Conservative benches. As I walked out of the chamber I met Anthony Howard, then lobby correspondent of the *New Statesman*. 'There,' I said, triumphant that his forebodings had been laid to rest. 'That's the end of it.' He did not look contrite: it was the press lobby rumours that contained the truth not the statement I had just heard. Within weeks John Profumo's political career had ended.

20 BUDGET DAY

Budget Day is a central feature of British politics. When the Chancellor emerges from his Number 11 Downing Street home sometime after 3 p.m., he holds aloft a slim, battered budget box which was used by Gladstone in the 1880s. Some traditions die hard, especially in the Treasury. We have Gladstone's box, but until recently his severe attitude to public spending was out of fashion.

The term 'budget' derives from 'bougette' an eighteenth-century French term for 'little bag'. A pamphlet in 1733 depicted Sir Robert Walpole, who was then both Prime Minister and Chancellor of the Exchequer, as a quack doctor opening his bag (or budget) of pills and potions. Even in those days, it seems, the economy was discussed in terms of health and fever and stimulus.

What awaits a Chancellor as he leaves a camera-crowded Downing Street and makes his way to the Commons? Budget Day is now traditionally a Tuesday. Question Time will have been conducted in a rather listless fashion. Even Prime Minister's Question Time will have been little more than a warm-up for the Chancellor. The lack of parliamentary liveliness is compensated for by the sense of occasion. Early in the morning members will have left 'prayer cards' on the benches, an occasional and predictable show of piety which ensures a reserved seat. From prayers onwards the chamber has been crowded. There is an undercurrent of gossip, largely related to budget prospects.

In past decades the sartorial splendour matched the day. It was Westminster's riposte to Royal Ascot. Things are now different from the time when Sir Gerald Nabarro and Sir Colin Thornton Kemsley used to appear in their black silk toppers. These two Tory members, complete with carnations, looked imposing and elegant whatever the passing vagaries of the economy might be. There have been less traditional approaches to budget dress. In the 1970s Charles Simeons, the Conservative MP for Luton, sported a jaunty boater, designed to remind us that Luton was the traditional manufacturing home of straw hats and possibly also to persuade us to renew the fashion – a brave but vain gesture. The Commons in those days was decidedly post-Edwardian. Stan Awbery, the Labour MP for Bristol Central, decided that the black silk topper needed a class and fashion challenge. He wore a docker's flat cap which suited him admirably, and was much appreciated. The sartorial parade in the 1960s and 1970s was completed by Leo Abse, Labour MP for Pontypool. His suits had a daring

The House of Commons altered so as to accommodate all its members. Punch *cartoon, 22 February 1890.*

peacock style and colour that made most MPs look like drab sparrows. Parliament has missed Leo Abse for many reasons and not least for the panache he showed on Budget Day. In the 1980s the general sartorial dreariness is only offset by the daring tax strategies of the Chancellor.

The House is impatient to hear the Chancellor the moment Prime Minister's Question Time is concluded at 3.30 p.m. Occasionally there are modest but unwelcome disruptions to the careful plans. The Budget is now broadcast live on radio. Expectant or fearful stockbrokers, merchant bankers and country solicitors cluster around their sets. To them a back-bench MP who has secured a ten-minute-rule bill will come as an irritant

'*Look out! Here comes Leo Abse!!*' Cartoon by *Emmwood,* Daily Mail, *1 November 1973.*

and not an amusing diversion. Government managers try to ensure that ten-minute-rule bills on Budget Day will be taken by back-benchers who will then waive the opportunity, as described in Chapter 9. However, there may be some urgent Question that, in the Speaker's judgement, requires a ministerial reply. This takes precedence over the Budget, and must be disposed of first.

In March 1968 I found myself in an unexpected and unsought disruptive role. Some months earlier there had been an outbreak of foot-and-mouth disease at Nantmawr, near Oswestry, which spread to become the worst such epidemic the United Kingdom has ever known, ravaging the dairy and pig industries. The disease appeared to have died down. Then a new infection was diagnosed and the nightmare prospect arose of a second outbreak unrelated to the first. The second infection, like the original one, occurred in my constituency. I decided I must ask the Speaker if I could question the Agriculture Minister, Budget Day or no Budget Day, and the Speaker agreed. The Chancellor, Roy Jenkins, had to wait while the Minister of Agriculture disposed of my question. The world outside also waited; and I hope they gained some inkling of what foot-and-mouth disease had done to the rural economy.

Once on his feet, the Chancellor performs a formidable task. He must undertake a wide-ranging survey of the economy enabling him to set out the background to the proposed tax changes, and also to explain what other economic policies he is proposing. Then comes the second section of his speech, which will awaken any MPs whose thoughts have been wandering. This concluding part of the speech will detail the precise tax changes he has in mind. This is when MPs make rapid economic and political calculations on the backs of envelopes. Within an hour or so they will be making their own 'budget judgements' to the national and local media. They will have to pit their instincts against a mass of Treasury statistics and often highly technical tax changes. It is a day for the carefree, and for bold assessments.

A clash between Gladstone and Disraeli, the two leaders who dominated British politics for a generation, on the occasion of Disraeli's first budget in 1852. When Lord Derby offered Disraeli the Chancellorship of the Exchequer, Disraeli said he knew nothing of financial questions. 'You know as much as Mr Canning did. They give you all the figures,' answered Lord Derby.

The Leader of the Opposition is in the most miserable position. He has to respond, not within the hour but instantly. He will have anticipated a substantial amount of what the Chancellor proposes, but it is near-certain that much will have come to him as total news. It is not an occasion on which a Leader of the Opposition can easily shine. Most have wisely used the occasion to make no more than general economic observations.

The length of the budget speech much concerns those crowded on the green benches in the Commons, and it affects the media who have the task of editing and commenting upon such important political material. Often our forebears varied considerably in their approach to Budget Day. Glad-

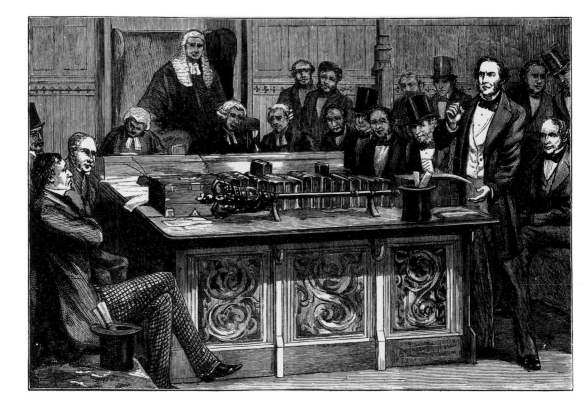

stone spoke for five hours when delivering his first budget in 1853. In contrast, his arch-rival Disraeli took no more than 45 minutes to review and judge the nation's financial affairs in 1867. Although his successor George Ward-Hunt detained the House a little longer the following year, *The Times* nonetheless commented on 'the apathy which awaited the budget last night' and continued:

> Within living memory there never has been such slackness of attend-
> ance at the Commons on such an occasion. The Strangers' Gallery
> itself was not filled. The more reserved places of resort and the body
> of the House itself exhibited an array of empty seats. Only the Ladies'
> Gallery appeared comfortably full. It was not MR HUNT's fault. It
> was the certainty of a deficiency which damped the ardour of the
> usual attendants upon the House of Commons. Men reasoned with
> themselves that they would learn only too soon what additional
> taxation they would be called upon to pay, and they were careless or
> indifferent about the details of an evil fortune they had no power to
> prevent.

Alas, such halcyon days of public unconcern did not last long. From the turn of the century onwards the Budget became an instrument of social policy. Taxation was no longer needed merely to furnish the armed forces and fund the modest role of Victorian government. The social spending of Lloyd George and most of his successors increased taxation and recast personal wealth. The irony is obvious. It took Gladstone five hours to spend very little, whereas a modern Chancellor spends around 40 per cent of the national output and does it regularly within a budget speech ranging between ninety minutes and two hours. I would opt for the economics of Gladstone coupled with Disraeli's 1867 brevity; a monetarist's dream ticket.

Occasionally an ambitious budget speech defeats its author. This hap-pened in 1909, when Lloyd George's budget had important social impli-cations and was bitterly contested by the Conservatives. Picture the crowded and intensely partisan Commons, as the dazzling Welsh poli-tician's oratory began to falter – as if Maria Callas had developed laryngitis while in full voice as Tosca. Hansard hardly conveys the drama of the occasion. The text of the budget speech reads: 'I cannot, therefore, safely calculate upon receiving more than £650,000 in 1909–10. (Sitting Sus-pended for Half an Hour) Mr Lloyd George (resuming at 23 minutes past six of the clock): I am exceedingly obliged to you, Sir, and to the House for the indulgence extended to me.' While Hansard's reporting was accurate, it was *The Times* that brought the incident to life in its parliamentary report for 30 April 1909:

At this point the Chancellor of the Exchequer paused. The right hon. gentleman had been addressing the crowded House for nearly three hours, and the strain was obviously telling upon his physical powers. His voice, too, in the later parts of his speech was growing weaker, and his words were more difficult to follow. During the pause

MR BALFOUR leant smilingly across the table separating the two front-benches and said something which was quite inaudible in the gallery. It was evident immediately, however, that the leader of the Opposition was suggesting an adjournment in order to give the Chancellor of the Exchequer an opportunity for a short rest, because there arose cries of 'Half an hour', and 'Give him an hour'.

MR ASQUITH interposed, and was understood to say there would be an adjournment for half an hour . . .

There has never been such a Budget Day drama since, although Winston Churchill, as Chancellor, did take a break during his speech in 1928.

A minor but entertaining diversion is to speculate what liquid refreshment the Chancellor will take during his budget speech, always a marathon by today's standards. The *Encyclopaedia of Parliament* states that a Chancellor 'is permitted to regale himself with the liquid refreshment of his choice'. There is now folklore and speculation about what beverages have sustained the Chancellor and thereby the economy. Disraeli is said to have favoured brandy and water; Goschen, who was Conservative Chancellor from 1886 to 1892, liked port; Gladstone drank sherry and beaten egg; Jim Callaghan, tonic water; and Stafford Cripps, plain water. The tipple seems to range as widely as the policies, and perhaps only Cripps is depressingly predictable.

I have never entertained the remotest wish to become Chancellor of the Exchequer, although I did have a happy spell in the Treasury as Chief Secretary. That experience may have kindled an ambition. Unlike Stafford Cripps I found plain water inappropriate as a companion through a speech and the long hours of attendance on the front bench. I envied the Chancellor's perk of some reinforced variant of Thames water. I had an excellent accomplice in Richard Page, my parliamentary private secretary. He would leave the chamber while I was chained to the front bench and return with a carafe of clear and sparkling liquid. It was weak vodka and tonic.

The Chancellor, however lengthy and however contentious his budget speech, is protected by the convention that he is not interrupted. The tradition is well founded. There will be time enough to debate and contest the policies in the general debate that follows the budget and in the Finance Bill. The most controversial tax changes may be greeted with a chorus of dismay, anger and incredulity, but MPs remain in their seats. Occasionally more exuberant and persistent MPs will bend the convention and get their views recorded in Hansard. Nancy Astor was such a gadfly to Churchill when he was at the Treasury between 1924 and 1929. Indeed, after Churchill had announced increases in National Insurance contributions in his 1925 Budget there was a minor storm. The Chairman of Ways and Means, who presides over the Budget debate rather than the Speaker, had to ask 'Hon. Members to allow the Right Hon. Gentleman to continue'.

These lapses from form continued sporadically. Philip Snowden, Chancellor of the Exchequer in 1931, was vigorously heckled during the closing passage of his budget speech. Only recently, however, have we had a budget speech thoroughly disrupted by deliberate barracking. On 15 March 1988 Alex Salmond, a Scottish National Party MP, interrupted so persistently that he got himself 'named' and had to leave the Chamber. Calm had barely been restored when the news of income tax cuts produced such a furious reaction from many Labour MPs that the sitting was suspended. Sage Tory members mournfully nodded their heads and told me this was just a dry run for the cameras; and that television would kill the Commons.

The presentation of the Budget starts a Commons process that dominates Westminster for the next three months or so. Any tax changes are immediately implemented under the Provisional Collection of Taxes Act. Meanwhile the budget will have initiated a four-day general economic debate which ends with the passing of the Budget resolutions that embody the new tax rates. These resolutions have immediate effect and last until early August. There is, therefore, a window of time between the announcement of the Budget and early August when the Commons must turn the major proposals into law. This is done by the Finance Bill which incorporates the detailed provisions of the Budget, and which is considered partly by the Commons as a whole and partly in the Finance Bill Standing Committee, which considers tax changes in great depth and provides an amiable berth for accountants, tax lawyers and other sound people in the City. It is the élite of standing committees, and an excellent apprenticeship for the new member wishing to learn the ways of the wise.

The general four-day debate on the budget, by contrast, is wide-ranging, political and usually good-natured. The length of the debate enables the opposition to choose the economic topics for consideration. The second day is opened by the leading opposition Treasury spokesman, who is countered by the Chief Secretary of the Treasury, a Cabinet Minister with responsibility for public spending. Subsequent days will be devoted to issues such as health spending, employment or trade. The final evening contains a second speech by the Chancellor who winds up the debate. It is a relaxed occasion.

Over the years I have often taken part in those debates, usually from the back-benches but on two occasions as Chief Secretary, when I was pitted against Denis Healey who led for Labour on Treasury matters. They were enjoyable days. My clearest memory is of the respect bordering on awe that Denis Healey commanded from the Treasury civil servants. He had been Chancellor only a few months earlier and memories were still green. The mandarins revered Healey's acute intellect but even more they marvelled at his enthusiasm for a taproom political brawl. I must have been a disappointment to them on both counts.

The drama of Budget Day is the culmination of immense, hard and largely secret work in Whitehall. I was at the Treasury when two budgets were prepared and presented by Geoffrey Howe. It was fascinating to watch how the public spending and revenue material was assembled both in total and in detail. Much time was spent in hearing representations on taxation. Keenly contested battles were fought over spending with Cabinet members. While one budget was being presented the next was already taking very general shape. The public spending component is generally known some months ahead of Budget Day, but the Chancellor falls into silence early in the New Year. Then he must decide on the borrowing element in the budget and, crucially, what tax changes to make.

It is a lonely decision. While the Prime Minister is naturally kept in touch, the Cabinet do not know the proposed tax changes until the morning of Budget Day. The reasons for such secrecy are evident. Fortunes could be made from advance knowledge of even minor tax changes. British public life has been well served by high standards of budget secrecy. The lapses have been exceedingly rare and have involved personal disaster for those concerned.

Jimmy Thomas, the railway union leader who left Labour to support the National Government in 1931, resigned in 1936. He was then a Cabinet Minister, and he had 'leaked' budget proposals. It was a sad end to a life of public service. Hugh Dalton committed a major indiscretion in 1947. As Chancellor of the Exchequer in Attlee's post-war Labour government, he was due to make a budget speech; on his way to the chamber and in a moment of incredible folly, he disclosed a few details to a journalist. There was no question at all of financial advantage: it was a matter of indiscretion and misjudgement. Dalton resigned, and although he had a post-budget ministerial life, the episode tarnished his career thereafter.

Budgets are major political events. The tragedy of a Thomas or the recklessness of a Dalton are offset by Chancellors who have triumphed with their budgets. Even so, Iain Macleod, leading Tory Minister in the 1960s and a shrewd observer of Westminster, remarked how fickle a Budget could be. The Chancellor cheered to the echo on a Tuesday afternoon could easily be discomfited by Wednesday's press. Fleet Street, and particularly the growing army of economic commentators, can be harsh and determined sceptics. The gratitude of those who benefit from tax reductions is rarely heard, the anguish of the disadvantaged is deafening.

Only three of Britain's ten post-war Prime Ministers have previously served as Chancellor of the Exchequer: Churchill, Macmillan and Callaghan. It is a surprising statistic in view of the vital economic and political significance of the Treasury.

The Commons has always been the forum of national debate. This involves the crucial concept of a 'loyal opposition' – effectively a government-in-waiting. It is natural, therefore, that the opposition has a recognised role in Parliament. The Leader of the Opposition and his Chief Whip are paid from public funds. Commons Standing Orders grant the opposition twenty days a session, irrespective of its length, when it may nominate the subject for debate. Seventeen of these days are at the disposal of the largest opposition party, three are available for the leader of the second largest opposition party. In effect these are shared by negotiation between the various smaller parties.

   The opposition's stake in the parliamentary timetable has a long history. Centuries ago Parliament 'supplied' the monarch with money provided he sought to redress their grievances. Parliament also began checking the 'estimates' of expenditure. Over the generations expenditure was transferred to the King's government in Parliament. This expenditure lay at the heart of much political controversy. The estimates of spending and its supply became the occasion for general debates, often highly critical of the government in power.

   Major reforms were undertaken in 1896 by Arthur Balfour, the leading Commons Conservative later to become Prime Minister. He summarised the position. 'While supply does not exist for the purpose of enforcing economy on the government, it does exist for the purpose of criticising the policy of the government, of controlling their administration, at home and abroad.' His reforms, and their implementation, led to the opposition controlling what was discussed on supply days. They became even greater days of political controversy. In 1982 logic triumphed. The fiction that supply days were about the examination of public spending was abandoned and most of these days were reclassified as Opposition Days, much more accurately describing their use and constitutional role.

   It was against this background that John Smith, Labour MP for Monklands East, rose to initiate an opposition day debate on 5 February 1986. He chose a topic on which the government would have preferred parliamentary silence. The motion deplored 'the willingness of the government to dispose of British Leyland's commercial vehicle enterprises ...'

   The political atmosphere was electric. The government benches were still uneasy over the damaging Westland episode which had resulted in two Cabinet resignations. The news that Ford might acquire Austin Rover and that General Motors might purchase Leyland Trucks and Land-Rover touched a raw nerve. Suspicion of United States commercial ambitions was not confined to the Labour left.

It was a good and aggressive debate which lasted around two-and-a-half hours. This timescale, known as an opposition half-day, makes the debate more compact, but obviously reduces the number of speakers. The Speaker made his usual appeal: 'This is a day on which brief contributions will be very much to the benefit of other Hon. Members.' Seven members were called to speak from the back-benches, and two each from the two front benches.

Often a member who knows he is unlikely to be called will make his point by the clever use of an intervention. All in the House knew the government's plans were opposed by the vociferous and redoubtable Birmingham MP, Anthony Beaumont-Dark, famous for firing with both barrels of publicity: Parliament and the Press Association. Today he was not called to speak in the debate. He intervened in John Smith's speech from the opposition front bench, referring to him as his 'Right Honourable and Learned friend'. Now, the House has its own code: 'Right Honourable' means Privy Councillor, and 'Learned' means Queen's Counsel. But friend! Party colleagues are 'friends', opponents are 'Members'. Tories at once seized the point. Their simulated disbelief and horror is recorded in Hansard as (Interruption). Beaumont-Dark retorted: 'In this instance we are either all friends together or we are all lost on the motorway.' We knew where he stood; and it wasn't in the government division lobby at the end of the debate. Labour could be content that they had selected a topic that had embarrassed the government and exposed political division.

Not all opposition days are quite so successful. A debate can turn traitor as it did in February 1977. The Conservative opposition had been pressing the Labour government on the unemployment issue. They decided to debate the subject region by region to get a good provincial press. But there was a difficulty.

The party, under Margaret Thatcher, was now committed to a policy of tight controls on public spending. This perhaps required that there should be caution in any arguments about public spending as a means of countering unemployment. And yet Conservatives from the south-west suddenly began to show an old-style faith in publicly-financed construction of roads, schools, hospitals and drains as a means of reducing the numbers of jobless.

By 8.12 p.m. the chamber is sparsely attended by a mere handful of members waiting to make their speeches. Edward du Cann, MP for Taunton, made up in content what he lacked in audience. To his prestige as a former Conservative Party Chairman he added the heretical view that there should be 'an announcement by the government that in the South

West they would henceforth embark on a great public works programme – as Keynes suggested – to build roads and hospitals'. This was too much for John Nott, opposition front-bencher and an architect of the new Tory economic faith. Publicly he chided Edward du Cann: 'My Right Hon. Friend should pay some attention to public expenditure in making his comments on increased public works.'

There were no subsequent Tory opposition debates on unemployment in the regions. If you are going to shoot yourself in the foot, do it in government time and not your own.

Between 1976 and 1979 I was a member of the shadow Cabinet and came to appreciate some of the problems of opposition days. If the government was doing badly, it was argued, why give them a chance to explain their case in parliament? Often embarrassing events rather than debate provide the most effective opposition. Furthermore, the research available to the opposition rarely matches the departmental support for a Minister. The case for caution can be endless. Opposition days, like all else in the Commons, have to be handled with instinct and skill, but the opportunities they provide are at the heart of parliamentary democracy.

Five days in each session are devoted to defence debates. Although these are not specifically provided for in the Standing Orders of the Commons, there is by convention a two-day debate on the annual Defence White Paper and a day on each of the three Services. Despite the huge budgets of the Departments of Health (£19.6 bn), Social Services (£46.4 bn) and Education (£17.2 bn), compared with Defence (£18.85 bn), there are no corresponding arrangements for them.

Defence debates are generally rather sedate – perhaps surprisingly, considering the fierce argument over nuclear weapons since the 1950s. Gallery observers of the debate on the Royal Air Force in February 1988 would have found the proceedings worthy rather than noisy. The debate was opened by the Minister of State for the Armed Forces, Ian Stewart, just after 4.30 p.m. He had an early tangle with Eric Heffer, left-wing Labour MP for Liverpool Walton, over air defences. Thereafter the debate was serious and orderly. The Speaker did not appeal for brevity: the opening speeches lasted nearly 90 minutes in all. A Conservative back-bencher, Neville Trotter, MP for Tynemouth, observing the technical nature of the debate, commented, 'we spend most of our time discussing equipment'. Sixteen members spoke and there was no division. On that occasion the Commons did not provide theatre, but critics should note that it was an informed treatment of a vital subject. The memory of 1940 and the nation's debt to the RAF still lingers.

There have been only two occasions since 1945 when the Commons have met on a Saturday, both in times of national emergency. One concerned the Anglo-French invasion of Egypt (the Suez crisis) in

November 1956, the other related to the Argentine seizure of the Falklands in April 1982, both events of great parliamentary moment. The pages of Hansard cannot begin to convey the noise and suspense of the Suez debates. The Commons was then divided more sharply than at any time since World War Two.

I was immensely fortunate to have a ringside seat for the Falklands debate. At that time I was Trade Secretary and had been involved in the early plans for requisitioning ships for the Task Force. The emergency debate started at 11 a.m. A three-hour debate had been arranged. This was vainly challenged by some back-benchers, who feared the time would be insufficient and largely devoted to the views of former Prime Ministers and Ministers. It was a great parliamentary occasion, but because of the issue rather than the speeches.

Michael Foot, at this time leading the Labour Party, had a difficult task. Many in his party were uneasy about the government's preparedness to use force. There were anxieties that he would want to appease these critics. As I listened to Michael Foot, the flow and cadences of his oratory reminded me of his intense opposition to Franco in pre-war days. In Galtieri he had found another Spanish-style dictator. 'It is a question of people who wish to be associated with this country and who have built their lives on the basis of association with this country. We have a moral duty, a political duty and every other kind of duty to ensure that this is sustained.' The House knew that Britain would be united in its determination to reverse the Argentinian occupation. Unlike the Saturday morning Suez debate, the Commons spoke with one voice and did not divide.

22 DEPARTMENTAL SELECT COMMITTEES

In July 1980 Sir Douglas Wass, Treasury mandarin-in-chief, made his first appearance before the Treasury and Civil Service Departmental Select Committee. He was following a recently established tradition. Sir Anthony Rawlinson, a senior Treasury official whose life was sadly and prematurely ended by a mountaineering accident, had been the first Treasury civil servant to give evidence to the Select Committee in December 1979.

These occasions created some interest at Westminster but even more in Fleet Street. There had long been a desire by the press to see senior civil servants under public cross-examination. The actual meeting at which Sir Douglas was present was somewhat low-key, but it initiated other occasions when, so great was the interest, that MPs had to vie with journalists for space in order to observe the duel between witness and parliamentary interrogators.

I have never attended a Treasury departmental select committee, although as Chief Secretary to the Treasury I was naturally only too well aware of the amount of work it generated. It was a matter of good Civil Service sense, as well as honour, to anticipate as many of the committee's questions as possible. The exchanges, although usually courteous, often had a sharp undertone.

Thus, when I became Trade Secretary and a Minister monitored by a departmental select committee, I decided on an essay in diplomacy. I invited the entire Trade select committee for a six o'clock drink. The committee chairman was a veteran Tory MP and Yorkshireman, Sir Donald Kaberry. In the mid-1950s, as Conservative Party vice-chairman, he had almost literally patted me on the head and sent me out into the world as a Central Office-approved parliamentary candidate. It seemed safe to open our discussion with a few reminiscences. My objective was plain. I wanted the committee as an ally. Did we need a common enemy? I dismissed from my mind the aptness of the Treasury for such a role. We discussed the importance of proper funding of our export promotion, and doubtless much else besides. I am sure the meeting had no influence upon the subsequent decisions of the committee, but we did get off to a good-natured start. I can also recall that in my short sojourn at the Trade Department I was never summoned to appear before Sir Donald and his team.

Departmental select committees have a fairly recent origin. They derive from a procedure committee report in the late 1970s which recommended that existing select committees covering a range of government activities should be replaced by committees each matching a government department. Frequently the recommendations of procedure committees lie dormant. On this occasion they found a champion in Norman St John Stevas, now Lord St John of Fawsley, who was Leader of the House in the early years of Mrs Thatcher's government. He commended the proposals as 'a necessary preliminary to the more effective scrutiny of government . . . an opportunity for closer examination of departmental policy . . . an important contribution to greater openness in government, of a kind that is in accord with our parliamentary arrangements and our constitutional tradition'.

With those ambitious words he set up fourteen departmental select committees covering most government departments. Within the decade these have become a familiar part of the Commons. They even have their own BBC radio programme, 'In Committee', which is broadcast on Sunday evenings by Radio Four.

The powers of departmental select committees are broadly similar to those of parliament itself. This includes the power of being able to send for 'persons, papers and records'; and there should be no inhibition on their investigating role. Nonetheless, there are conventions which qualify these powers. A Minister answers for the policy of his department, and since civil servants answer to him rather than to the committee, he nominates which civil servants should appear. There is also the convention that civil servants do not disclose the advice they give to ministers but only answer questions upon agreed departmental policy. Finally there is a long-standing and general convention that the Prime Minister answers to the House and not to individual committees. These conventions came under scrutiny during the Defence Committee investigation into the defence implications of the future of Westland Helicopters and especially when it considered the government's decision-making in this area.

Equipped with such powers the departmental select committees have undertaken a growing range of duties. In the 1983–7 parliament 306 reports were published, and a host of recommendations were made. The committees operate by influence: they cannot compel the implementation of their proposals. Therefore they must build up goodwill, and cultivate relationships with Ministers. This approach is matched by a wish to have all-party consensus within the committee. The chairman works patiently for a report that can be agreed by all members irrespective of party loyalty. This involves sacrifice, and a compromise report is often preferred to one which reveals divisions within the committee.

A good example of this was the select committee report on resourcing the National Health Service, published in March 1988. It was a contentious issue that commanded general support. The chairman, Frank Field, Labour

MP for Birkenhead, was widely applauded for his courtesy and tact in handling the topic.

The general view is that an agreed report is likely to have greater influence. Occasionally the contentious nature of the subject makes this impossible. Had Solomon been chairman of the Energy committee in the 1986–7 session there would still have been sharp party division over a report on the coal industry in the wake of the epoch-making coal-miners' strike. The report was carried on a straight party vote.

Select committees are relatively modest in composition. Thirteen have eleven members each, and the remaining one, on Scotland, – now in limbo – had thirteen members. The membership is decided by the Committee of Selection which chooses standing committees (see Chapter 12). Vacancies for Conservative members are advertised in the weekly Whip sent to all Tory MPs. Membership is genuinely back-bench, since it excludes Ministers, parliamentary private secretaries and opposition front-bench spokesmen.

The work of select committees often means studying issues where more than one department is involved. The Westland issue was a case in point, involving both the Trade and Defence departments. A liaison committee had been formed consisting of all the committee chairmen. It was my task, as Leader of the House, to keep in close and informal touch with the chairman of the liaison committee Terence Higgins, MP for Worthing and former Conservative Treasury Minister. Our task was to minimise friction between the committees and Whitehall. I can recall only a few problems, one of which involved management consultants. They felt it was unethical to provide certain information requested by a select committee. Eventually it was given, but not published in the committee's report.

As Leader of the House I would also see the departmental select committee chairmen individually. This would be a mainly social twenty minutes in the early evening. Very occasionally I would receive helpful early notice of some impending problem. Time spent with Terence Higgins and the committee chairmen, however lacking in immediacy, was never wasted. It helped smooth the relationship between the committees and Whitehall.

The central role of select committees was confirmed when the government chose to refer the Westland affair to the Defence select committee rather than to any other form of enquiry. It is arguable that the committee would have conducted its own enquiry in any case, for it is already clear that select committees are likely to make their own decision to investigate any major political event. Sometimes it has been argued that select committees should have wider powers, so that they could help in framing legislation. It would be a significant departure and could involve co-operation with the department on its parliamentary programme. This would nudge the committees towards the status of US Congressional Committees which play an active part in law-making. I very much doubt if this will happen in the near future. The select committees have established themselves effectively within their current terms of reference. There is still much to do in the task of providing a Commons role in investigating government departments. That work would be prejudiced rather than aided by seeking a law-making partnership with Whitehall.

Media influence may well change the status and ambitions of the departmental select committees. There is something compelling about a cross-examination. Some members, for example John Gilbert, the Dudley Labour MP, and Nick Budgen, his Tory Wolverhampton neighbour, are masters in the Perry Mason class. Gilbert earned his reputation in the Westland enquiry, and Budgen dealt robustly with Treasury spokesmen over the European budget. The members sit in a horseshoe pattern, the chairman facing the witness. The exchanges tend to be succinct, and often the clashes are dramatic. This procedure goes to the heart of politics and should be more widely reported in our national media. Select committees are open to the public in the same way as standing committees, unless they decide to hold their meetings in private.

One select committee deserves honourable mention even though it is outside the departmental network. The Public Accounts Committee was

Committee of the House of Commons to enquire into the state of the Army before Sebastopol, during the Crimean War, 1855. The horse-shoe seating is currently used by Select Committees.

established in the 1860s by Gladstone, an austere practitioner of economy. The committee reports on audits of government expenditure. It is assisted by the Comptroller and Auditor General (C and AG) an officer of the Commons and head of the National Audit Office. This body has 900 qualified investigators. The NAO's task is not only to see that public money has been spent on the purposes Parliament intended but also to ensure that the underlying policy is being carried out with proper economy and efficiency and to proper effect. NAO reports are considered by the committee which reports in turn to the House. Debate may follow.

The Public Accounts Committee meets regularly, usually under the chairmanship of a member with Treasury experience. In November 1964 I became a member of the committee, a valuable political apprenticeship. The C and AG was in attendance, and also a representative of the Treasury. At successive sessions MPs, sitting in their horseshoe formation, would interview the accounting officers of government departments. We would have before us papers prepared by the C and AG which highlighted examples of suggested waste. The chairman, John Boyd-Carpenter, former Tory Minister, always led the cross-examination with both courtesy and incisiveness. Then members of the committee took up the questions.

I sat next to the C and AG, Sir Edmund Compton. That was a great privilege. He would whisper to me what he knew would be searching questions. 'Ask him if this was the first time it happened.' With a studied, casual air I would pass on the question which would devastatingly reveal the full negligence of the case. It was the classic instance of an MP's work being as good as his research assistant. Altogether I served on the committee for three years, from November 1964 until the end of the 1966–7 session. I believe I learned a tolerable amount about Whitehall, and I am sure Whitehall had a circumspect view of the PAC.

23 SEATED AND COVERED

Where you sit, and what you wear, are most important in the Commons. Both are governed by convention, but the rules are occasionally breached or changed. Dame Irene Ward, a Conservative MP, was a veteran champion of the North-East, and was unhappy with the government's economic policy. During the 1962–3 session she flouted convention and firmly planted herself on the government front bench (the Treasury bench): doubtless she hoped for an informal word with the Prime Minister, Harold Macmillan. Decorum and conformity had to be restored. The Chief Whip obliged with a quiet word requesting her to move.

Indeed, knowledge of the seating in parliament is essential to its understanding. The chamber can seat almost 350 members. For most of the time that is more than adequate for those attending its business, but on great parliamentary occasions there is a sense of crowding as many of the 650 members compete for seats. Members have even been known to sit on the floor in the gangways.

The chamber, reflecting the original architecture of St Stephen's Chapel, has two sides, each with five rows of benches and each divided by a gangway. The government and its supporters sit on the Speaker's right, members of the opposition on his left. The front bench on the government side above the gangway (i.e. nearest the Speaker) is occupied by the Cabinet and other members of the government depending upon availability of space. The Chief Whip sits in the corner seat furthest from the Speaker, strategically placed to survey what is happening and to exchange stage whispers with the opposition Chief Whip. The Prime Minister, when attending, sits close to the despatch box which is used by the government Minister who is addressing the House. The Foreign Secretary, Chancellor of the Exchequer and Home Secretary have some claim to sit at the centre of affairs, and the Leader of the House usually sits next to the Chief Whip. Sitting on the government front bench is a mixture of Tory traditions of hierarchy and the squeeze and scramble of the free market.

Speaking from the front bench has the advantage that the copious notes that chain Ministers to their departments can be rested on the despatch box. Sustained by the box and the notes, and with only the immediate view of the opposition front bench, a wily Minister can develop tunnel vision and selective deafness. This enables him neither to see nor hear would-be interruptions – particularly from behind. The despatch box undoubtedly provides moral and physical support.

The second government bench above the gangway is usually occupied by parliamentary private secretaries. These MPs have their feet on the first rung of the ministerial ladder. They are paid nothing in addition to their MPs' salaries but are expected to vote with the government. They act as general 'confidants' to their Ministers and gain some knowledge of how Whitehall works. As Trade Secretary I had an excellent PPS. However, he voted against some foolish government measure. Although I pleaded on his behalf, discipline took its course and he was sacked. Then the fates were even harsher. He was promoted to the Home Office.

During debates Ministers and PPSs are often in whispered consultation, and frequently the PPS will go to the civil servants seated in their 'box' behind the Speaker's chair to obtain information to be used in the debate. The most dramatic instance of civil servants feverishly trying to send information to a Minister is recorded in the diaries of Sir Henry (Chips) Channon, Tory MP for Southend before the war. He tells how officials tried to pass to the front bench messages just received from Hitler and Mussolini. Neville Chamberlain, the Prime Minister, was already addressing the Commons; eventually the messages were passed to him, having been delayed because the benches were so crowded. The Commons watched and waited. Chamberlain read the papers, hastily conferred with his neighbours, and then announced the Munich meeting with Hitler. History had been made.

The remaining three government benches above the gangway contain a cross-section of supporters. They may not make history, but they have ringside seats.

The government front bench below the gangway is one of the most valuable pieces of real estate in the Commons. It is traditionally the home of former Prime Ministers from the ruling party. In my earliest days as an MP, Sir Winston Churchill still sat in the corner seat below the gangway, a shadow of his former greatness but a presence nevertheless. Edward Heath later occupied that seat, morosely observing the rule of upstarts. The bench is shared with a mixture of former Ministers and back-bench characters.

The four benches behind also contain government supporters, sometimes including the more independent-minded. 'Below the gangway' has a connotation, albeit tenuous, of outspokenness. In the 1970 Parliament I sat in the third row below the gangway and had two colourful Tories as near neighbours, both, alas, now dead. Neil Marten, MP for Banbury, combined a superb war record, great personal charm and a buccaneering opposition to British membership of the European Community. My other neighbour was Sir Harry Legge-Bourke, who represented the Isle of Ely. I served under his chairmanship on the executive of the 1922 Committee. (This group represents all Conservative back-benchers.) He was every inch a soldier, and the epitome of loyalty. This, however, did not prevent him from speaking candidly.

Amid the government benches will be found Westminster's three Democratic Unionist MPs from Ulster. With Ian Paisley as their leader they add voice and variety to proceedings.

To the Speaker's immediate left is the opposition front bench. They 'shadow' the government: the Leader of the Opposition sits across from the Prime Minister and the opposition Chief Whip sits in the corner seat eyeing his counterpart the government Chief Whip. The other opposition benches behind the 'shadows' and above the gangway are occupied by back-bench MPs.

Below the gangway there is great variety. The front bench is at present occupied by left-wing freebooters such as Dennis Canavan, Dennis Skinner, Bob Cryer and Brian Sedgemore. When the Social Democrats were formed there was a great struggle for the possession of this bench. Today it accommodates David Owen and his two supporters as well as the standard-bearers of traditional socialism. The bench occupies a strategic position in the chamber. From his corner seat Dennis Skinner can address the Prime Minister, Edward Heath, or others deserving his advice, *sotto voce* or louder. Some of his wisdom gets into Hansard, much more is lost.

The second bench below the gangway is occupied by the Social and Liberal Democrats, with Paddy Ashdown, their leader, in the corner seat. In leaner Liberal days there has been room for others on this bench. I sat there in the 1964 and 1966 parliaments. I liked the company, but never developed an enthusiasm for their paving-stone politics. The bench behind them is occupied by members of the Scottish National Party, Plaid Cymru, and the Northern Ireland Social and Democratic Labour Party. Behind them sit the Official Unionists. When Enoch Powell was a Member he occupied the corner seat and his powerful and daunting presence was well captured by June Mendoza in her painting of the chamber. There is a good deal of in-filling undertaken by MPs of the main opposition party on the benches only partially occupied by the smaller parties.

The relatively neat division between government and opposition has not always been maintained. The 1931 General Election returned 554 supporters for the National Government out of 615 seats. The government majority occupied much of the opposition side, and they included the younger and more radical Tory MPs such as Harold Macmillan. They were dubbed the 'Tory Mountain', following the most extreme faction in the French National Assembly after the Revolution in 1789. This was one of the few departures from seating conventions, but it was unavoidable in this instance. Another was the latitude given to Asquith, the former Liberal leader and Prime Minister, after he had lost his place on the front bench in 1916. He was still allowed to speak from the despatch box, presumably because after many years in office he found it difficult and unfamiliar to speak from the back-benches.

The Commons conducts its business with government and opposition facing each other. Therefore any major change in party loyalty involves 'crossing the floor' and sitting opposite your former position. This drama is avoided in many parliaments elsewhere in the world where a member needs merely to nudge a few degrees around the semi-circle of seats. Churchill crossed the floor from Conservative to Liberal in 1904 and recrossed to the Conservatives in the 1920s. For most once is enough.

I have witnessed only one flamboyant crossing of the floor. Christopher Brocklebank-Fowler was Conservative MP for Norfolk North-West. In March 1981 he concluded a Commons speech by saying he intended to join the Social Democratic Party. He collected his notes and walked from a seat on the rear government benches, down the gangway and across the floor, to a doubtless pre-warmed seat among his new colleagues. It was an effective gesture, but he lost his seat to a Tory at the next General Election.

Dress has always been conventional rather than formal in the House of Commons. The Speaker, the Serjeant at Arms and the Clerks have remained firmly in the eighteenth century. The House generally dresses to middle-class standards. This applies to women MPs no less than to their male counterparts. Nancy Astor was as sartorially sober as she was teetotal. The Victorians dressed almost uniformly in dark frock-coats and top hats. There was apprehension if not outrage when the Socialist leader Keir Hardie, after his General Election victory in 1892, arrived at Parliament wearing a cloth cap and tweed jacket. (He was also conveyed on a two-horse brake with a trumpeter on the box.)

In the inter-war years many MPs wore a black coat and pinstriped trousers. The old parliamentary social customs, however, had been shattered by the trauma of World War One, and the rapid rise of the Labour Party after 1918. Nonetheless, in the evenings most Conservative MPs would attend Commons divisions wearing white tie and tails, having come straight from dinner parties. Today dinner-jackets are often worn as the consequence of worthy corporate festivities.

However, there is a convention that Ministers do not sit on the front bench in dinner-jackets. The Chief Whip, Michael Jopling, recently reminded me of the point. One evening I had been eating for Britain, having changed in the office. I returned to the House and discovered, contrary to all expectations, there was procedural mayhem. The view was that the Leader of the House should put in an appearance – and pretty quick. I tore off my black tie and dinner-jacket. Trousers and shirt belonged to the evening; jacket and tie to the day. In this 'black-and-tan' outfit I went to face the House and the storm eventually blew over. The Chief Whip was right: a dinner-jacket would have compounded anger with ridicule.

Although today's Commons is not a fashion show, the spectator can occasionally be rewarded. Some years ago Hugh Dykes and Robert Adley, both Tory MPs, startled the House by attending Questions in their Chinese Maoist blue cotton suits. They looked very impressive, but I do not believe they repeated the performance. Dennis Canavan, Labour MP, frequently wears a safari suit. I now take that to be a sign that summer has started, since I can get so few confirming signals elsewhere. Jeremy Corbyn, the left-wing Labour MP for Islington North, dresses with enviable casualness. Frequently he discards his tie and wears a bush shirt. This causes great irritation to a number of Conservatives, but I suspect it is his liberation politics rather than his gear that causes so much anguish. Occasionally a Member may sport a T-shirt to promote some political cause.

I have always been singularly unimaginative about clothes, although I once lapsed from this happy condition. In the 1960s I went to the United States for a lecture tour, taking only my habitual city suits and shirts. I stayed in New York with friends from the worlds of publishing and theatre – not a political soul among them. 'John,' they protested, 'you can't go on wearing shirts like that!' I returned with the latest thing – a turtle-neck sweater. I wore it in the Commons, for one day. My friends were polite. Then I met in the lobby Andrew Faulds, Labour MP for Smethwick and an actor. At that time I hardly knew him. He greeted me approvingly: 'Good Heavens! How splendid! What made you do it?' Then I knew my American friends had been well-meaning, and quite wrong. I have conformed ever since.

The House today is dressed conventionally but without distinction; Sir Nicholas Fairbairn apart, none of us merits attention from the fashion and gossip magazines. We sit at present under a Speaker who comes from a distinguished family of tailors. As he looks down upon us, I wonder if he judges that it is only our manners that need mending.

The question of parliamentary headgear is another topic that is bound by tradition. Right through the nineteenth century, Members customarily kept their hats on in the chamber, removing them only when they rose to address the House. Occasionally a period of procedural storm is stilled by the ritual of raising a point of order while a division is in progress. Members are then walking about the chamber on their way to the lobbies, and the normal way of raising a point of order, by standing and saying, 'Mr Speaker, on a point of order ...' becomes ineffective. The protester is one of a crowd. The Commons has got round this difficulty by requiring those seeking to raise points of order during a division to observe two conventions normally forbidden to a member: speaking while remaining seated and speaking while wearing a hat. By doing both at once, an MP can hardly fail to attract the Speaker's attention.

Any hat can be worn by an MP to meet this qualification, but a

'Yes, I'm determined to catch the Speaker's eye this season!' Cartoon by Lee, Evening News, 1 February 1938.

handkerchief, newspaper or Order Paper placed on the head will not do. Hats, however, are rarely worn these days and now a quaint ritual has to be enacted. The Serjeant at Arms keeps two collapsible opera hats, one at either end of the chamber. When a hat is needed the Serjeant produces it and it is passed, often unceremoniously, to the protesting member. The hat is snapped open by the strong springs inside and donned by the member. As one point of order often releases a torrent of subsequent protests, the battered opera hat is rapidly passed around the Commons by members displaying the nervous excitement of children playing a Christmas game of pass the parcel.

An opera hat, in my opinion, is not intended to flatter. Most MPs look mildly incongruous as it perches around their ears. Anger often turns to mirth. A jaunty angle adds a touch of rakishness to the proceedings. Dennis Skinner, Labour MP for Bolsover, hides his considerable political sophistication behind the mask of an impudent political street urchin. When he puts on the hat a cheer goes up, followed by the predictable cry of 'Artful Dodger'.

I once sat on a Procedure Committee which solemnly reviewed the 'opera hat procedure'. I am glad to say we were resolved to maintain the present arrangements. But what happens when we have a Sikh MP? Will he be required to perch this bizarre headgear on top of his turban? Such an eventuality would have all the makings of farce in trying to maintain a time-honoured principle.

On 13 April 1988 the House held an emergency debate on the Social Security rates. Labour had successfully forced a debate immediately the Commons returned from the Easter recess, by applying for a Standing Order No. 20 debate which the Speaker had granted. The amended Social Security system was not working well. Tory MPs knew from their postbags that unintended hardship had been caused. Robin Cook, from Labour's front bench, made an effective debating onslaught. John Moore, Secretary of State for Health and Social Services, was in an unenviable position. The policy was being changed, but its new form had still to be decided, and he was coping with the aftermath of an illness that had badly affected his voice. He could barely do more than whisper a case which was actually far stronger than his critics believed.

Fortune seemed to have dealt the Labour front bench all the aces; but then a joker was played. Dave Nellist, articulate militant Labour MP for Coventry South-East, in his fury created a classic case of disorder. He stood up and insisted on shouting his challenge and questions at the Health and Social Services Secretary. The luckless John Moore had been deserted by his voice but not by his friends. They bayed back at Nellist and demanded he be called to order and restrained from speech-wrecking tactics. The Speaker initially disregarded their advice, no doubt hoping the parliamentary squall would blow over. It did not. He issued warnings to the recalcitrant Member. Eventually – amidst the babble – he announced: 'I must now ask the Hon. Member for Coventry, South-East, to leave the Chamber.' Dave Nellist was in no mood for hints or requests. Martyrdom beckoned and he remained firmly in his place. The reluctant Speaker then 'named' the errant Member. The Leader of the House at once moved that the offending Member be suspended. It was resolved by an instant division with no debate. Dave Nellist was suspended by 270 votes to 32.

It had been an excellent interlude for the Conservative Party. The division had knocked at least fifteen minutes out of the debate, nearly ten per cent of total time, as well as effectively breaking up the rhythm of the argument which had been strongly in favour of the opposition. It created deserved sympathy for John Moore, struggling as he was with both Treasury colleagues and his failing voice. Finally, Nellist had flagrantly defied the interests of his leader and front-bench colleagues. If I had been a member of the Carlton Club, the home of High Tories, I would have nominated him for membership. Indeed, such was the catalogue of Labour misfortune that flowed from the Nellist episode that one wonders why politicians engage in any disorder at all. We do, of course, but not on anything like the scale the public supposes.

The House of Commons has a strong sense of order and courtesy. Personal names are hardly ever used in the chamber and only then by the Speaker. Members address one another as 'Honourable' unless they are members of the Privy Council, when they are known as 'Right Honourable'. Within the same political party members are known as 'friends', opponents merely as 'members'. Queen's Counsel are called 'learned' and commissioned officers are called 'gallant'. It is a ritual almost universally observed although occasionally the courtesies come through gritted teeth.

Standing Orders are the printed rules which regulate the procedure, debate, and conduct of MPs in the Commons. Erskine May defined Standing Orders in 1844 as being 'for the permanent guidance and order of their proceedings; which, if not vacated or rescinded, endure from one Parliament to another, and are of equal force in all-binding upon the proceedings of the House by which they were agreed to, as continual bye-laws, until their operation is concluded by another vote of the House upon the same matter.'

The decision of the Commons to have rules which survived the end of a Parliament can be traced back at least to the late sixteenth century. The phrase 'Standing Order' was used on 7 February 1678, when it gave permanence to a resolution that 'all Protections and written Certificates' issued by MPs were 'void in Law'. This meant that MPs could not transfer the privilege of freedom from arrest then enjoyed by a Member's personal servant to anyone who had in some way come by the necessary written 'protection'. In the same year, the Whig Members being in dispute with the Tory Speaker over attempts to exclude James, Duke of York, from succession to the throne, another Standing Order was created which said that 'Mr Speaker shall not at any time adjourn the House, without a question first put, if it be insisted upon.' There was a steady growth in the number of Standing Orders during the eighteenth century, and the total stood at 46 by 1774.

The modern character of Standing Orders derives from the last century. There were two major reasons for this. The growing importance of government necessitated greater ministerial control over business. Between 1832 and 1878 Orders were confirmed that gave the government rights over the order of business and the distribution of the time of the House. After 1878 there were further and far-reaching Orders as a consequence of the obstructionist tactics of Irish Nationalist MPs. These included measures passed in 1887 enabling the House to impose predetermined time limits on the passage of a bill (guillotine) and to cut short a debate (closure).

It is now inconceivable that the government could plan its business

A disturbance in the House, 1893. How much quieter things are today!

without these measures of last resort. At the end of the nineteenth century there were nearly 100 Standing Orders relating to public business, but not covering the modest area of private bills. In 1986 the number had risen to 146.

There is a powerful belief that in recent times Parliament has become noisy and ill-mannered. Some even think there was a golden age of near-silence and good manners way back in the undiscovered past. I doubt it. Uncouth manners and rough language have long disfigured Westminster. Pepys records in his diary for 19 December 1666 that 'Sir Allen Broderick and Sir Allen Apsley did both come drunk the other day into the House, and did both speak for half an hour together, and could not be either laughed, or pulled, or bid to sit down and hold their peace.' Down the centuries echo the vain and croaking cries of 'Order, Order' at this inebriate display.

Local government taxation excites powerful parliamentary opinion. The 1988 debates on the community charge were courtesy itself compared with the Commons reception of the Municipal Corporation Bill in 1833. The *Morning Post* then reported that 'the most confusing sounds, mysteriously blended, issued from all corners of the House ... a sort of drone like humming, having almost the sound of distant hand organs or bagpipes issued from the back benches ... a single voice from the Ministerial benches imitated very accurately the yelp of a kennel hound.'

We still have physical reminders of dangerous days in the Commons. Swords were worn as part of fashionable dress as late as the eighteenth century. MPs were forbidden to carry swords or other offensive weapons into the chamber. This injunction avoided the risk of MPs being drawn into actual conflict. A short loop of red tape was provided in the MPs cloakroom, where they could hang their swords, and remains to this day. I use it for my umbrella.

The red stripes on the carpet of the Commons Chamber – the same colour as the ribbons in the cloakroom – act as a further safeguard. They are two sword-lengths apart and MPs were forbidden to step across them when addressing the House. The idea was that if any MP had managed to smuggle a sword into the chamber, these red lines would prevent his coming close enough to strike his opponents.

Today's behaviour is but a shadow of the disorder and fracas of the past. There was an unhappy incident in April 1938 when Emmanuel Shinwell, the Labour firebrand and later elder statesman, stung by an epithet, crossed the floor and hit Commander Bower, Conservative MP for Cleveland, across the head. The blow permanently impaired Bower's hearing.

Shinwell had a short fuse. In the 1960s I listened to an altercation between him and Cyril Osborne, the Conservative MP for Louth. They were standing just behind the Speaker's chair. The mutters became snarls, and Shinwell squared up for a passage of arms. 'Don't be a fool, Manny,' said Osborne apprehensively, 'you're an old man.' Happily for all, a peace-keeping force arrived. Some years later I went to a party celebrating Shinwell's one-hundredth birthday. Even then he looked and sounded as if he relished a fight to the finish.

As Leader of the House it was occasionally my task to move the suspension of a Member after he had been 'named' by the Speaker. I carried in my wallet a tatty piece of paper which bore the form of words: 'That ... be suspended from the service of the House.' When first given the paper I pencilled in the name of the first member I expected to require my use of the formula: 'Ian Paisley'. It was a gross calumny. Throughout my period as Leader of the House I never had to quote his name. I apologise; but I doubt that he will bear me a grudge. He is too skilled and too innate a politician not to know when a rough house in the Commons reads well in the Ballymena press.

The penalty for a named member is relatively modest. The first naming for an incident in any one session involves suspension for five days, the second suspension lasts twenty days, and third and subsequent suspensions

last until they are revoked by the House. Throughout the period of
suspension a member continues to be paid and to receive his parliamentary
allowances. The punishment is that he is not allowed within the precincts
of the Palace of Westminster; the only quixotic exception being to attend
a committee on private bills. Suspension is often premeditated, and
occasionally the media have been alerted to an intended unruly protest.
Cynics may observe that this form of parliamentary martyrdom comes
very cheap indeed.

*'Order! Order!' Cartoon by
Heath in* Punch, *29 April
1988.*

It is of great benefit when the Speaker can disperse a spasm of angry abuse with a flash of humour. On one occasion there were heated recriminations and name-calling. Parentage was questioned. Outrage, real or simulated, followed. Speaker 'Shakes' Morrison intervened. Wearily and patiently he is alleged to have observed: 'I always understood that "bastard" was a North-Country term of endearment.' The incident became part of Westminster folklore, and was recalled by Speaker Selwyn Lloyd on 20 May 1969 in the following parliamentary exchanges:

> Mr Burden: On a point of order. Is it in order for the Leader of the Liberal Party, the Right Hon. Member for Devon North [Mr Thorpe], to call Conservative Hon. Members 'mean bastards'?
> Hon. Members: Shame. Withdraw.
> Mr Speaker: I did not hear the Right Hon. Gentleman make that remark.
> Hon Members: We did.
> Mr Speaker: I hope, if the Right Hon. Gentleman did use that expression, that he will withdraw it; although one of my predecessors in the Chair once ruled that the word was a term of endearment ...
> Mr Thorpe: If it may in any way be thought that I used the expression as a term of endearment towards the Conservative Party, I unequivocally withdraw it.
> Hon. Members: Oh.
> Mr Speaker: Order. I take it that the Right Hon. Gentleman has literally, if not spiritually, withdrawn it.
> Mr Thorpe *indicated assent*.

In 1971 Labour conducted a furious demonstration against the Industrial Relations Bill. A phalanx of MPs gathered in front of the mace, determined to bring proceedings to an end. They stood shoulder to shoulder, resolute in anger but not entirely clear what they should do next. Speaker Selwyn Lloyd rose superbly to the inherent nonsense of the situation. 'Oh dear,' he sighed. 'This is getting as boring as a standing ovation.' The House, in due course, recovered its sense of order and proportion. Business proceeded and the Commons resumed its normal practice. Members were seated, speakers were courteous, endless and detailed issues were debated in an earnest and conversational way. The business continued for hours. Nothing for Fleet Street to write about.

25 LOBBYING

There is no guide to how one may effectively lobby an MP. Some members are decidedly not lobby fodder – for either the Whips Office or their constituents. Lobbying, however, is an essential part of Westminster life, and has existed since the early days when parliament passed legislation affecting and regulating trade and commerce. Commons decisions constantly reflect public and professional lobbying. As long as government spends money and makes law there will be lobbyists. Indeed, attempts to influence the decisions of MPs are inherent in democratic politics.

The mass lobby is the kind of popular pressure that most easily catches the public imagination. It also makes a physical impact at Westminster. The demonstrators mill around in the Central Lobby, usually festooned with badges proclaiming their cause. CND has a long record of such lobbying. Sometimes the demonstration is related to an intended act of government, but usually it is a general protest against current defence and foreign policies. Often demonstrators will send in 'green cards' asking their MP to see them. These are delivered by House of Commons messengers. Many members are called and a surprising number respond. Somewhat harassed MPs are then surrounded by small groups of articulate zealots propounding nuclear or animal or environmental issues. It makes rather good Westminster theatre and an enjoyable day out for the demonstrators, but I doubt if many opinions are swayed.

Much more effective is the co-ordinated lobby involving correspondence and visits to MPs' surgeries. These are the occasions when an MP makes himself available in his constituency to meet individual electors and if possible to help with their problems. A well-organised lobby ensures that all these letters are individually written and do not bear the anonymous stamp of the word-processor. Both the letter and the surgery visitor state the objections to a particular government policy and request the Member's support at Westminster.

The lobby against the reform of Sunday trading laws was exceptionally well organised. It brought together churchmen, trade unionists and a substantial section of the public who felt there was enough pressure in life without turning Sunday into another Saturday. Like most other MPs I received several hundred letters. I believe most people wanted reform of Sunday trading, and therefore I reckon that the proposed bill was defeated on its second reading as a result of the most effective and mannerly lobbying by a minority of the electorate, albeit a sizeable one. I commend

The Members' Lobby, 1875: a composite photograph of behatted and whiskered MPs.

their professionalism. Many of the radical protesters could take a leaf from their lobbying book.

Every MP has his own reactions to lobbying. I find personal lobbying the most effective, and it makes most impact when the lobbyists use the constituency surgery, or some other means of personal contact, for the purpose of arguing their point. I am slightly cynical when teachers, nurses and so on take time away from work to visit me in London when we can as well meet in Shropshire, unless, of course, the purpose is to attract publicity rather than to inform MPs of the arguments.

The National Farmers Union has a great reputation for effective lobbying. Farmers, rendered pessimists by the adversity of the elements and the waywardness of politicians, rarely believe this. Nonetheless it is true. There is a close and effective relationship between NFU headquarters and its rural membership. Economic and legal staff are well able to brief MPs on the complexities of farming in the European Community, and the same headquarters organises branch members to meet and write to their own MPs.

The NFU in North Shropshire has an arrangement whereby every autumn my wife and I are taken on a different farm walk. We do a rural grand tour which includes the milking parlour, the fields where barley has been harvested, and those where potatoes are being lifted, back to the farm, the empty pig units ('no money in pigs') and the slurry lagoon. There follows a superb farmhouse tea. Then comes: 'What about the Irish getting a special milk quota?' 'What about dairy inspection charges?' 'There will be a world *shortage* of cereals just when you're taking land out of production!' After salmon sandwiches, ham sandwiches, fruit salad, and home-made currant cake, my defences are low. I am being lobbied, but there are worse ways of being subjected to persuasion.

Over the years there have developed firms of professional lobbyists, or pressure groups. In his book *Directory of Pressure Groups and Representative Organisations* Peter Shipley has reckoned that in 1900 there were about 109 bodies that could have been identified as pressure groups, by 1939 there were almost 250 and by 1979 there were 628. The figure is certainly higher today, and includes groups representing the nursing profession such as the Royal College of Nursing, the Navy League, which presses the need for powerful sea defence, and publishers fearful of the imposition of Value Added Tax on books. The term 'lobbyist' need not be hostile. The Friends of the Earth will tell me of the shortcomings of civil nuclear power. British Nuclear Fuels will tell me of its benefits. Both argue in good faith, and ultimately I must use my voice and vote with the benefit of their 'pressure', 'lobbying' or 'information'. When I was shadow Energy spokesman in 1976 opposing Tony Benn, then Secretary of State for Energy, I was superbly briefed by the oil companies, particularly on the tax treatment appropriate to encourage the development of high-cost oil fields and a production depletion policy that would not discourage new exploration. I knew they were arguing their own case and it was my responsibility to take that into account.

There has been some anxiety that MPs, because there is a tradition of their having part-time work outside the House, would have their judgement subverted by these 'outside interests'. In the past, Members would 'declare their interest' when speaking in a debate, but because of the speedy nature of Question Time no one was expected to declare an interest before putting a supplementary question. I do not believe the House of Commons is a financially corrupt place. The notorious Horatio Bottomley, twice elected as an MP and expelled from the House in 1922 after receiving a prison sentence for fraud, is a rare exception. But Westminster is anxious to appear above suspicion. In 1975 a voluntary register of interest, available to the public and press, was instituted by resolution of the House. My own entry reads:

BIFFEN, Rt. Hon. John (North Shropshire)

1. Directorships — Glynwed International PLC (non-executive).
J. Bibby & Sons PLC (currently a subsidiary of Barlow Rand) (from 3.8.88) (non-executive).
Rockware Group (non-executive) (from September 1988).

2. Employment or Office	Member of the Panel of the Association for Protection of the Investor.
3. Trades or Professions, etc.	Occasional paid contributions to radio, television and newspapers, and also occasional talks.
6. Overseas travel	September 1987, to Malta sponsored by the Maltese Government. November 1987, to the United States, sponsored by the British American Parliamentary Group.

The decision was made to use a resolution of the House rather than pass a law. This was because it would be extremely difficult to construct a legal definition of 'business interest'. The fear was that the difficulties of definition would make the exercise nonsensical. The registration of Members' tax returns was also discarded largely for the same reasons.

If the register is operated in the spirit of the Commons resolution it is probably as reasonable a way as any of informing the public of MPs' outside interests. There are obvious reforms which might be considered. One is whether the interests of an MP's spouse should also be shown. Mrs Thatcher gave an oblique lead in this matter on the occasion of the debate on the second reading of the Control of Pollution Bill on 17 June 1974. She said: 'I start by declaring an interest. Either I or my family have been associated with the petro-chemical or agro-chemical industry for some time. The interests are mainly through my husband. I am not sure whether marriage is an interest which one ought to declare, but I am being on the safe side in doing so.'

The register is operated by a select committee under the chairmanship of Sir Geoffrey Johnson Smith. In the 1983–7 parliament the register was extended in very general terms to cover the interests of secretaries and research assistants, parliamentary journalists, and all party and registered groups. These registers are available for inspection by MPs only.

An area of current concern is the work of professional parliamentary lobbyists and the use that they may make of MPs and their staff. The problem is not unique to the United Kingdom. Lobbying is far more developed in the United States, where Congress introduced a Register of Lobbyists as long ago as 1946. Inevitably it has encountered problems of definition. Such problems would happen here. Would lobbying by the Child Poverty Action Group fall into the same category as lobbying by British Aerospace? Both seek my voice, and the former more often my vote. The debate is likely to continue, but I feel that open declaration is at its heart. Attempts at close definition could be self-defeating. The present

law concerning charities is a warning of the difficulties of framing specific definitions.

Meanwhile the activities of members are subject to the scrutiny of the resourceful Andrew Roth, a professional parliamentary commentator, and his independent organisation, Parliamentary Profile Services Ltd. His parliamentary profiles give a comprehensive list of all the known commercial and political activities of MPs. I can recall, as Leader of the House, being interested to know whether or not an MP drawn early in the private members' ballot might introduce a bill concerning abortion. An imperfect but immediate test was religion. What was the faith of Tom Clarke, Labour MP for Monklands West? The parliamentary reference books such as Vacher's, Dod's, *Times Guide to the House of Commons* all failed in the hour of need, but Roth had the answer. Tom Clarke was a Roman Catholic. In the event he brought in a bill to help the disabled. The value of Andrew Roth, however, goes wider. He has collected a

Andrew Roth, as portrayed in his own Parliamentary Profiles.

wide-ranging body of information on members' commercial interests which he up-dates. The relationship between interest and political behaviour must, of course, be a matter of conjecture and of personal judgement.

Members of Parliament, unlike Ministers or senior civil servants, are rarely in a position to take a decision of commercial consequence. In that sense they are unlike even local government councillors. The system of collective party loyalty and the operation of the Whips makes it difficult for lobbyists to detach enough members to affect the outcome of a vote. These factors encourage me to welcome the most open declaration of interest simply because I believe that, in the main, MPs should have nothing to hide.

The last word should rest with the great historian Lord Acton, who wrote: 'Power corrupts, and absolute power corrupts absolutely.' He was not thinking of a sun-drenched holiday financed by a building contractor. He had in mind the manner in which keen independence of judgement and democratic obligation can become subverted by the pleasures of office. No parliamentary register can protect the public from that.

I was in the Commons on the afternoon of 17 April 1969 when the Prime Minister, Harold Wilson, hurried through his lines announcing the abandonment of plans to reform the House of Lords. His gabbled words drew the interjection of Enoch Powell: 'Eat them slowly.' Once more the Lords had been preserved from major reform.

This book is about the Commons. Nonetheless, it shares the Palace of Westminster and the powers of government with the House of Lords, always referred to as 'the other place' in Commons debate. The Lords and Commons in earliest times both developed out of the King's court. The status of the Lords derived from the medieval system of feudal overlordship. Over the centuries their power was restricted by that of the knights and burgesses who represented the Commons. By the eighteenth century the Cabinet had clearly succeeded the Lords as principal advisers to the monarch. Kenneth Bradshaw and David Pring, Clerks to the Commons and historians of Parliament, have argued: 'Once the King had acknowledged the compelling nature of the advice given by ministers with authority rooted in a majority of the House of Commons, the government was able to ensure that in the last resort the House of Lords gave way to the will of the Commons.'

The dominance of the Commons was underlined by the extension of the franchise and by the growing importance of government. Even so, the House of Lords continues to have an important function in the administration: it is not a rubber stamp. It has modest powers to delay legislation and undoubted influence; some Cabinet ministers sit in the Lords. It continues to be dominated by hereditary membership. Radical reform, often promised, has proved difficult to achieve and abolition seems more distant than ever.

The powers, procedure and composition of 'the other place' each merit consideration. The powers are strictly limited in relation to the Commons. Their lordships are complementary rather than partners in government. Money is at the heart of power. There was inevitable rivalry between the Lords and Commons over which House should be dominant in this vital area. In 1671 and 1678 the Commons passed resolutions denying the House of Lords the right to alter bills of 'aids and supplies'. The Lords power of rejection, as opposed to alteration, was retained but rarely used.

The financial issue was decisively resolved in the 1911 Parliament Act, which followed Lloyd George's budget battles of 1909. The Act divided legislation between money bills, which dealt only with taxation and related financial matters, and others. The Speaker of the Commons was given the authority to decide which was a money bill. The House of Lords could not amend a money bill, and Royal Assent could be given even if the consent of the Lords had been withheld.

The House of Lords has the power to amend other bills, and these amendments are then further considered by the Commons. Since 1979 the power has been widely used. During the sessions from 1979/80 to 1987/8 the government suffered 124 defeats in the Lords, the vast majority invoking amendments to government bills. The figures tell us more about the rough-hewn nature of Commons legislation than they do of a resurgence of power in the Lords. The great majority of all the amendments passed were moved by the government in response to persuasive Lords arguments, departmental alterations to bills, or the fulfilling of promises made in the Commons.

Some Lords amendments have been made in defiance of the government, for example in relation to proposed changes in local government law and the abolition of the Greater London Council. More recently the Lords have voted against certain health charges in the Medicines Act. The spectacle of a House of Lords in disagreement with a Conservative government is not necessarily unhappy and certainly not menacing. The Parliament Act enables the Lords to exercise a modest delaying power to enable reflection. The independent judgement of the Lords would soon rust if it were not exercised.

Under the Parliament Act 1949, the Lords may delay a non-money bill until it has been passed in two successive sessions in the Commons. This power is rarely used. The Lords also used their delaying power with Labour's Aircraft and Shipbuilding Industries Bill, 1975, which sought to nationalise these concerns. They secured a compromise and the exclusion of ship repairers from the bill.

These two modest delays to Labour legislation and the recent amending of Conservative legislation do not constitute any serious challenge to the Commons. Britain is mercifully free from a constitution where there is potential deadlock between the two strong chambers of government, and where both have derived authority from direct election. The powers of the Lords are exercisable because they are modest. The non-elective membership of the Lords also means that the exercise of their power is not seen as a democratic challenge. Thus Britain has the convenience of a two-chamber parliament with none of its potential rivalry and tension.

The Lords procedures that buttress their powers are broadly similar to those of the Commons, but there are major differences. Their Lordships have a much more spacious and ornate chamber, which has fairly easily

adapted to the television cameras. The leather benches are red, in contrast
to the Commons green. The Lord Chancellor presides over their deliberations and he sits on a square, heavily upholstered red cloth seat called
the Woolsack, a reminder of the days when sheep and the wool trade
played a major role in the English economy. The Lord Chancellor is
unique in being required to perform in all three arms of government. He
has an executive role as a member of the Cabinet; a legislative function
while presiding over the House of Lords; and legal responsibilities as head
of the judiciary. The present Lord Chancellor, Lord Mackay of Clashfern,
has the unusual distinction of being a Scots lawyer. From 1979 to 1987 the
post was occupied by Lord Hailsham, whose learning, wit and robust
politics are already a legend.

The Lord Chancellor presides over the House with relatively little
formal discipline. The broad form of debate is the same as that for the
Commons but the differences are noteworthy. The committee stage of a
bill is taken by the Lords as a whole, not remitted to a standing committee
as is usually the case in the Commons. About a quarter of government
bills are introduced in the Lords before being sent to the Commons. This
is an example of how the Lords shares the legislative work with the
Commons to ensure that neither chamber is overburdened. The Lords
have only a limited number of select committees, but unlike the Commons
the Lords Committee on the European Community can judge the merits
of Commission proposals and not merely their importance. The Lords
cannot veto EC measures. The House of Commons EC Scrutiny Committee can only judge EC documents on their importance (sewage control
is more important than tin-tack dimensions) and make proposals for their
consideration by the House; the Lords EC Committee can say if they
think a proposal is wrong-headed or foolish besides being important or
otherwise.

Decisions in the Lords are occasionally reached by judging the strength
of the voices, but the usual procedure is to use voting lobbies as in the
Commons. The votes are counted as 'Contents' and 'Not-contents' as
opposed to 'Ayes' and 'Noes'. Question Time in the Lords is significantly
different from its Commons counterpart. Lords questions are limited to
four 'starred' questions to Ministers. They lead to a more protracted and
less partisan consideration of the topic than the quicker technique of the
Commons.

The House of Lords has fewer than 90 public business Standing Orders
compared with around 150 for the Commons. This difference is partly
explained by the absence of Irish Nationalist peers in the last century.
While Parnell and his Irish Home Rulers were wrecking the business of
the Commons, the Lordly calm proceeded. Another difference from the
Commons predates the Irish Home Rulers. The Lords address each other,

and not the chair, when they speak. The Lord Chancellor has very few powers in comparison to the Commons Speaker. He performs the formal function of putting the question to the vote, but little else. He cannot arbitrate on points of order and he cannot adjourn the House.

The order of debate is normally resolved by the peers wishing to take part, and a list of intending speakers is published before the debate. Some peers not on the list even stay to listen to the debate. Such arrangements seem profoundly civilised after the bustle and partisanship of the Commons. I do not believe it is merely the Irish factor that explains the difference.

Finally, there is the composition of the Lords. This issue still remains more contentious than either powers or procedure. In the seventeenth century membership fluctuated between 70 and 150. There were marked increases following the Acts of Union with Scotland (1707) and Ireland (1801). The expansion of peerages continued in the last century and this. More than 260 hereditary peers were created between 1912 and 1964.

In 1958 the Life Peerages Act was passed. This enabled the granting of a peerage for only the lifetime of the recipient, a measure which has significantly affected the character of the Upper House. It has brought many qualities to the Lords, but they are mostly possessed by those who have retired or are of retiring age. There are few young peers, and these are mainly the hereditary element.

The present House of Lords potentially consists of about 1,200 members, but a considerably smaller number are politically active. Around 200 peers play no part at all and many others play only an occasional role. There are more than 700 hereditary peers. These still form the core of the House of Lords membership, but their influence if not their numbers is matched by the growing number of life peers. The Upper House is also distinguished by two long-standing special-interest groups. The first of these is the Lords Spiritual, church leaders drawn exclusively from the Church of England, numbering 26 archbishops and bishops. In the Middle Ages the church accounted for about half the Lords membership. Today that figure is 2 per cent, but the recent preparedness of Lords Spiritual to speak out on social issues has earned them unusual media attention. In 1988 the Chief Rabbi, Dr Immanuel Jakobovits was made a life peer. The innovation was widely acclaimed.

The second specialist group consists of the Judicial Life Peers, or Law Lords. There are about twenty of these. Their work is related to the role of the House of Lords as the highest court of appeal for civil cases in the United Kingdom and for criminal cases in England, Wales and Northern Ireland. (The position in respect of Scottish criminal cases is different.)

There are currently more than 330 life peers as a consequence of the 1958 Act. Many are former politicians, but they also include former civil servants, businessmen and trade union leaders. Life peers are usually created twice a year and announced in the Honours List. Opposition parties are consulted about recommendations they would like to make. The House of Lords is now probably more élitist and representative of 'establishment opinion' than ever before. The retired Whitehall leadership is replacing the traditional Tory landowner. If capital punishment again became an issue in the Lords, I judge that the life peer vote, unlike that of the hereditary peers, would be clearly opposed to re-introduction.

Those attending the House of Lords, hereditary or otherwise, can claim a daily allowance. In addition they are entitled to travel expenses similar but not identical to those claimed in the Commons.

The House of Lords works assiduously, even though the conditions are less onerous than the Commons. In the 1985–6 session the Lords sat for 165 days. Of the 1000 who play some part in the Lords' work, 268 peers attended on at least 100 days. These members constitute the working nucleus of the House of Lords. Their number includes rather more life peers than hereditary peers. The assumed allegiances of peers taking some part in Lords business were judged in April 1989 as: Conservative 444;

HAVING PASSED THE COMMITTEE STAGE IN THE COMMONS, MR. SILVERMAN'S BILL TO ABOLISH HANGING WILL COME UP FOR THE THIRD READING, AFTER WHICH IT GOES TO THE LORDS.

THE BACKWOODSMEN

END DEATH PENALTY BILL

*'Kind hearts and coronets!':
Sidney Silverman and the bill
to abolish capital punishment.
Cartoon by Vicky,* Daily
Mirror, *31 May 1956.*

Labour 116; Democrats 60; SDP 23; and independents or crossbenchers, taking no party Whip, 246. The only Communist sitting in Parliament is Lord Milford, a hereditary peer, who has unsuccessfully stood for the Commons. Recent years have demonstrated the crucial role played by crossbenchers in House of Lords votes. Management of Lords government business is not a matter of mere arithmetic. Lord Whitelaw valiantly turned his political experience to the challenge of leading the Lords in the 1983 Parliament. His skills are now being matched by Lord Belstead who sits in the Cabinet as Leader of the House of Lords.

The effective, as opposed to the nominal, membership of the Lords does much to dispel the fear that the chamber is anachronistic and Conservative-dominated. It is, of course, still possible for the Conservatives to rely upon their ultimate majority of so-called 'backwoodsmen' when a crucial vote is impending; but the need relatively rarely arises. The working members do a constructive job; the sleeping members disturb no one. Many institutions would relish such a balance.

The powers, procedures and composition of the House of Lords cause me little anxiety, let alone reforming zeal. There are all too many other political dragons to slay. At one time their Lordships' existence seemed in peril. There was an ominous clash between the Asquith Liberal government and the peers before World War One, when the Lords foolishly attempted to challenge a major social reform programme. 'Six hundred men chosen accidentally from among the unemployed', thundered Lloyd George. Ironically, he was to add handsomely to their numbers before he fell from office, when he was Liberal Prime Minister with Conservative support between 1916 and 1922. The reformers discovered it was easier to prescribe destruction than replacement. The post-World War Two Attlee government tinkered with the Lords' powers. Then came Richard Crossman. He had a vaulting ambition, but it was hardly conceived in anger. His reform would have provided a House of Lords composed of members with many fine qualities, but ultimately chosen by the leaderships of the political parties. It was too clever. The dangers of patronage were obvious enough for both Michael Foot and Enoch Powell, and they talked the bill into the sunset. Since then we have coped with an unreformed House of Lords. Now it is quite often stubbing the toes of a Tory government. Furthermore, like old men in a hurry, the House of Lords has beaten the Commons in the race to the television screens. Who says there are no surprises?

PART IV

Running
the Show

27 THE COMMONS COMMISSION

About once a month there takes place a meeting of the House of Commons Commission. It is an informal occasion for what is, at least technically, a matter of substantial administrative importance. The Speaker and five commission members gather in the Speaker's high-ceilinged room over-looking the Thames. Officers of the House, such as the catering manager, who may be needed to deal with specific matters on the agenda sit in the corridor outside awaiting their summons.

Around the table will be seated the Speaker in the chair, the Leader of the House, a nominee of the Leader of the Opposition, and three members appointed by a resolution of the House: usually a senior back-bencher from each of the two main parties and a representative from the minor parties. The Clerk of the House will also be in attendance, and a member of the Clerk's department takes notes. The meetings take place in the late afternoon and are friendly but business-like. Tea is never served. There is not a vestige of party political controversy in the conduct of affairs. I was a member of the commission for five years, 1982–7, and by far the most time-consuming activity was the patient attempt to get a comprehensive regrading of staff.

The House of Commons Commission is a body whose existence is barely known to the public and whose work is not well known even within the Commons, although a commission member does take occasional oral questions in the chamber. It was brought into being to replace the rather ill-defined and parallel responsibilities being undertaken by different organ-isations within the House. Speaker Selwyn Lloyd set up an inquiry into these affairs in 1974, entrusting the task to Sir Edmund Compton, a distinguished public servant formerly C and AG. The Compton Report suggested that those in charge of the House, including the Clerk, should pay more attention to administration than to parliamentary procedure.

Implicit in the Compton findings was the centralisation of Commons administration, with a Secretary General in overall charge. This rec-ommendation was further considered by a Committee of Members under the chairmanship of Arthur Bottomley, the former Labour Minister and Middlesbrough MP who now sits in the Lords as Lord Bottomley. The Commons, often enthusiastic in reforming others, was immensely cautious in changing its own organisation. The Bottomley committee rejected a centralised structure of administration. It suggested rationalising the exist-ing six independent departments with the Clerk of the House carrying ultimate authority as accounting officer. This proposal was adopted by the House, and the House of Commons (Administration) Act 1978 established the commission as a statutory body.

The commission has wide powers over the staffing and expenditure of the six departments responsible for Commons services. It approves and lays before Parliament the annual estimate for Commons administration, and the heads of the six departments form a board of management which answers to the Commission. The departments represented are, Clerk's, Serjeant at Arms, Library, Administration (including Fees Office), Hansard, and Refreshment. The Commission is under a statutory requirement to ensure that numbers, pay, pensions and grading of staff should be kept broadly in line with those in the Home Civil Service. 'The Commission', therefore, is the answer to the question 'Who runs the show?' In practice, however, the board of management effectively operates the services of the Commons, only referring matters of strategic importance to the Commission. For example, only very senior staff appointments would be discussed by the Commission, and even then the decision may formally rest with the Crown or the Speaker.

The cost of the Commons is substantial and increasing. Estimated expenditure in 1988–9 is just short of £26.5 million. This excludes MPs' salaries and allowances which are carried on a separate vote. It does, however, include some ancillary services provided outside the six departments answering to the Commission.

Relations with the Treasury are courteous rather than cordial. The House of Commons has escaped the Treasury discipline of cash limits, preferring to apply its own cost standards. Some MPs suspect government motives where financial control is concerned. This view was put by David Alton, Liberal MP for Mossley Hill, who demanded in the Commons on 27 June 1988: 'Has the Commission been under pressure from the government to impose strict cash limits? Does he [Alan Beith] agree that such limits would have the effect of gagging potential critics, which would be undesirable for the conduct of the affairs of the House?' When I look around the Commons and observe Dennis Skinner, Tony Benn, Edward Heath and other government critics I cannot think they would be curbed by Commons cash limits.

David Alton's question was put to the MP who answers for the Commission about three times every session. He was, in fact, querying his fellow-Liberal Alan Beith, the MP for Berwick. Beith has been a member of the Commission since its inception, and currently answers for it in the House of Commons. This role almost merits an entry in the *Guinness Book of Records*, for he is the only Liberal to have answered parliamentary questions since the departure of Liberal Ministers from the coalition government in 1945.

The Commission is a substantial employer with a payroll in excess of nine hundred. The largest number are employed in the Refreshment Department followed by the department of the Serjeant at Arms, which is in charge of housekeeping as well as order, security and ceremonial. As such it has wrestled with the task of imposing order on a patchwork quilt of pay and conditions, commissioning consultants' reports and negotiating with the Whitley Council, which represents all the major Civil Service unions.

The Clerk of the House bears an ancient office, tracing unbroken succession back to Robert de Melton in 1363. The post is a Crown appointment, although over the past century and a quarter only one Clerk has been appointed who had not previously served in the Clerk's Department, whose members in turn are recruited through open competitive examinations. Now his role has changed: he is the Commission's chief accounting officer. A Clerk is no longer valued solely on account of his mastery of Commons procedure and his understanding of precedent. He is also expected to show the administrative skills that will enable him to take the chair of the management committee. Clerks of the House from past generations would have been astonished at such a development. It is one more example of how the form of Parliament has an unchanging appearance; but the reality adjusts to the contemporary demands of a working democratic national Parliament. A modern Spy cartoon would show the Clerk of the House with wig and formal dress, but bearing a copy of Erskine May in one hand, and a management consultant's report in the other.

The House of Commons Commission operates with a low profile. Many employers might wish that they too could conduct their affairs with such modest public attention. The Commission is available to answer parliamentary questions. Few are asked. This reasonably happy state of affairs is not a result of lethargy: that general quality is rare at Westminster. It comes about because the Commission does its work quietly and patiently, and seeks a partnership with all those who work at Westminster to make the business of the Commons effective.

Charles Irving, Conservative MP for Cheltenham, is the present Chairman of the Catering Sub-Committee of the Commons Services Committee, elected to the post by fellow MPs. He is well equipped to carry out his voluntary duties, having a distinguished former career as a hotelier. The title is extensive and so are his duties. He is responsible for the catering arrangements for all who work in the House of Commons and not just the provisioning of MPs. He is assisted by the General Manager, John Smillie, and a staff of nearly 1000. These figures disclose the magnitude of the Commons as a working organisation. It dispels any idea that Westminster has remained intimate and club-like. Mr Smillie claims that 3000 meals a day are served in the Commons, only exceeded in London by Harrods.

The catering chairmanship has attracted a range of colourful characters. One was Sir William Steward, Conservative Member for Woolwich West 1950–59, and proprietor of Veeraswamy's Restaurant in Swallow Street, near Piccadilly Circus. It also marked a stage in the commercial career of Robert Maxwell while he was Labour MP for Buckingham. Bessie Braddock, the redoubtable Liverpool Labour MP, was chairman from December 1965 to March 1967.

The task of Commons catering is to feed MPs, officers of the House, MPs' staff, others employed on the premises, and visitors accompanied by MPs. There are no catering facilities, not even a cup of tea, for the visitor to the Commons unaccompanied by an MP. The numbers themselves are formidable. The further and more onerous requirement is that this task should be carried out as long as the House is sitting, whatever the time of day or night. Inevitably this makes forward planning exceedingly difficult. Every MP's spouse will sympathise with the task of Charles Irving.

Altogether there are 26 House of Commons Refreshment Department outlets, including nine bars. In general they cater for the different groups who regularly attend the Commons. The Members Smoking Room is legendary. It is next to the Library and overlooks the Thames. The room retains a Victorian atmosphere, with its leather upholstery and scattered newspapers. From the walls Charles James Fox and Edmund Burke look down upon today's small change of political gossip. The Members Dining Room is on the same floor. It is essentially for MPs, although officers of the House have a table. Conservative and Labour MPs eat at opposite ends of the room, the Social and Liberal Democrats have their own table. The government Chief Whip also has his own table to which he invites members. Once again we eat with history, for the walls are lined with past heroes including Sir Robert Walpole and Pitt the Younger. We also eat under the paternal guidance of Charles Irving who has now supplied low-calorie and vegetarian bills of fare.

Institutions have their characters. When I was elected in 1961 the Members dining room had a magnificent red-haired Irish lady cashier with great presence. Her consuming interest was the turf. She assumed, wrongly I think, that most Tory MPs had the shrewdest tips from the best trainers and graced the smartest race courses. I had none of these attributes, but an Oswestry farmer trainer had a locally fancied horse called Merry Deal. Nonchalantly I passed on the tip: the horse won at a handsome price. I had only been in the House a few weeks, but from that moment I had made a reputation as undeserved and spurious as any I subsequently earned in the chamber.

Next to the Members dining room is the Strangers Dining Room where MPs can take guests. The Members Tea Room is also on the same floor as the chamber. It has a cafeteria service and the atmosphere is quite informal. It was in this room in March 1987 that John Prescott, MP for Hull, delivered a message of fraternal dissent to James Callaghan over the latter's views on defence. The tea room used to have a transport café atmosphere which has been altered by capital spending and an emphasis on such healthy foods as salads. I still go there, remaining loyal to my sausages and baked beans, surrounded by younger MPs who eat yoghurt. It is an excellent place for political gossip.

The Harcourt Room is on a lower floor, below the chamber and on the same level as the terrace. Members may take visitors there. It is named after Lewis Harcourt who was First Commissioner of Works in 1906, and is used as a grill-room. The pictures include one of Sir Winston Churchill's paintings of Venice. In recent years a Welsh harpist has played on two evenings a week. This delightful innovation caused a squall, with Enoch

Powell among the protesters. The predictable Early Day Motion was tabled:

> That, in the opinion of this House, it is insufferable that musical performances be permitted in any place of refreshment in the precincts; and neither the Services Committee nor any sub-committee of that Committee has approval of this House in permitting, or purporting to permit, such performances, whether generally or for a limited period.

The critics did not prevail, and I will wager there would be an outcry if our harpist now left. Along the corridor leading to the Harcourt Room there are a number of private dining rooms, which can be booked by Members for private dinners on behalf of outside bodies; but the MP must be present at the function. These rooms are in great demand and the

Edwardian elegance on the Terrace of the House of Commons, 1909. Painting by Milly Childers.

Banqueting Office takes bookings for the twelve months ahead on 1 September each year.

There are two cafeterias, one for Members and one for Strangers, at the Westminster Bridge end on the terrace level. Visitors accompanied by a Member can visit the Strangers Cafeteria. It is often used by MPs' employees with Westminster passes who also use a cafeteria off Westminster Hall.

During the summer months a marquee is set up on the terrace where buffet lunch and tea are served. The Press Gallery have their own dining and cafeteria facilities.

The sale of alcohol in the Commons is permitted without a licence. A 1935 Court Ruling established that the matter fell within the House's right to regulate its own internal affairs. I have two favourite bars. Annie's is on the floor below the chamber. It is intimate and restricted to MPs and journalists. Close by is the Strangers Bar, known as the Kremlin, which

The House of Commons sales kiosk, which – relative to its space – achieves a remarkably high turnover. MPs, staff and visitors to the House may all use the kiosk.

is said to have been so named after Labour MPs who frequented it a couple of generations ago. I am sorry that their mild plans for social reform should have earned so sharp a reaction. However, they brought with them Federation Ale, from the working men's clubs of the North. Members can entertain visitors in the Kremlin, and may very exceptionally discover a left-wing Labour MP.

The numbers using the Commons and the available facilities lead some to imagine that the catering is profitable. This assumption overlooks the tremendous cost of providing refreshments at all hours when the House is sitting. There is also the factor that many of the cafeterias have to price meals for Members' employees and other staff who have little chance to eat economically elsewhere.

Charles Irving has shown his commercial skill by the exploitation of the sales kiosk in the corridor leading to the Strangers Cafeteria. Visitors can buy a range of Commons souvenirs, from Scotch to key rings. Also on offer are tins of 'Commons Humbug' and 'Commons Fudge', which have proved great favourites. The kiosk measures only 2.44 by 4.57 metres, and now has a turnover of just under £1 million a year. I am told this is the highest sales/space ratio for any retailing concern in Europe. Overall the refreshment department has a turnover of about £3 million.

On the walls of Charles Irving's room is a portrait of John Bellamy, the pioneer caterer and a legend in Commons history. Pitt's dying words in 1806 are reputed to have been: 'I think I could eat one of Bellamy's veal pies.' Bellamy had been appointed Deputy Housekeeper in the Palace of Westminster in 1773. He was persuaded to provide food on the premises, and did so with evident success. Bellamys, father and son, fed the Commons until 1834 when their kitchen was gutted in the fire. It was described by Charles Dickens in *Sketches by Boz*.

> When you have taken your seat in the kitchen, and duly noticed the large fire and roasting jack at one end of the room – the little table for washing glasses and draining jugs at the other – the damask table cloth and bare floor – the plate and china on the tables, and the gridiron on the fire; and a few other anomalies peculiar to the place – we will point out to your notice two or three of the people present whose station or absurdities render them the most worthy of remark.

As Leader of the House I had a very general and tenuous responsibility for the Services Committee and its catering offshoot. I had no wish to make my role more tangible. My only mass catering experience had been as a National Serviceman, when my period in the kitchen had been clouded by making tea in unwashed buckets earlier used for peeling onions. At one moment I feared the authorities would allow my misdemeanour to be resolved by lynch law rather than formal discipline. It was with these memories that I was summoned to visit the Commons kitchens one steaming hot summer when a catering walk-out threatened to add to other difficulties. The spectre of lynch law reappeared. The staff were working in appalling heat, and eventually an understanding was reached with the promise of a major capital spending programme to improve working conditions.

Today's capital spending and building programmes follow past attempts to improve facilities. After the great fire a new Commons was constructed which had more ample kitchens than those described by Dickens. In 1848 a Select Committee was appointed to enquire into 'proposed arrangements for the kitchen, eating and accommodation rooms for Members'. It set up arrangements for a catering committee not dissimilar from those now operating. By 1900 twenty cooks were employed. The story since then has been one of steady expansion. The Commons is eating more. If Charles Irving has his way it will eat healthily and, who knows, one day even profitably.

28 HANSARD AND REPORTING PARLIAMENT

After making a speech I remain for a while on the benches listening to the debate. After a few moments an envelope is passed to me from the official Hansard reporters with the terse request: 'notes and quotations'. Sometime thereafter I visit the official reporters' room in order to check my speech. I hope the 'notes and quotations' will have helped those who have struggled to convert my amiable ramblings into concise and challenging prose. I go through their text meticulously, but only occasionally suggest amendments, usually to shorten the sentences.

Hansard provides a remarkable service to MPs. It is the reporting, printing and publication organisation which ensures that the official report of the Commons business until 10 p.m. is available next morning. In addition to reporting the main business of the Commons, Hansard also publishes the proceedings of the standing committees.

The task of reporting Commons daily business is carried out from the front row of the Press Gallery, directly above the Speaker's chair. Although the proceedings are recorded on tape, the essential task is carried out by Hansard reporters, for no tape can identify interruptions. One reporter is responsible for covering business at any one time, and a replacement reporter usually sits alongside, ready to take over without any break. A typical rota consists of fourteen reporters taking five- and ten-minute turns, which are then dictated to high-speed typists. Many of the reporters still use shorthand, at extraordinary speeds of up to 250 words a minute. Some MPs must fully test this skill. I do not know if a league table is kept of those speaking with speed and coherence. I would have awarded a rosette to the late Leslie Hale, Labour MP for Oldham West. He spoke with passion and humour, at the speed of a machine gun. Most of us stumble along well within Hansard speeds.

Hansard printing is done on their presses just off the Old Kent Road. Messengers come to the House of Commons every half-hour during the day to collect the typescript. The day's proceedings, up to between 10 and 11 p.m. are printed that night, leaving the presses at around 5 to 6 a.m. This ensures that MPs can read Hansard in the morning before the day's Commons business begins at 2.30 p.m.

Hansard is also produced as a weekly collection of the daily reporting, and a fortnightly report is produced as a bound volume. I have kept the bound Hansards ever since I became an MP. They make an impressive showing, but they also provide useful political reference when I am

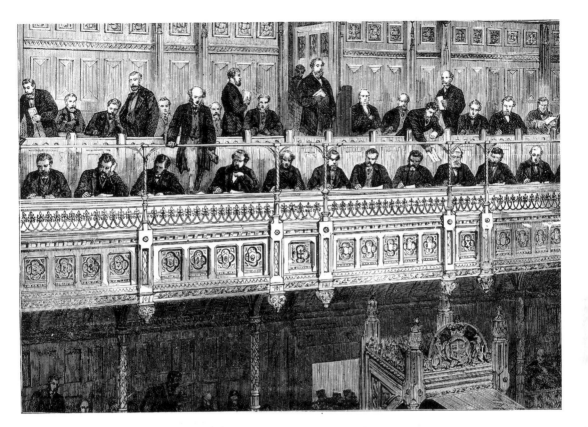

The Press Gallery in 1882.

working in Shropshire. MPs receive Hansard free of charge, but for the public an annual subscription costs more than £600. It has never become a best-seller. Indeed, the current subsidy on Hansard is nearly £5.2 million. Penguin Books produced commercially their own slim and heavily edited Hansard early in World War Two. I bought a copy on a second-hand stall in Taunton, and it helped inspire my schoolboy enthusiasm for politics. Many large public libraries stock Hansard, and details about this can be obtained from the House of Commons Public Information Office which was established as part of the Library in 1978.

Hansard is now integral to the working of Parliament. It seems incredible that there were ever difficulties in getting Parliament reported, and yet the idea of even relatively open government only came about over the centuries. MPs were originally concerned that their business should be conducted in secrecy because they wished to conceal their plans from the monarch. Furthermore, they did not think there was any need for their affairs to be known by the general public.

Sir Symonds D'Ewes, an MP for Suffolk in the early seventeenth century, collected from official and other sources a full account of all Elizabeth's Parliaments, both minutes (the Journal) and, where he could, speeches. Eventually, the Clerk was forbidden to record speeches in the Journal. Cromwell, however, saw advantages from publicity. He ordered broadsheets on government actions and policy to be printed and posted in Westminster Hall, Whitehall, and the Mansion House. He also ordered the publication of 'Daily Occurrences in Parliament', but characteristically ordered the severest punishment for anyone making an unofficial report.

Through the late seventeenth and eighteenth centuries unofficial reporting of parliamentary business steadily developed, in newsletters and broadsheets. Parliament was ambivalent about the practice. It was so widespread that attempts to prevent it proved ineffectual and MPs eventually gave up the struggle. A Frenchman, Abel Boyer, in 1711 started the magazine, *The Political State of Great Britain*. Soon some MPs were sending him their speeches for inclusion. Reporting was still formally forbidden, and publications like the *Gentleman's Magazine* resorted to wafer-thin disguises for political leaders: 'Sir Rubs Waleup' answered for Walpole, 'Plemham' was Pelham and 'Pulnib' concealed Pulteney.

Meanwhile newspapers were appointing specifically political writers. Edward Cave, proprietor of the *Gentleman's Magazine*, hired Samuel Johnson as a parliamentary correspondent. Johnson boasted he never sat in the gallery: only the unkind would suggest the tradition has lingered on. High literary standards were maintained by Samuel Taylor Coleridge, who from 1799 to 1800 was parliamentary reporter for the *Morning Post*.

Commons reserve towards the press throughout this period is illustrated by the lack of reporting facilities for political writers. Note-taking was forbidden and even today it is forbidden to take notes while in the Strangers Gallery. Legendary reporters in the eighteenth century, such as 'Memory' Woodfall and William Radcliffe, would observe the proceedings and then return to their offices or go to the printers and give a précis of what they had heard.

Newspaper reporters were first officially allocated seats in the Commons Public Gallery in 1803. William Cobbett, later to become a Tory MP as well as a journalist, had been carrying substantial accounts of what was happening in Parliament in his weekly *Political Register* since the year before and continued to do so until his death in 1835. He also published *Parliamentary Debates*, reports taken from his and other newspapers until he went bankrupt in 1811, when he sold his interest to Thomas Curson Hansard, son of Luke Hansard, printer to the House of Commons.

Initially Hansard was a private organisation, but eventually it was engulfed by financial difficulties. Assistance was provided by Stationery Office purchases of the reports and the Treasury also provided a subsidy. In 1909, following a Select Committee recommendation, Hansard was taken over by the House of Commons which became responsible for the staffing.

Luke Hansard (1752–1828), printer to the House of Commons and father of T. C. Hansard, first printer of the 1803 debates by Samuel Lane.

The public's knowledge of Parliament comes not from Hansard, but from newspapers, radio and television. The increase in the popular vote helped break down any lingering reluctance on the part of Parliament to admit, let alone encourage, press reporting. After the House of Commons fire in 1834, the Commons provided a small reporters' gallery above the Speaker's chair in the temporary chamber. Charles Dickens was one of the parliamentary journalists who worked there. He wrote the form of shorthand used by Gurneys, the business that supplies today's select committee transcribers. Dickens left the press gallery in 1836 to start writing *The Pickwick Papers*.

The chamber's provision for the press was enlarged after the bombing in 1941.

In his book *The Great Palace: The Story of Parliament*, Christopher Jones recalls an event which brings out the hazards of tampering with Westminster tradition. The Commons Press Gallery was very much a male preserve. In 1890 the *Woman's Penny Paper* wanted Miss Julia Blain to work in the gallery. A Bateman cartoon would be needed to describe the reaction of the House authorities. The Serjeant at Arms, supported by the Speaker, said it was quite impossible to admit women to the Press Gallery, which would lead to 'consequences which at present it is difficult to conceive'. The walls did not tumble until after World War One.

Perhaps the clearest indication that the press were welcomed rather than merely tolerated came in 1902, when it was decided to change Question Time to a fixed slot early in the afternoon to take account of press deadlines. Arthur Balfour, then Conservative Prime Minister, wistfully observed: 'We must arrange our proceedings, I presume, so that they may be reported in the newspapers that have currency all over the country.'

As Leader of the House I had a close and enjoyable link with the press representatives at Westminster collectively known as the 'lobby'. On

The Reporters' Room at the House of Commons, 1867. By this date the press reporting of Parliament had come of age and proper facilities were provided.

Thursday afternoon, when I had concluded 'next week's business' in the Commons, I would repair to a small room on the upper committee floor. This was press territory. The press journalists, or lobby correspondents, had an elected chairman who presided over the meeting. I would be accompanied by my parliamentary private secretary, Richard Page, the head of my private office, and also a would-be 'minder' from Number 10. My role was to answer questions. These were often related to next week's business, but they could range as widely as the journalists wished. I felt I was living dangerously. These lobby journalists were the eyes and ears of Westminster. The fact that the meeting was 'on lobby terms', meaning that my remarks would be attributed only to 'a government spokesman' meant little. In Whitehall and places close to Westminster everyone would know who had blundered.

I thoroughly enjoyed the weekly battle of wits. Once the episode was over I would retire to my room for a scotch and an immediate inquest with Richard Page. I felt as though I had just about survived a rodeo bucking bronco session – bruised but still in the saddle. I hope my time with the lobby epitomised what the relationship between politician and press should be: good-natured, mutually respectful, but never cosy.

Settling MPs' pay has been a miserable parliamentary experience. The Commons is rarely at its best when dealing with so self-conscious a matter. In recent years pay and allowance proposals have been made by an outside body, the Top Salaries Review Board (TSRB), the membership of which is mainly made up of senior businessmen. I still recollect the duty I had on 19 July 1983 of trying to persuade the House to accept a lower figure than that proposed. The government felt that MPs' pay was such a prominent issue that it would have a disproportionate impact upon public sector pay elsewhere. The debate started at 10 p.m. and finished six hours and seven votes later. Although the TSRB proposals were not carried, the government's plans were mangled. Ministers supported the government line, otherwise there was a free vote. It was a long and chaotic evening, but ironically its outcome was central to our present system whereby pay and allowances are linked to those outside Parliament and subject to periodic review.

Parliamentary pay has an uncertain history. In the thirteenth century boroughs and shires paid wages to their representatives in the Commons. Knights received four shillings a day, citizens and burgesses two shillings. These rates remained in force throughout the Middle Ages. The poet Andrew Marvell, Member for Kingston upon Hull from 1659 until his death in 1678, is reputed to have been the last person to receive a wage from his electors.

There was a system of fining MPs who did not attend the House. Absence, presumably for the session, rated a penalty of £20 in the days of Queen Elizabeth I. This practice persisted in the seventeenth century, particularly as some MPs preferred to absent themselves from Parliaments which dealt with such painful issues as then divided the Crown from the Commons. The last known fine for non-attendance was imposed in 1831. How civilized and gentle seem the disciplinary processes of our current Whips Offices.

The payment of MPs had ceased by the end of the seventeenth century. its passing was suitably regretted, just as its reintroduction early this century was greeted with dismay. Samuel Pepys wrote in his diary for 30 March 1668: 'At dinner . . . all concluded that the bane of Parliament hath been the leaving off the old custom of the places allowing wages to those that served them in Parliament, by which they chose men that understood their

'It's an unofficial strike for more pay for MPs. Wouldn't try to cross the picket line, Sir, they're in an ugly mood!' Cartoon by Lee, Evening News, 16 June 1952.

business and would attend it, and they could expect an account from, which now they cannot.'

In the eighteenth and much of the nineteenth centuries, therefore, only the wealthy could afford to become MPs. A seat in the Commons was a lucrative investment, since it often led to sinecure offices and pensions: far from expecting to be paid to enter Parliament, men were prepared to spend large sums to get themselves elected. Alongside pressure for the extension of the franchise there were increasing demands for the payment

'I only get elected for the fishing.' Cartoon by Lee, Evening News, 12 June 1936.

of MPs to open membership of the House to a wider social range. The Chartist movement advocated such a course in 1838, and at the turn of the century the cause was championed by Keir Hardie and the infant Labour party. Eventually, in 1911, a Commons resolution was passed by 265 votes to 173 which entitled MPs to draw £400 per annum from public funds. A factor in this decision was the 1909 Osborne judgement, which ruled that the trade union levy to support Labour MPs was illegal. The then Chancellor of the Exchequer, Lloyd George, summarised the case for change:

> When we offer £400 a year as payment for Members of Parliament it is not a recognition of the magnitude of the service, it is not a remuneration, it is not a recompense, it is not even a salary. It is just an allowance, to enable men to come here, men who would render incalculable service to the State, and whom it would be an incalculable loss to the State not to have here, but who cannot be here because their means do not allow it. It is purely an allowance to enable us to

open the door to great and honourable public service to these men, for whom this country will be all the richer, all the greater, and all the stronger for the unknown vicissitudes which it has to face by having them there to aid us by their counsel, by their courage, and by their resource. (Hansard, 1911, vol. 29, col. 1383).

Since that date the principle of MPs' pay has not been challenged, although the rate was cut as part of the National Government's economies in 1931. It was restored to the £400 level in 1935, again increased before World War Two, and raised to £1000 in 1946. There have been many increases, recommendations, reviews and abated recommendations concerning both pay and allowances since the war.

The key change was the decision in 1971 to refer MPs' pay, allowances, and pensions to the TSRB, while insisting that final decisions should remain with Parliament. The TSRB was first chaired by Lord Boyle, a former Cabinet Minister, and subsequently by Lord Plowden, whose distinguished career spanned the Civil Service and private industry. The recommendations have occasionally been scaled down by government, but essentially they now provide the framework of pay, allowances and pensions that are paid at Westminster.

Pay. An MP receives a basic salary of just over £24,000 (at 1 January 1989). The salary is reviewed annually in line with a point in the Senior Principal scale of the Civil Service. Ministers receive approximately 75 per cent of their MP's salary in addition to their ministerial salary, and also the allowances paid to MPs (see below).

Additional Costs Allowance is paid to reimburse an MP for identifiable additional costs of living in the constituency as well as in London. A claim is submitted to the Fees Office listing major items. Additional Costs are paid free of tax under Section 28 of the Finance Act 1984, and no additional expenses may be claimed against tax. The allowance is reviewed annually and has a Civil Service link. It stood at a maximum of £8957 in August 1988. Ministers may claim this allowance in full.

London Supplement is paid to meet the extra cost of living in London, and is taxable. Those eligible to receive the supplement are MPs with Inner London constituencies and MPs who receive a lower rate salary, namely Ministers. In August 1988 the London supplement was £1222 per annum.

Office allowance is paid for secretarial and research assistance and for office equipment and sundries. Salaries are paid direct by the Fees Office, otherwise MPs detail their expenses which they then claim from the Fees Office. The allowance is reviewed annually and has a Civil Service link. In August 1988 it stood at £22,588 per annum. Ministers may claim the allowance in full.

Motor Mileage is paid to MPs for driving carried out on constituency business and between Westminster and the constituency. The allowance is related to engine capacity and overall mileage, and calculated on a formula recommended by an independent enquiry chaired by Lord Peyton of Yeovil in 1984. MPs submit a form detailing the motor mileage claimed, and this is mutually agreed with the Fees Office.

Travel Warrants. MPs may use unlimited free rail warrants between Westminster and stations in or adjacent to their constituencies. A limited number of warrants are also available for spouses, secretaries/research assistants and children. Child warrants are taxable.

Resettlement Grant is payable to anyone who ceases to be an MP at a General Election, while under the age of 65. The amount varies and is based on age and length of service. The purpose of the grant is to provide short-term alleviation of the financial effects of an MP leaving the House. MPs do not qualify for redundancy payments. The grant is a lump sum, varying from 50 per cent of one year's salary for MPs serving up to 10 years to 100 per cent for MPs aged 55–64 with 15 or more years of service.

Pensions. MPs pay 9 per cent of their salary, and receive index-linked pensions now based upon one year's contribution buying a pension of one-fiftieth of the final salary and which provides for widows at the rate of one-half the MPs' pension.

Most MPs would argue that a major advantage of the above arrangements is that they are annually adjusted and have an acceptable point of reference with the outside world. I doubt if the standards of pay or allowances would strike those in industry and commerce as unduly generous; however, the system does rest heavily on self-assessment as far as allowances are concerned. The present practice is to have all factors in pay, pensions and allowances reviewed once every four years or so by the TSRB.

While the story of Westminster pay stretches back to the Middle Ages, discontent over office accommodation is much more recent. When I entered the Commons in 1961 I was given an ample locker opposite the Members dining room. During the Oswestry by-election Mrs Mary Rose had written suggesting she might be my part-time secretary. She was a wise and protective soul and just what a fledgling member needed. I nestled under her wing. My devotion was only mildly strained when she visited my bachelor home in the 1970 General Election and reorganised my kitchen while I was out canvassing. For a decade Mary Rose and I dealt with the letters of Oswestry and the nation with the aid of a cupboard. Dictation was carried out on any bench or chair that could be secured in a corridor. Looking back today, I simply cannot believe the conditions prevailing then.

Members have a substantial and growing work-load. They claim to need regular research assistance, as well as more space and more privacy for themselves and their staff. The Palace of Westminster is only capable of modest adaptation. A nineteenth-century Gothic palace cannot easily be transformed into a twentieth-century office block.

The Commons have reacted by developing adjacent buildings as offices for MPs and their staff. These include Old Palace Yard, Abbey Gardens, St Stephen's House and the buildings on the Embankment named after the architect Richard Norman Shaw. There are plans to make use of buildings in Cannon Row, close by, and eventually the parliamentary building being developed behind the façade of Bridge Street will provide accommodation for MPs' secretaries as well as additional library and refreshment facilities. The time beckons when generally adequate accommodation will be available. I hope MPs will not opt to spend their time in a bijou office rather than on the leather benches of the chamber.

The House of Commons is a blend of the traditional and the functional. That is especially true of the library. It is a combination of a gentleman's private library and a research department with computer technology. Strategically located on the same floor as the chamber and less than a minute away, it is adjacent to the Members tea room and smoking room. Quite properly, it is at the heart of the Commons.

The origins of the Commons library stretch back to the very first manuscript minutes of the House, the Journal, which dates from 1547, and the accumulated bills and papers laid on the Table which successive Clerks stored away. Eventually the Commons began to take an interest in its records and in 1742 ordered that the Journal should be printed. The Journal, together with a growing number of books, tracts and public documents, provided the embryo library.

In 1802 Speaker Abbot used the amassed material to establish the basis of the library, and his successor Speaker Manners–Sutton set aside a room to house the growing volume of books and records. The first Librarian, Benjamin Spiller, was appointed in 1818. Thereafter accommodation was improved and in 1828 the House voted £2000 to equip a new room 'with such books as might be deemed useful for Members of this House'. Thomas Babington Macaulay, the great Whig historian and MP, did much of his literary work from the Commons library, and William Gladstone served on the first library committee.

About 60 per cent of the books were rescued from the great fire in 1834, but virtually all the manuscript material was lost. The Commons was rebuilt with a new library which came into use in 1852. Originally it consisted of three magnificent rooms overlooking the river front of the Palace. Each room measures 16.76 metres by 9.14 metres and some 6.1 metres high. Shortly thereafter two more rooms were added. Finally an adjacent room long used by the Speaker as his own library was incorporated in 1967. These rooms constitute the library we have today. A branch exists in the Norman Shaw buildings.

Generations of Commons scribblers much less renowned than Macaulay have used the library's quiet, albeit not silent, atmosphere to write articles, books and speeches. The walls are lined with books from floor to ceiling. Tall ladders have to be used to reach the topmost shelves, since there is no gallery. The four main rooms are provided with writing tables and stationery, magazine racks and superbly comfortable armchairs. Before the present improvement in Members' accommodation, these chairs provided valuable berths for late-night and all-night sittings.

Specialist staff in the library can assist Members, or their research assistants, with practically every political topic. For example, I decided in the spring of 1988 that I wanted to speak on economic affairs. I knew what was to be the theme of my speech, but I did not have the statistics to demonstrate my argument. I asked the library staff if they could provide me with evidence on a number of items such as prices, incomes, and bank credits. I was duly provided with the material which, happily, confirmed my arguments. Without the library my speech would have been instinct and assertion; that paste was, I hope, converted into the pearls of persuasive logic.

The excellent reputation of the library research work explains why there has been a steady growth in its staff and budget. The staff currently number around 150, divided between research, 43; parliamentary section, around 80; and the Vote Office, 30. The Research Division deals currently with 8000 written enquiries a year from MPs and their staff and several thousand oral briefings. The growth in demand for library services is closely related to the rising number of research assistants. In 1978 the Commons library logged 144 requests for information from research assistants. In 1984 there were around 17,000.

The Parliamentary Division's four sections provide heterogeneous services including answering quick reference queries and enquiries from outside Parliament; an international affairs section deals with both reference and in-depth queries; and it runs the computer and technical services of the library. Since 1980 the work of the library, and particularly its research, has been assisted by a computer retrieval system (POLIS). The current overall cost of the library is just short of £3 million per year, consisting mainly of staff costs.

Library research activities should not overshadow its traditional role of providing MPs with access to a fine stock of books. The present book stock is 150,000 volumes, including 18,000 volumes of parliamentary papers of all descriptions which alone amount to a further 150,000 separate items. The library also subscribes to 1600 periodical titles and more than 100 national daily and regional newspapers.

The Vote Office also falls within the responsibility of the library. Its work originated in the late seventeenth century and provided for the delivery to Members' homes of the papers and parliamentary Acts they needed to carry out their duties. The Vote Office now delivers these papers direct to MPs living within a three-mile radius of the Palace of Westminster, and by post to others. There are also three places within the Commons where papers may be collected from Vote Office staff.

The library, for all its modern facilities echoes with history. One memorable incident was the ill-fated attempt in 1867 by Matthew Arnold (then Professor of Poetry at Oxford) to become Commons librarian. He wrote to Gladstone: 'Several Members of the House of Commons of both parties have kindly undertaken to recommend my application to the Speaker; but I need not say of what inestimable value your recommendation would be.' Arnold's entreaties did him little good: the Speaker appointed a Mr Howard. Members of the Library Committee in the nineteenth century included Peel, Palmerston, Russell, Gladstone and Disraeli – all Prime Ministers.

Much mention has been made in this book of Erskine May, later Lord Farnborough. His bust stands by the entrance to 'D' room in the library. He joined the library in 1831 at the age of sixteen, and stayed for fifteen years before eventually becoming the Clerk of the House and also making his name as an authority on Commons procedures and precedents. He was a voracious reader, and his notebook records that, having read 59 books in 1834 and 100 books in 1835, he hoped to 'continue to increase in this proportion annually'.

There is a custom that Commons authors deposit a signed copy of their publications with the library and over the generations a substantial stock of books has accumulated. Mercifully, not all Westminster authors confine themselves to economics and politics: titles range from *The Cornish Edwardians* by David Mudd, MP for Falmouth and Camborne, to *Top Hat and Tails*, a biography of Jack Buchanan by Michael Marshall, MP for Arundel. They would make a fascinating and popular exhibition. The star attraction would surely be the signed war memoirs of Winston Churchill which are now kept under lock and key.

PART V

A Personal
Perspective

31 A WEEK IS A LONG TIME

The timescales of Parliament vary. Politics is so immediate that the session, usually lasting a year, seems to stretch to infinity. On the other hand a day is but the movement of a parliamentary camera shutter, and crises are only fleetingly caught. Between the day and the session Westminster has judged that a natural working unit is the parliamentary week.

Each Thursday the Leader of the House announces next week's business, and MPs have a chance to assess the burden of the workload ahead. No week is typical, but all have the potential to be quite unpredictable whatever the planning. Harold Wilson once coined the phrase that 'in politics a week is a long time'. He was right on two counts. Firstly, political events can be so fast-moving that Monday's drama has become Friday's footnote. Secondly, there are weeks when the House has to deal with solid legislation day after day into the early hours; then Friday seems to arrive slowly.

MPs have inadequate facilities to deal with their long hours. Their rooms, and not all have one, are modestly furnished. There is the comfort of the library chairs and the conviviality of the smoking room. The debating chamber is air-conditioned and encourages those who prefer the debate to drowsy rest. For MPs protracted working, or 'waiting', hours are a trial, and an imposition upon their families. One day this may be changed by procedural reform, but currently the prospects are poor.

On Fridays MPs receive a written Whip detailing the next week's business outlined by the Leader of the House. There is a convention that parliamentary Whips may not be published for twenty years. Therefore I reproduce below the business for the week 4–11 July 1988 which was published in *The Times* on Friday, 1 July. This outlines only the main business and does not include many of the items which are taken late at night.

PARLIAMENT NEXT WEEK
The main business in the Commons next week will be:
Monday: Legal Aid Bill, remaining stages, North Killingholme Cargo Terminal Bill, second reading. Debate on prevention of pollution.
Tuesday: Debate on Opposition motion on the health service.
Wednesday: Debates on SNP motion on the political situation in Scotland and on SLD motion on pensioners.

'Really, Sir! I appreciate that you must be on call for every division now, but you can't SLEEP here, y'know!' This cartoon by Lee in the Evening News (1 March 1950) shows an all-night sitting and the woeful lack of facilities in the Commons.

Thursday: Debates on estimates on defence, on housing and on environmental and planning services.

Friday: Private members' Bills: Malicious Communications Bill and Access to Medical Records Bill, Lords amendments. Landlord and Tenant Bill, third reading.

The main business in the Lords is expected to be:

Monday and Tuesday: Local Government Finance Bill, report, third and fourth days.

Wednesday: British Steel Bill, report. Housing (Scotland) Bill, report, first day.

Thursday: Education Reform Bill, third reading.

Friday: Debate on reform of EEC structural funds.

The Commons business suggests there will be an active week, with emphasis upon general debates such as that on the National Health Service. Considerable time will also be spent on legislation, and variety will be provided by a Church of England measure and a Northern Ireland Order. The House would normally finish its substantive business at 10 p.m. (followed by the half-hour adjournment debate) unless the '10 o'clock rule' is suspended, in which case business can run without limit. The programme for 4–11 July suggests that the Commons could run very late on Monday and Wednesday, until 1 a.m. on Tuesday and 11.30 p.m. on Wednesday. Happily these dire forecasts are not always realised, and often one can 'pair' with a political opponent (as explained in Chapter 13) where the business is of two-line importance.

Indeed, my immediate task after studying next week's Whip is to discuss with a Labour MP when we both may be away in the evening. Many MPs make such 'pairing' arrangements because they wish to fulfil evening engagements, often political, outside the Commons. Others are particularly anxious to pair after the major votes at 10 p.m. in the hope of getting some beauty sleep. I try to pair as much as possible to avoid late-night business. I doubt if I would now enjoy even an all-night May Ball, let alone keeping the early morning watch for some modest government order.

Nowadays I have a relatively restricted parliamentary programme. I am not a member of a departmental select committee. Nonetheless I am a diligent attender at the Commons and rarely travel away from Westminster. I often go to the back-bench Conservative parliamentary committees; although the meetings, broadly related to government departmental activities, are confidential, they can be dramatic as well as informative. Many a government crisis is played out in the parliamentary committee as well as in Whitehall. A similar committee structure exists for both the Conservative and Labour parties. The confidentiality means that neither the dates nor the proceedings appears in the press except during moments of high drama, when investigative journalism triumphs over political reticence. The diaries of Henry (Chips) Channon and Harold Nicolson have now unlocked the secrets of the Conservative parliamentary Foreign Affairs committee and its passionate debates over appeasement in the 1930s. Similarly Robert Skidelsky, in his biography of Sir Oswald Mosley, gives a dramatic account of the Labour parliamentary meeting where Mosley, having resigned from the Labour Cabinet, challenged his erstwhile colleagues on their unemployment policy. Mosley was convincing but impetuous. He was outmanoeuvred and soon thereafter left the Labour Party. His formidable talents were subsequently dissipated in right-wing fringe politics.

This incident is a reminder that high politics in the Palace of Westminster are not confined to the floor of the Commons. Some of the richest political occasions are locked away in the rooms where the weekly party meetings take place. The week of 4–11 July 1988 was, by contrast, 'worthy'. Douglas Hurd, Home Secretary, addressed the Urban and Inner Cities Committee; and Lord Harris of High Cross, a free market economist, addressed the Finance Committee. There was not a mention of either in the press.

My weekly diary usually includes one speaking engagement, normally arranged by the Conservative Party. These take place in London because of my work in the Commons. A generation ago there was a sharp decline in the number of political meetings. The old-style public gathering, complete with hecklers, has practically vanished. Most Tory politics are now taken with a meal. They are useful in making contacts and learning of problems I would not encounter in a rural constituency.

MPs receive many visitors during the week, particularly if their constituencies are in London. Obviously fewer constituents visit Westminster from Shropshire than from Surbiton, but I also get quite a number of visitors on account of my interest in economics and my general political activities. During the week in question I gave dinner in the Commons to an American professor from Illinois who was researching the political philosophies of Rousseau and Burke. Our table talk made a change from the sharp controversies over the community charge legislation.

I love the Commons dearly, but I cannot pretend that 4–11 July was a memorable week. Nonetheless it was quite a representative one: a description of Parliament's work does not lend itself to endless drama. The week's agenda reads like a laundry list, ranging from a Bill on Electricity (Financial Provisions) (Scotland) to a ten-minute-rule bill to curb smoking in taxi cabs. None of these items made *The Times* list of 'main' business. The parliamentary party committees had such dull business that they kept their secrets locked. Perhaps most unkindly, all this unnewsworthy business required long hours and confinement to the Palace.

And yet I would never complain. The Commons, mercifully, develops a charm quite independent of its agenda. It still has about it something of both the London Club and the eighteenth-century coffee house. There is a Westminster mood that is created merely by MPs being together and mixing with the lobby journalists. That mood has to be taken into account by the Whips and by government. The Westminster working week, with its long hours and lack of defined tasks, would be the despair of management consultants. Wisely they have not been commissioned to report on our ways to the Procedure Committee. The House of Commons is not an ants' nest of eager junior executives working ceaselessly to climb the rungs of government. MPs are at Westminster to look and listen, and perhaps occasionally to speak. They should provide a critical audience for government, and constantly assert that MPs are not an extension of the government, even though they sustain it.

Finally no politician's work is merely life at Westminster. The constituency is a vital dimension of politics, and like many MPs I live in my own parliamentary division, North Shropshire. Westminster's work done, on Friday my wife and I drive to our home in the border village of Llanyblodwel. It is distinguished by a superb sixteenth-century inn, the Horseshoe, the river Tanat, and a church remarkably restored by its incumbent, John Parker, in the 1840s. The whole world looks much saner from the Tanat Valley.

A weekend, while relaxing, is rarely a total rest from politics. Surgeries or advice bureaux have to be undertaken in the six market towns that fall within the constituency. There are frequent Conservative fund-raising events providing the temptations of tombola and the welcome opportunity to buy home-made cakes. Visits must be made to hospitals, schools, farms and factories. The constituency must be diligently waited upon throughout the year. I am ever mindful of A.E. Housman's lines:

You and I must keep from shame
In London streets the Shropshire name.

So the political week, dominated by Westminster and underpinned by the constituency, rolls into months and beyond. Indeed soon the sessions extend into the lifetime of a Parliament, and towards the process of democratic renewal, a General Election. Whether the judgement is on the political day, week, or session, I know of no other career so varied or satisfying. Harold Wilson may well have been right that 'a week is a long time', but for me it is simply not long enough.

A popular general misconception is that a noisy and widely reported Question Time constitutes a busy day's work. This is not the case. I give below a work diary based on actual incidents but not necessarily on the same day when Parliament is sitting. No day is typical, and MPs' interests are diverse. My diary is influenced by the fact that I have some outside business interests and also that I am not a member of any standing or select committees. Whilst my day is not typical it conveys something of an MP's long hours and his need to be a good listener.

During the week I live in Battersea. When I ceased to have a ministerial car a friendly neighbour included me in her school run. At 8.15 a.m. the day begins, knees under chin, in a mature Citroën *deux chevaux*. The ten-minute walk from the Westminster Cathedral Choir School to the Commons is almost my only exercise.

My first call is the Members' post office situated near the chamber, where I collect my daily bundle of mail and go to my room. I am fortunate in having a sizeable room near the chamber furnished with a desk, table, armchair, sofa and filing cabinet. I have installed my own fridge, and so the daily toil is lubricated by a stream of iced Malvern water. My post is modest compared with that of MPs with larger and more urban constituencies. Over 40 per cent of my items of mail are circulars and information sheets that range from the US Chamber of Commerce to *India Weekly*, as well as a handful of crank letters. They are put aside.

Replies to constituents' problems from government departments and public authorities account for about 15 per cent of the mail, and 10 per cent consists of letters from constituents, mainly requiring approaches to Whitehall or local authorities. One letter demands action to preserve the tropical rain forests. Many constituency problems are dealt with at surgeries rather than through the post. The remaining mail consists of political invitations, House of Commons matters, newspapers and, finally, letters from the general public. One of these – a prize – is from Finchley and commends my views on the European Community.

This amount of mail is modest and manageable. Dealing with it usually takes me about an hour. I deal with the letters immediately I have finished reading them. My secretary is able to answer many letters without guidance, but where necessary I draft by hand the answer I require. I would always answer technical agricultural problems myself. My secretary works in a run-down building on the Thames Embankment, five minutes' walk away. Her tatty working conditions would not be tolerated in most commercial organisations.

My next task is to read the newspapers. Since my room has neither radio nor television I rely on newspapers to keep me informed on national and local issues. My daily national reading is the *Independent*. I try to cover most major reporting including the City pages. I also glance at other papers in the Commons library. My other regular paper is the *Shropshire Star*. Its circulation in the constituency is believed to outstrip any of the nationals and it has a good coverage of local events.

Later in the morning I might visit the library, or my secretary, or have coffee and discuss the small change of politics in the Members' tea room. There will also be a succession of telephone calls, often from the media. These can take up a considerable amount of time.

At 11 a.m. I have a meeting with the chairman of the Shropshire National Farmers Union. I meet him in the Central Lobby and take him to my room. The troubles of farming are focused on the need for a Green Pound revaluation, the MCA (Monetary Compensatory Arrangements) difficulties for the pig industry, and uncertainties concerning set-aside schemes which take land out of production. The meeting last 45 minutes. Again I resolve to lobby the Minister of Agriculture even though decisions on these matters rest not with him but with Brussels.

The meeting over, I try to snatch some much-needed time to pause and think about the issues that have been raised. I must shortly leave the Commons for my lunch engagement as the guest of a major insurance company in the City. It is a courteous but brisk occasion. There are about half-a-dozen executives present, and I am the only guest. The food is excellent, but the quality of the wine is academic since I am teetotal until 6 p.m.

I bolt my food in order to take questions from my hosts. They come thick and fast, about insurance and the European Community, the possible changes in the UK tax laws on insurance, and the scope for insurance in providing care for the elderly. Then the pitch is varied. Will Mrs Thatcher lead the Conservatives next time? Who would she like to follow her? I enjoy fielding the questions; but for me these are never relaxed occasions. Lunch has not been free.

I return to Westminster in order to hear the bulk of Question Time, followed by statements and possibly the opening of a debate. This is the part of the day that I devote to the chamber. It is usually well attended, and there is often the chance of having a word with fellow-MPs.

On this particular day, a Tuesday, I plan to attend two meetings organised by back-bench Conservative MPs. At 5 p.m. I will go to Committee Room 14 and listen to Neville Wallace of the British Poultry Federation. The chairman of these 'party groups' are elected annually. The

'The major and minor events of a day at St Stephen's':
Illustrated London News,
1908.

attendance varies but is usually modest, between twelve and twenty. The meeting is extremely informal but is conducted in confidence. It is an excellent occasion to learn from those, like Neville Wallace, who are experts in their subject. The meeting may last for an hour.

Next I go to the party Finance committee chaired by Sir William Clark, MP for Croydon South. The attendance for this meeting is higher than for agriculture. The speaker is the financial journalist Christopher Fildes. He makes his compelling argument with a dry wit. Again the meeting is conducted in strict confidence.

These two meetings, unknown to the general public, have taken the heart out of the afternoon. It is now 7 p.m. I collect my dictation from the letter board in the Members lobby and go to my room. I sign the letters, mark up my own forward diary with the day's new commitments and make any telephone calls possibly arising from messages left with my secretary.

The day is beginning to run away, and the temperance rule can be breached. A few yards away is Annie's bar, strictly for MPs and journalists. I drop in for a glass of Federation Ale and such political wisdom as may be on offer.

At 8 p.m. I must be in the Central Lobby to meet my wife and guests, a publisher friend and his Australian wife. We have a table in the Harcourt dining-room. It is one of the nights when we can eat to the accompaniment of the Welsh harpist. The table soon becomes an oasis in the Westminster wilderness with talk of publishing, the theatre and country activities.

At 10 p.m. the division is called. MPs proceed to cast their votes and to resume their never-ending political discussion and tactics as they walk through the lobbies. At about 10.30 p.m. it is fairly safe to leave and I join the queue for a taxi. The chamber is echoing to the pleas of the lone MP who has the adjournment debate, and I have now completed my working day, all of which has been spent in the Commons with the exception of lunch. Some of the time has been taken up by waiting upon events and some in casual political conversation. Much of the time has been spent listening, little in speaking. The day has lasted nearly fourteen hours. Soon the police will intone: 'Who goes home?'

33 EVOLUTION OR ECLIPSE

In 1972 the United Kingdom signed the Treaty of Rome and joined the European Community (EC). Since that date Westminster has sought to adapt its law-making role to the Community's requirements.

The major EC institutions are the Council of Ministers (comprising Ministers from the member states), and the European Commission, which is appointed by the Member States, the larger having two Commissioners and the smaller, one. In addition there is an elected European Parliament and the European Court of Justice, which acts as an interpreter of Community legislation. EC law is made by the Council of Ministers, acting upon proposals from the EC Commission. Ministers from the governments of the various member states, in effect, act as law-makers. National Parliaments have no direct role in making these laws, which are made by Ministers and unamendable by the Commons. They apply throughout the Community, Britain included. These laws have as much force as any Act of Parliament.

Against this background the Economic Secretary to the Treasury, Peter Lilley, came to the Commons on 21 June 1988 with disagreeable news. The European Court, which is the legal guardian of the Treaty of Rome, had ruled that Britain must levy Value Added Tax on a number of items including the construction of industrial and commercial buildings and industrial water and sewerage services. The European Commission, a body of hybrid politicians/administrators whose task it is to ensure Community common practice, had successfully taken the United Kingdom to court.

I doubt that Peter Lilley expected to find the Commons passive and philosophical about the government's defeat. Certainly he was subjected to prolonged and vigorous questioning. Supporters and opponents of Community membership were both hostile. There were three points of concern. In the first instance the decision seemed pedantic: industrial buildings and sewerage services are hardly exportable, so harmonisation was not necessary. Secondly, the House of Commons has for centuries been the only authority that could tax the British people. Value Added Tax is a highly sensitive political issue, the Labour party giving it lower significance in revenue raising than the Conservatives. Finally, the decision to broaden the imposition of Value Added Tax had come not from Community politicians, but from Community judges. Taxes decided by judges with no possibility of amendment by Parliament were wholly alien to the Commons. For generations Westminster had been making the law, not being bound by it.

Peter Lilley put a calm and measured case. It did not convince John Marek, his Labour shadow, and MP for Wrexham, who tartly observed: 'Yet again new taxes are to be imposed on the public against the wishes of Government and Parliament.' Peter Shore, Labour MP for Bethnal Green and Stepney and veteran Euro-sceptic, observed: 'Is this not another brutal reminder of the extent to which the House has ceased to be master of its own affairs?' John Redwood, Conservative MP for Wokingham and a Commons catch from the Downing Street 'think tank', judged that 'there is a widespread feeling on both sides of the House that we have already surrendered too many powers.' There was much more of the same. And certainly there will be still more. The three points of anxiety – the pedantry of the tax changes, the unacceptability of Community-enforced taxation, and the role of the European Court – will continue to cause unease at Westminster.

How has this come about? The Treaty of Rome, which established the EC, sets out the aims and objectives of the Community and defines the powers and functions of its institutions. There are three types of Community law: directives, regulations, and decisions. Directives are binding in their aim, but national latitude is allowed in implementation. Community regulations are binding throughout all member states, and are directly applicable. Decisions are binding on particular individuals, companies or member states.

From the outset the British Parliament recognised that the provisions of the Treaty of Rome would be a challenge to traditional law-making. A committee was set up in the 1972–3 session of Parliament under the chairmanship of an outstanding lawyer, the late Sir John Foster, MP for Northwich. It recommended that a Commons committee should be established to consider all EC Commission proposals before they reached the Council of Ministers, where the British government was represented. The special Commons committee would assess the importance of the documents in requiring debate, rather than their merits, and report their views to the House. This proposal was adopted.

In May 1974 the Select Committee on European Secondary Legislation (Scrutiny Committee) was established. It has sixteen members and is appointed for the lifetime of a parliament. The present chairman is Labour MP for Newham South, Nigel Spearing. (I knew him slightly at University. When we met nearly thirty years later in the Commons I could swear he still had the same bicycle.)

The Scrutiny Committee has an onerous task. It has to deal with about 700 EC documents a year. The filtering process requires careful evaluation and cannot be rushed. Some documents are recommended by the Scrutiny

Committee for consideration by a Standing Committee on European Community documents. Its membership is modest and can hold two-and-a-half-hour debates, usually in the morning, to consider these documents. Many, however, concern issues that demand full Commons attention.

There are two major problems concerning the Commons and the EC. The first is the amount of Westminster time that can be given to prospective Community law. The growth of EC law has not diminished the law-making appetite of the British government. In the 1983–4 session there were sixteen debates on EC documents lasting a total of 26 hours, but much of this time was spent very late at night. It would be churlish to disparage the arrangements, but they will be wholly inadequate if EC powers are increased with greater economic ambitions and an enlarged Community.

The second difficulty concerns how the debate should be used. Generally the House likes a specific debate. However, it has been reluctant to mandate Ministers ahead of a Council meeting where Euro-horsetrading is graced as 'negotiations'. Council meetings often resolve so many matters simultaneously within a flexible agenda that it is unrealistic for the Commons to mandate Ministers. The Westminster debate will collect the voices rather than record votes. It is, therefore, natural that many motions are 'to take note' of the documents. Westminster voices can, however, grow faint once the Minister is locked in noisy discourse with eleven other Ministers and numerous advisers. Furthermore the decisions, once made, are set in Euro-concrete with no prospect of amendment. It is certain that the frustrations produced by this situation will make for continuing anxiety and debate.

There is a tenuous analogy between EC law and the use of what is termed 'delegated legislation'. This comes from Acts which have been passed by Parliament. Many contain provisions which, while not in the main legislation, may be made law by subsequent orders or statutory instruments (SIs). Currently about 2000 SIs are made annually. Most of these are technical and non-controversial but many are of significance. For example, the whole of the legislation providing for the scope and design of road signs and markings was enacted by means of SIs under the Road Traffic General Directions Act of 1967. EC law is not mandated by parliamentary Acts, and it covers issues generally far more far-reaching than delegated legislation.

Some essentially non-controversial SIs are not subjected to any parliamentary procedure. Others will cease to have effect if the House passes a motion for their annulment. This is referred to as a negative procedure. The motion is known as a 'prayer' or request because of its wording which asks 'that an humble Address be presented to Her Majesty, praying that the ... Order be annulled'. Finally, some Acts require that a motion approving any relevant SI must be passed by the House before they come into force. This is called the affirmative procedure.

This modern system of considering SIs arose from the 1950s. The Conservative opposition in the 1950–51 parliament used considerable parliamentary time to debate these measures with damaging and vexatious effect. In the mid-1950s more civilised counsels prevailed. Debates are now generally limited to 90 minutes late in the evening. A Scrutiny Committee was also established to report upon SIs. It cannot report upon the alleged merits of SIs, but it can judge whether the Minister is correct in his exercise of power and whether the proposed SI is outside the scope of the parent Act. In 1973–4 Standing Committees were also set up specifically to discuss SIs and to relieve the pressure for debates in the House. This is one instance of where there is some analogy between the treatment of SI and EC business.

The decision on which negative procedure SIs should be debated on the floor of the House is agreed between the business managers of the government and opposition. These SIs frequently lead to vigorous parliamentary debate, as they can express the essence rather than the technicalities of policy. I remember nostalgically the keen debates on Labour's prices and incomes policy between 1966 and 1968. The main Act decided that every instance of government regulation of pay or price should be authorised by an Order. The result was that the policy was debated in miniature almost weekly, and against the background of growing trade union and Labour Party unease. It was just one example of how a rather technical form of law-making can spring into political life. Above all it demonstrated that SIs cannot have a disembodied life beyond the influence of the Commons. The same considerations will eventually apply to laws that bind the British but which stem from Brussels.

The House of Commons has weathered so much turbulence in the past that it is reasonable to ask why there should now be anxieties about its future. It is certainly worth while to recall its achievements.

Over the centuries power has been won from the Crown, and is now exercised through the political parties responding to the popular vote. That is the working reality of Westminster, and it should not be obscured by the historical trappings. Its continuing effectiveness will depend upon power being exercised by an executive which answers to a Parliament resting upon a popular vote. The procedures of Parliament have a vital role in ensuring that those relationships proceed effectively. Above all they must ensure that Westminster is not insulated from the economic and social changes that beset the nation generally. The charm of the past and proper reverence for tradition must not convert the Commons into a museum.

Meanwhile popular support for Parliament remains strong. This is crucial and does not appear to be at risk. There is no sign that responsibility at election time is being replaced by apathy and indifference. In the last General Election there was a turnout of 75.3 per cent. This was less than the post-war record of 84 per cent in 1950, but well above the figures scored in presidential elections in the United States. Parliament continues to have an authority derived from a substantial popular vote.

Secondly, there is no doubt that the political party is still performing its indispensable role linking government and electorate. All the parties represented at Westminster are conscious of their need to be professional in the skills of communication and vote-winning. It is now inconceivable that the major parties would fail to fight any seat at a general or by-election. The numbers seriously seeking election to the Commons remain as high as ever, the demand far exceeding the seats available. This is hardly the sign of an institution in decline.

Some people believe, however, that there is a danger that parliamentary procedures have rusted away, and no longer enable the Commons and the government to do their job. This is a long-standing challenge and is sometimes valid. The doors of Westminster should always rattle with the protests of the deprived. Parliament's laws and taxes have a social as well as an economic purpose. At Westminster we are all heirs to Disraeli's concept of 'One Nation'. The way we conduct parliament's business should enable us to reflect the world outside and not retreat into a narrow Westminster enclave. In actuality, remoteness is not a serious danger to parliament.

Where, then, lie the developments and dangers that make Westminster's future uncertain? Once again we return to the European Community.

When in 1972 the Commons debated and passed the European Communities Act, two singularly effective voices sounded a warning, those of Enoch Powell and Michael Foot. Both had a reverence for and understanding of the Commons that transcended any party politics. Powell argued in the second reading debate of the European Communities Bill: 'For this House lacking the necessary authority . . . legislatively to give away the independence and sovereignty of this House now and for the future is an unthinkable act. Even if there were not those outside to whom we have to render account, the very stones of this place would cry out against us if we dared such a thing.' Such a thing was dared.

The emerging consequences can now be perceived. The European Court has the authority to make essentially political decisions such as extending VAT to charities. That, however, is more than matched by the growing power of the European Council of Ministers and the ambitions of the European Parliament in Strasbourg. The Council of Ministers is the more powerful. Its judgements range widely in scale and importance. A Council decision set in train the Single European Act which is designed to increase substantially the political authority of the Community; on the other hand, in 1987 a Council decision was so specialised as to affect only the collection of Italian agricultural statistics. The meetings are private, at least nominally. We do not know with what skill or determination the British Minister has fought for the national case. Once the arguments are concluded, Council decisions are announced at Westminster. The decisions often have law-making implications, and Parliament can only accept; it cannot veto, amend or qualify. This is an affront to the status patiently acquired by the Commons over the generations. It is an unsatisfactory situation and will remain so until MPs insist upon being able to qualify this recent transfer of power to Ministers.

The transfer of law-making away from national Parliaments (including the House of Commons) has few friends. Some of those propose that the European Community needs new continental institutions rather than co-operation between national Parliaments. They argue that the decline of the House of Commons should be offset by greater powers for the European Parliament at Strasbourg. Doubtless this argument will continue. Meanwhile it is worth assessing some of the relative merits as between the proven practice of Westminster and the Strasbourg blueprint. The first relates to popular esteem. The test is popular demand. Is there general enthusiasm to have taxing and law-making carried out by a European Parliament representing a Community population of 320 million?

In the United Kingdom this process involves Euro-constituencies with electorates of more than 530,000, compared with a Commons figure of less than 67,000. Does the public want larger constituencies? Furthermore, politics at Strasbourg are based upon loose alliances of parties from different countries which shift and change according to the issue under debate. The voter is not able to identify parties with policies and performance. Perhaps it is hardly surprising that many of the European parliamentary divisions do not record the individual votes of members. The Commons would be hooted off the parliamentary stage if it behaved in such a way.

The European partnership was debated in general terms and launched with goodwill more than thirty years ago. Now the detailed reality is becoming apparent. From the outset a central role was assigned to the Council of Ministers and to the European Parliament. Even so, I do not believe that European co-operation can be happily secured at the cost of the House of Commons and national Parliaments. Westminster's patient work of centuries should have an integral role in European partnership. It should not be set aside out of a fashionable concern to increase the power of government and in the unproven belief that continental size can secure social contentment and economic success. A proper regard for our national institutions should make possible, not confound, partnership with our neighbours. The stones of Westminster tell us so.

SELECT BIBLIOGRAPHY

REFERENCE BOOKS

Butler, D., and Butler, G.: *British Political Facts 1900–1985* (Macmillan, 6th ed, 1986)

Dod's *Parliamentary Companion* (Dod's Parliamentary Companion Ltd.), published annually

Manual of Proceedings in the Public Business (HMSO, 14th ed, 1987)

May, Sir T. Erskine: *The Law, Privileges, Proceedings and Usage of Parliament* (Butterworth, 20th ed, 1983)

Roth, Andrew: *Parliamentary Profiles* (Parliamentary Profile Services Ltd.)

The Times Guide to the House of Commons 1987 (Times Newspapers Ltd., 1987), published following each General Election

Vacher's *Parliamentary Companion* (A.S. Kerswill Ltd.), published quarterly

GENERAL

Bradshaw, K.A. and Pring, D.A.M.: *Parliament and Congress* (Quartet, 3rd ed, 1981)

Cormack, Patrick: *Westminster: Palace and Parliament* (Frederick Warne, 1981)

de Smith, S., Street, S., and Brazier, R.: *Constitutional and Administrative Law* (Penguin, 1985)

Fell, Sir B.H., Mackenzie, K.R., and Sands, R.B.: *The Houses of Parliament* (Eyre and Spottiswoode, 13th ed, 1977)

Jones, Christopher: *The Great Palace: The Story of Parliament* (BBC Publications, 1983)

Norton, Philip: *The Commons in Perspective* (Martin Robertson, 1981)

Norton, Philip: *Parliament in the 1980s* (Basil Blackwell, 1985)

Silk, Paul: *How Parliament Works* (Longman, 1987)

Walkland, S.A.: *The House of Commons in the Twentieth Century* (Clarendon Press, 1979)

Walkland, S.A.: *The Legislative Process in Great Britain* (George Allen and Unwin, 1968)

Walkland, S.A., and Ryle, M. (eds): *The Commons Today* (Fontana, rev. ed, 1981)

Wilding, N., and Laundy, P.: *An Encyclopaedia of Parliament* (Cassell, 1958)

GLOSSARY

This short glossary is intended only as a brief guide to some of the terms commonly used in descriptions of the House of Commons. Further details will be found in the relevant chapters.

BLACK ROD: The shortened title of an official of the House of Lords, whose full title is Gentleman Usher of the Black Rod. He fulfils a similar role to that of the Serjeant at Arms in the House of Commons. Black Rod's appointment dates from the reign of Henry VIII, when he was to be chief of all the ushers of the kingdom and to have care and custody of the doors of the 'High Court of Parliament'. His title derives from the short ebony rod of office, surmounted by a golden lion rampant. (See Chapter 16.)

CHILTERN HUNDREDS: An MP is technically not allowed to resign his or her seat. As a result, any MP wishing to relinquish his or her seat in the Commons between general elections must follow a curious procedure, known as 'applying for the Chiltern Hundreds'. The office of steward or bailiff of the Three Chiltern Hundreds of Stoke, Desborough and Burnham nominally continues as an office of profit under the Crown, although it has actually ceased to exist. Since no MP is allowed to hold an office of profit under the Crown (other than ministerial offices as authorised by statute), applying for this nominal sinecure means that the MP must relinquish his or her seat. The custom apparently dates from around 1750. (See Chapter 18.)

CLOSURE: This is the procedure by which a Commons debate can be terminated, by a majority vote (which must include at least 100 affirmative votes), although all MPs wishing to speak may not have done so. Until the late nineteenth century, there was no means of limiting the length of debate, a situation which the Irish Nationalist MPs were able to exploit to prolong debates and thereby obstruct government business. The closure was introduced as a result of Speaker Brand's personal initiative on 2 February 1881, when he terminated a sitting which had lasted $41\frac{1}{2}$ hours. In 1882, the closure was incorporated in Standing Orders, and became a permanent feature of Commons proceedings. See also 'Guillotine', below. (See Chapter 4.)

DESPATCH BOX: Two Despatch Boxes are placed on the Table of the House at the far end from the Speaker, one on the government side and the other on the opposition side. Ministers and opposition front-benchers addressing the House use the despatch box as a convenient rest for their notes, and will sometimes thump their hand against it as they make their point. (See Chapter 23.) The present despatch boxes are a gift of the New Zealand government. They were presented when the chamber was rebuilt after the wartime bombing.

DIVISION: Occurs when a vote is called if the outcome cannot be settled merely by the cries of 'Aye' and 'No' from MPs present in the chamber. The Speaker orders that a formal vote be taken, and MPs are alerted throughout the palace of Westminster and surrounding buildings by the ringing of bells. MPs then vote by walking through two lobbies on either side of the chamber, one for those MPs wishing to vote for the question, and the other for those wishing to vote against: the House has literally divided. (See Chapter 11.)

EDM: Early Day Motions are technically motions for debate, which MPs table for debate on an 'early day', i.e. in the near future. In fact, very few are ever debated, and EDMs are now used almost exclusively as a means of airing an issue, expressing an opinion, or demonstrating the strength of back-bench feeling on a particular topic. (See Chapter 9.)

GUILLOTINE: A development of the closure (q.v.), which is applied to various stages of a bill. Its aim is to expedite the passage of a bill by proposing a timetable allotting a certain amount of time to each stage of a bill – or, in committees and at report stage, to specified clauses of the bill. The result is that at the end of each allotted period of time, the debate on the relevant stage, or group of clauses, is concluded and the necessary votes taken. This can mean that specific clauses in a bill are approved without detailed discussion. Whereas a closure motion can only be proposed while a debate is actually in progress, a 'guillotine' motion has to be agreed to before the beginning of the debate which it is designed to limit. (See Chapter 12.)

HANSARD: The name given to the official report of parliamentary debates. It takes its name from the printer, Thomas Curson Hansard (son of the printer to the Commons, Luke Hansard) who in 1811 bought the business of reporting parliamentary debates from William Cobbett. (See Chapter 28.)

LEADER OF THE HOUSE: A Cabinet Minister, who announces the forth-coming business in the Commons each week and works closely with the Chief Whip – they are often referred to as the government's 'business managers'. The Leader of the House endeavours to ensure that the Government's business is transacted, while the interest of the House in ensuring full debate and expression of all shades of opinion is also respected. The title appears to date from the mid-nineteenth century, and when the Prime Minister was a member of the House of Lords (as was sometimes the case until 1902), the leading government spokesman in the Commons was known as the Leader of the House. Until 1942, Prime Ministers sitting in the Commons were also known by this title. Gladstone maintained that the Leader of the House 'suggests, and in a great degree fixes, the course of all principal matters of business, super- vises and keeps in harmony the actions of his colleagues, takes the initiative in matters of ceremonial procedure, and advises the House in every difficulty as it arises'. (See also Chapter 14.)

'NAMING' AN MP: If an MP disobeys the authority of the Speaker by abusing the rules of the House (e.g. refusing to withdraw offensive language), the Speaker can order the MP to leave the Chamber for the rest of the day's sitting. If the MP persists in abusing the rules of the House, the Speaker refers the matter to the House by rising and saying, 'I name Mr ..., for disregarding the authority of the Chair' (or for persistently and wilfully obstructing the business of the House by abusing its rules, or some similar offence). The Leader of the House then moves that the MP be suspended from the service of the House. (See Chapter 24.)

POINTS OF ORDER: If a Member wishes to raise a query concerning procedure or the rules of debate, he or she stands up and catches the Speaker's eye by saying 'On a point of order, Mr Speaker.' The Speaker will then allow the MP to raise the point of order, except during Question Time when points of order can only be raised once questions have finished. The Speaker's judgement on any point of order is final.

PPS: It is a common source of confusion that two members of a Minister's team are both known by the initials 'PPS'. When civil servants use the term PPS, they are usually referring to the head of a Minister's Private Office, the Principal Private Secretary. When MPs or parliamentary journalists talk about a Minister's PPS, they usually mean the Par- liamentary Private Secretary – generally a young back-bencher, who serves as the eyes and ears for a Minister in the Commons, ensuring that the Minister knows the mood of the House and also that other MPs are kept informed of the Minister's thinking. The job of Parliamentary Private Secretary is unpaid, but is regarded as the first rung on the ladder to ministerial office. (See Chapter 23.)

PRIVATE MEMBER'S BILL: Introduced by a backbench MP, as distinct from government bills which are piloted through the House by a Minister. Government and private members' bills are known as public bills, because they relate to matters of public policy and apply to the country in general. (See Chapter 10.)

PRIVATE BILL: This type of legislation confers particular powers or benefits on a specific individual or organisation, e.g. local authorities, companies, etc., and therefore does not apply to the country in general. (See Chapter 10.)

PRIVY COUNCILLOR: There are around 300 members of the Privy Council, who are entitled to the prefix 'Right Honourable' or to use the initials 'PC' after their name. A Privy Councillor is required to take the special Privy Councillor's oath in addition to the oath of allegiance. Today, all Cabinet Ministers become Privy Councillors by convention, and also some of the more senior Ministers outside the Cabinet are appointed. Other Privy Councillors include the Leader of the Opposition, the two archbishops, the Speaker of the House of Commons, the Lord Chief Justice, leading statesmen from Commonwealth countries, and other eminent politicians, lawyers and members of the clergy. The Privy Council was formerly the most important government body, but was superseded by the Cabinet. Its present-day functions are largely formal, giving effect to Proclamations (e.g. summoning, proroguing and dissolving Parliament) and Orders in Council (e.g. setting up a new Government Department), which are issued by the Crown under statutory or prerogative powers. Almost invariably, a member of the Privy Council remains so for life.

QUEEN'S SPEECH: A new session of Parliament opens with the speech from the throne in the House of Lords, which is usually delivered by the monarch. The speech is drafted by the government of the day, and sets out its proposed programme of legislation for the coming session. (See Chapter 16.)

QUESTION TIME: The period before the day's main public business when MPs question Ministers and receive oral replies. Usually lasts from a little after 2.35 until 3.30 p.m., and Ministers reply from the despatch box on a rota so that over a period of about four weeks MPs have the chance to question Ministers in every government department. Prime Minister's Questions are held twice weekly, on Tuesdays and Thursdays, between 3.15 and 3.30 p.m. (See Chapters 5 and 6.)

SECOND READING: The major debate on the principles of a bill, when its general purpose and implications are discussed. At the opening of the debate, the MP (in the case of a government bill, the Minister) responsible for the legislation proposes the motion 'That the Bill be now read a second time'. At the end of the debate, a vote is taken, and if a bill is given a Second Reading, it moves on to the Committee Stage, where matters of detail are discussed. (See Chapter 11.)

SERJEANT AT ARMS: Appointed by the Crown, but the servant of the Commons. Responsible for the maintenance of law and order throughout the precincts of the House of Commons, he takes into custody 'Strangers' who misconduct themselves in the House. He ensures the attendance of people summoned to appear before the Commons and its committees, and he sees that the Speaker's instructions are carried out (e.g. that an MP named by the Speaker and suspended by the House leaves the precincts of the House). His mace, which he carries on ceremonial occasions, has become the symbol of the power and privileges of the House of Commons. He is also housekeeper of the House of Commons. (See Chapter 2.)

SESSION (OF PARLIAMENT): Lasts usually around a year, and generally from November till October the following year. A session opens with the Queen's Speech, and is concluded with the prorogation of Parliament. Sometimes a session can last longer than twelve months – e.g. the sessions of 1983–4 and 1987–8, which both opened in the summer (after June General Elections) and lasted through until the October of the following year. The sessions of 1982–3 and 1986–7 were both cut short by the calling of General Elections in June 1983 and June 1987. (See Chapter 16.)

STANDING COMMITTEE: Debates the committee stage of a public bill. Before 1882, this was taken in Committee of the whole House, but under pressure of business bills have increasingly been referred to smaller committees of MPs. The committee stage of bills dealing with constitutional issues is by custom taken in Committee of the whole House. When a bill is referred to a standing committee, it is said to have been sent 'upstairs', as the committee rooms are located on the floor above the chamber. (See Chapter 12.)

STANDING ORDERS: The rules of the House of Commons, which regulate debates in the House, proceedings on public money, procedure in Committees and the conduct of MPs. (See Chapter 8.)

STRANGERS (GALLERY): Anyone within the precincts of the palace of Westminster who is neither a peer, an MP, nor an officer of one of the Houses of Parliament. The term 'Stranger' makes a clear distinction between a member and a non-member, non-members being allowed on the premises only on tolerance and not as of right. The galleries above the chamber where seats are available for the public are thus termed 'Strangers Galleries'. The term is also used in the wording of the motion to clear the galleries, not usually motivated by a desire to cloak debate in secrecy, but a ploy to delay proceedings. An MP states 'I spy strangers', and the Speaker has to put the question, 'That strangers do withdraw'. The House then votes on whether the galleries should be cleared. (See Chapter 4.)

WHIP: This can refer both to a document, and to one of a small number of specially appointed MPs within each of the parties represented in the Commons. The document is sent out each week to MPs in each party, and details the coming week's business. Each item of business is underlined according to its importance i.e. by one, two or three lines, representing degrees of pressure on MPs to attend. MPs known as 'Whips' derive their name from the 'whippers-in' of the fox-hunt, and are appointed in their respective parties with the prime function of ensuring that their fellow-MPs attend and vote as required. (See Chapter 13.)

ILLUSTRATION CREDITS

BLACK AND WHITE PICTURES

Reproduced by kind permission of the Speaker and the Advisory Committee of Works of Art in the House of Commons: pp 8 (PSA 1669), 9 (PSA 1665), 14 (PSA 3067), 24 (PSA 2953), 25 (PSA 2712), 28 (PSA 631), 76 (PSA 2952), 160 (PSA 370), 178 (PSA 623), 185 (PSA 2734)

Reproduced by courtesy of The Centre for the Study of Cartoons and Caricature at the University of Kent: pp viii, ix, 31, 33, 79, 93, 95, 120, 129, 142, 151, 163, 169, 189, 190, 200

Illustrated London News: pp 18, 23, 32, 54, 61, 72 (both), 73, 96, 112, 113, 123, 130, 144, 183, 186, 206

Punch Library: pp 85, 128, 157

The Mansell Collection: pp 12, 177

Mary Evans Picture Library: p 155

Popperfoto: p 4

Chief Whip's Office: p 81

© *Observer*/Trog: p 124

Parliamentary Profiles: p 164

COLOUR PICTURES

Sir Thomas More refusing to grant Wolsey a subsidy in 1523 PSA 2596

Westminster Hall depicted in 1819 Fotomas Index

Charles James Fox by Anton Hickel Fotomas Index

Baron Lionel de Rothschild being presented to the House of Commons Fotomas Index

The House of Commons viewed from Old Palace Yard PSA 1639

St Stephen's Crypt PSA 1601

Leo Amery MP speaking in the debate on defence on 7 May 1940 PSA 2936

Introduction of Lady Astor as the first woman member of the House of Commons Reproduced by permission of Plymouth City Museums and Art Gallery

The State Opening of Parliament by Queen Victoria Fotomas Index

Black Rod PSA GCN 24422/3

Serjeant at Arms Susan Griggs Agency

The Members' Tea Room PSA G29831/2

The House of Commons by June Mendoza

'The other picture' by A. T. Festing

Photographs given PSA reference numbers are reproduced by kind permission of the Speaker and the Advisory Committee of Works of Art in the House of Commons

All photographs not mentioned above were photographed by Grafton Books, with the kind permission of the Speaker

INDEX